Notes from an Italian Garden

Notes from an Italian Garden

JOAN MARBLE

Illustrated by Corinna Sargood

WILLIAM MORROW 75 YEARS OF PUBLISHING
An Imprint of HarperCollins*Publishers*

This book was originally published in Great Britain in 2000
by Doubleday, a division of Transworld Publishers.

FIRST U.S. EDITION

Library of Congress Cataloging-in-Publication Data

Marble, Joan.
Notes from an Italian garden / Joan Marble ;
illustrated by Corinna Sargood—1st us ed.
p.   cm.
Includes bibliographical references (p.).
ISBN 0-06-018574-0
1. Gardens—Italy—Canale.   2. Gardening—Italy—Canale.
3. Marble, Joan—Homes and haunts—Italy—Canale.   I. Title.
SB455 .M367   2001
635'.0945'63—dc21   00-058098

01   02   03   04   05   10   9   8   7   6   5   4   3   2   1

For Robert, Jenny and Henry,
with love

Contents

Illustrations

Notes from an Italian Garden

Introduction

THE FIRST TIME WE WENT TO INSPECT OUR LAND IN Canale after signing the papers, we were astonished to find a rainbow arching from our olive grove to the woods across the ravine. For once, I thought, Nature has got her signals straight. I had been yearning for a field of my own for a very long time – and here it was at the end of a rainbow.

When I was eight years old I had had my own garden full of pansies and snapdragons behind our house near Boston, and when I went away to Smith College I was planning to be a landscape architect. But though I love flowers and long, dreamy landscapes, I found that the finer details in the horticultural textbooks, about monocotyledons and xerophytic plants, put me instantly to sleep; so I ended up studying English instead and that led to journalism.

In Washington, where I worked for the United Press International, I was lucky to find a house in Georgetown with a back garden full of yellow roses and tulips. I left this garden intending to take only a short trip to Egypt but I never returned because in Cairo I met Robert Cook, a genial American sculptor working in Rome who had gone out to Egypt to see the antiquities. We were married some months later in the Campidoglio in Rome and then we started a family, and for years I did all my gardening in pots on Roman terraces. But there came a point when the yearning for a real garden grew so strong that we went out and found a patch of old Etruscan land which we have cherished ever since.

Our rationale was that a country home would be wonderful for our two children – but although they were initially charmed by the tree climbing and horse-riding, their enthusiasm tailed off as they turned fourteen and fifteen and had more exciting things to do in Rome. (Their affection for the place was to return much later.)

But Robert and I were smitten from the first. Robert had been very much a city fellow while he worked at his Via Margutta studio in Rome. He loved to carve olive wood or walnut, although he didn't know an olive tree from a mimosa. But once he got out to the country, he gradually became interested in planting trees and cooking fig jam and achieved limited local fame as the best grafter of fruit trees in the area. Farmers came from all over asking him to lend a hand.

For my part, I discovered to my surprise that there was a big difference between making a garden in New England and one in Canale, and I slowly got myself an education in Mediterranean gardening. In doing this I met all kinds of gardeners, from a farmer's wife who grew glorious tree peonies in oil drums to a countess who made ends meet by renting out the family chapel for local weddings and holding the receptions in her lovely rose garden.

This introduction to village life gave us a more intimate view of Italian character and customs than we could ever have acquired in Rome. Roman families are tightly knit and tend to turn inwards, whereas in Canale, although we were always *stranieri* (foreigners), we were never *forestieri*, which means 'unknown people' or 'outsiders'. We were part of the town almost from the word go, and over the years we learned much about the flora and fauna of the place and about its sturdy inhabitants who have remained surprisingly resilient, even buoyant, despite the fact that their area of southern Etruria remained virtually frozen in a feudal system until the dawn of the twentieth century. Even today they are still attached to customs – ancient attitudes – that go back in an almost uninterrupted line to the days of the Etruscans themselves.

'I think I've found my permanent outfit,' Robert used to say after we settled in. This was a reference to his days in the army when he was constantly being moved from one model-making unit to another. So that was it: Canale had become our permanent outfit, a place where we could settle down at last.

One of its greatest attractions was our awareness that we were not the first people to inhabit and work this piece of earth. Long ago – perhaps as long as three thousand years ago – other people worked and cherished this land, and every time we plant our seeds by the moon we know it is the same moon that the Etruscans saw rising from the woods of Manziana, and whenever we dig up a fragment of a pink terracotta pot, or cross the old Etruscan bridge to get fresh ricotta from the shepherd across the creek, we are reminded of the clever people who came before us. Those early Etruscans cleared the swamps of the Maremma and built miles of underground water conduits, a few of which are still used today, and they also treated the forests with care, coppicing parcels of the woods at regular intervals so the land was never eroded and nature could renew itself. We cannot claim to have Etruscan blood in our veins, as do some of the citizens of Canale; but we hope that a bit of their spirit, and their passionate regard for nature, may help us now and again as we tend our modest plot.

January

The Lure of Etruria

I FELL IN LOVE WITH ETRURIA ONE CHILLY EVENING IN THE middle of winter. They were having a New Year's Eve festival in a little town near Campagnano, and a group of local boys dressed in Renaissance costumes were marching in a torchlight parade down the main street. As I stood there in the cold watching the flames lurching to the sky and silhouetting the bare limbs of the plane trees, I realized that I felt very much at home in this ancient place. If ever we should decide to move to the country, this was the kind of place I would choose.

One figure who caught my eye was a young man holding a flaming torch, which he would use to light the festival bonfire. He was wearing a green velvet tunic and beige tights and he marched ahead of five other youths who were carrying bundles of branches for the fire. It was his profile that attracted my attention. The line from the forehead ran almost straight to the nose with barely a dent at the bridge. The eyes were large and almond-shaped and the mouth turned up at the edges in a faintly self-mocking smile. The face seemed familiar to me and then I realized that I had seen a profile very like it on the wall of an Etruscan tomb at Tarquinia. These ghosts from the past flicker into your consciousness whenever you wander through the scrabbly little towns of central Italy – when a farm lady setting down her basket of eggs at the market in Barbarano has her black hair curled like the dancer's ringlets on an Etruscan chalice, or when a mason's helper climbs on to a roof balancing a load of cement on his shoulder, his back perfectly straight and his legs showing the over-developed calf just below the knee that is so typically Etruscan.

In some places in old Etruria the people still pronounce the first letter 'C' as if it were an 'H' ('*casa*' becomes '*hasa*'), which was an Etruscan way of speaking. The design of many farmhouses still copies the Etruscan floor plan and the farmers continue to dig with a mattock, plant by the moon, and coppice their trees every twenty years. They are also first-rate metalworkers as were the Etruscans, who were attracted to the area because of iron and copper in the hills.

In their heyday, from the eighth to the third centuries BC, the Etruscans were among the most powerful people on earth. Their territory was called Tuscia which comes from the Greek and means 'tower' and their borders extended from the Tiber valley to the Tyrrhenian Sea, with outposts as far north as the Po and as far south as Naples. Energetic and enterprising, these early people smelted the metals that they found in the

Tolfa hills, developed miles of rugged roads so that carts could rumble to all the villages in the Etruscan League and invented excellent systems of irrigation which carried water through miles and miles of hand-dug tunnels criss-crossing their bumpy landscape. Etruscan galleys plied the Mediterranean carrying fine wine, metals, hand-painted vases and statues to the Greeks and Carthaginians and their gold jewellery was very much in demand, especially the breastplates, and exquisite earrings made by welding hundreds of tiny pin-drops of gold into natural shapes, a granulation technique that has never been duplicated since.

Even in their social relations the Etruscans seemed ahead of their times. Etruscan tomb paintings in Tarquinia show women happily sitting next to men at banqueting tables wearing lovely lacy dresses and holding aloft chalices of wine. And stone coffins are often decorated with sitting figures of man and wife where the woman is depicted as every bit as important as her husband.

But despite their manifest talents and social graces the Etruscans had one fatal blind spot: they refused to pay attention to the strange-speaking lowlanders who clustered in a village called Rome close by their southern border on the Tiber river. The Romans possessed little in the way of art or culture, in their 'shanty town on the Palatine', but they were a practical and persistent bunch and while the Etruscans amused themselves with their arts and their gods and glorious dinner parties, the Romans honed their martial skills and polished their spears. Eventually, in 396 BC, they were strong enough to march on the Etruscan stronghold at

Veio and bring their proud neighbours to heel.

This defeat marked the beginning of a long decline for the Etruscans. In the first years it wasn't so bad; the Romans were proud of the civilization they had conquered, and copied everything they could, from their art to their religion, law, institutions and military organization. They also invited Etruscan diviners to their palaces in Rome to read entrails and stars and advise them about the future. In the first century AD, the Emperor Claudius wrote a book in eight parts telling of the wonders of the Etruscan civilization, but sadly for all of us the book was lost and a great fund of Etruscan knowledge slipped into oblivion.

After this the Roman enthusiasm began to cool, and by the time Rome was converted to Christianity the Etruscan culture was disappearing fast. The Emperor Honorius ordered the burning of all Etruscan books and the destruction was so thorough that we have no source of reference for both Etruscan and Latin words. Thus we can read the letters which the Etruscans carved into their tombs and temples, odd Greek letters which seem to be written backwards, but the texts are so limited that they tell almost nothing of Etruscan lore or legends. To show their further disrespect, the Romans erased the old name of Tuscia from the maps. The northern section of Etruria was absorbed into Tuscany, while the southern part (where we live) was renamed Latium and recently modernized to the awkward Lazio.

The area of northern Etruria went on to greater things, with the eventual rise of cultural centres such as Florence and Siena, but our section of southern Etruria (or what is also known confusingly as northern Lazio) never recovered its former glory. The heavy hand of absentee landlords and the attendant poverty kept the area frozen in a state of permanent misery, with the fine old irrigation systems abandoned and the population decimated by malaria and the Black Death. A further blow was dealt during the eighth century when the Lombards rolled down from the north and seized a hunk of the old Etruria around Sutri, which they presented to the Vatican. The Pope incorporated the land into The Papal States but did almost nothing to improve the lot of the miserable inhabitants and so the Renaissance, which ennobled Florence and Siena and Rome, had far less impact on the hapless towns of southern Etruria.

The countryside struggled on for centuries, a wild and hostile place, full of gorges, empty streambeds, deep volcanic lakes and abandoned castles. Wandering shepherds lived in grass huts, leading their flocks to the hills in summer and back to the lowland pastures in winter. It was a hunting ground for brigands and highwaymen, and officials who had to travel through it were warned to go in broad daylight and carry arms to avoid kidnapping or murder. The papal government was corrupt and incompetent. To the Vatican princes the challenge was not embellishment or rebuilding but pacification, and whenever the inhabitants made trouble French mercenaries were sent in to subdue them. To this day, the people of northern Lazio are strongly anti-clerical and wary of foreigners.

A few new churches and fortified castles were built during the years of Vatican control but these contributed little to human welfare and even in the nineteenth century James Skene, a Scottish watercolourist who passed through, complained that the people were so poor that they could scarcely manage to scratch a few seeds into the harsh and barren soil. When they ploughed, he wrote, the farmers climbed up on to their wooden ploughs drawn by starving oxen to save themselves from walking. The poet Shelley was one of the few travellers who had a good word for the territory. In a letter to a friend in 1818 he wrote: 'We arrived at Rome across the much-belied "Campagna di Roma", a place I confess infinitely to my taste.'

It is odd indeed that an area which is so close to Rome should suffer such neglect, but in fact this is often the fate of lands lying in the shadow of a great capital. The princes of the city preferred to live within the protective walls of their splendid palaces and when they ventured into the country on weekend boar hunts or for jousting they went heavily armed and ready for trouble. Their aim was to keep the country people as poor and ignorant as possible, working at only the most menial jobs. The natives very quickly learned that while they should keep their shoulders hunched to resist incursions from the north, they should also turn their faces to the south with winning smiles and outstretched hands in the hope that some of the bounties from the city would fall upon them. These twin compulsions to resist authority but also to scoop up its benefits have fostered a complex, not to say schizophrenic, personality among the citizens of southern Etruria. Inhabitants of other areas regard them as difficult and a little forbidding.

To add to their problems, malaria was endemic in the area around the central Italian lakes and to this day many cautious Italians consider these lakes unhealthy. It was only in the Forties and Fifties when malaria was eliminated with liberal doses of DDT that a few outsiders, mostly Germans and English, began to settle around the lake shores. Italians themselves still prefer to spend their holidays by the sea, where they claim the iodine and salt in the air (along with unmentioned gulps of carbon monoxide) refresh their lungs and restore their livers. Thus the fame of the Lazio area is circumscribed and tourist buses on their way from Assisi or Florence to Rome zip through Etruria without a pause.

When you tell non-Italians you live in Lazio, they tend to look perplexed and say, 'Lazio? Now just where is that? Is it part of Tuscany?'

Actually, those of us who love southern Etruria are quite happy with this obscurity. We do not envy the citizens of Florence who struggle to walk through the centre of their city because of the numbers of tourists. Nor would we change places with the long-suffering Venetians whose lovely piazzas are jammed with day-trippers eating salami sandwiches and throwing ice-cream wrappers into the canals.

Like the princess who guessed that her frog was really a handsome prince, we know that our corner of Etruria is really a jewel of rare beauty, and has a mystic quality tied to its ancient Etruscan roots. We feel this beauty every time we walk through the pastures and woods which stretch towards the Tolfa hills, or whenever we pass little stone villages built on top of open ravines whose sides are honeycombed with the cave tombs of vanished Etruscans. We feel it too when we look out to the hills beyond these villages and see herds of white longhorn cattle – the same kind of cattle that were painted on the walls of the prehistoric caves at Lascaux. And we feel it when we see the pigs rooting through the autumn forests in search of acorns.

I will always be happy that we found the area when we did, in 1964, while it was still an unknown backwater, for we were able to catch – just before it began to disappear – a way of life that had gone on virtually unchanged since the Dark Ages, and sometimes much longer.

It wasn't, I might add, any special inside knowledge that led us to Etruria. We wanted to have a garden with a peony bush and some olive trees and since we do not like autostradas we decided to hunt for something fairly close to the city. So we drew a circle around Rome to include everything that lay inside the thirty-mile zone. The choices were not all that difficult. The south and southeast of Rome, which included the popular Alban Hills resorts of Frascati and Albano, had already been gobbled up. The western approaches which led to the airport and the Roman seaport of Ostia had become unkempt dormitory areas for Rome. To the east there was Tivoli and the approaches to the Apennines, but the landscape seemed bleak. So that left the area to the north of Rome, with its big volcanic lakes and tumbled Etruscan ruins, and after we saw the winter parade at Campagnano we decided that this might indeed be home.

Real estate agents were not common back in those days but after asking around we were told that there was one very rustic agent out in the town of Bracciano. He was a Sardinian and his name was Puddu. He had a one-room office on the main square in Bracciano, and although he could neither read nor write, he had a part-time secretary who could. Physically he was unimpressive, a small man who wore velvet suits made of *pelle del diavolo* (devil's cloth), a kind of corduroy without stripes. He had a small head, always covered by a hat, and a hard squint, probably from looking for a long time at distant horizons or far-off watercourses. His right hand was missing several finger joints, reportedly the result of some unpleasantness in Sardinia, and he had a swivel tooth which gave him a lisp and caused all his 'l's to come out as 'r's.

Whenever he took us around in his old red Renault, Puddu carried a stout wooden stick or staff which we came to realize was not a walking stick but his official badge of office. In rural Italy a man with a staff is immediately recognizable as the *mediatore*, the man who has the power to organize and supervise any exchange of goods, whether it is horses and donkeys or houses and land. According to folklore specialists, the staff was derived from the crook of the Etruscan priests and later adopted by the Christian Church as a symbol of the power given to bishops to lead their flocks.

Puddu listened to us with a good bit of impatience when we told him that we wanted to find an old *casa colonica* (country house) possibly with a view of the lake, and a walk-in fireplace.

Finding an old house, Puddu warned us, was '*morto difficile*'. For a moment I thought he was warning us about a difficult death. What he really meant was that it was *molto* (with an 'l') *difficile* to find an old farmhouse in open Lazio countryside, and he was right.

Peasants in Etruria were not accustomed to building houses out in the open. It was too dangerous. They preferred to huddle in close to the high walls of a fortified castle or church, thus absorbing warmth and protection from the wealthy landlord. This practice was so common that it had a special name, *incastellazione* (putting the people into the castle), but the result was that if the farmers owned or rented a tiny piece of land outside the town, they had to ride out on a donkey every day to tend their vines and pick their olives, carrying most of their equipment with them.

Things had been different in Tuscany. There the countryside was more settled; farmers were richer than in Lazio and were protected by a network of forest guardians, gamekeepers and village police so that they were able to build houses in the countryside long before farmers around Rome even built chicken coops. These Tuscan country farmhouses known as *casali*, with their massive walls and great pitched roofs of hand-turned tiles, give the landscape a more developed and substantial look, and the owners often had the foresight to plant long rows of cypress trees leading to their house and to terrace the vineyards and plant shade trees around their farm buildings. Lazio, by contrast, has been less subdued by man; the forests and ravines and *garrigue* (prickly heath-like countryside) remain as nature made them.

'Forget about the *casa colonica*,' Puddu said. 'I'll find you a piece of land *morto berro*, and then for a few hundred thousand lire you can build your own *casa colonica*.'

We soon learned to beware of Puddu's figures; his estimates of what it would cost to build a small house were too low by about 200 per cent while his estimates of what the property would soon be worth were just as erroneous on the high side. He also had a breezy way of assuring us of essential services. We were looking at a strip of olive grove overlooking the lake one day and I asked him if we might have difficulty drilling for water.

'You don't need to dig a well here,' he said airily. 'There's an aqueduct over there, so you can get all your water free.'

I discovered years later that the aqueduct was a special line that carried lake water from Bracciano to the port of Civitavecchia, and we could no more attach to it than we could hook on to the gas pipeline from Russia.

One day when we were looking at another piece of property on the Tolfa road, I remarked that it might be difficult to get ENEL to bring electricity that long distance.

'No problem, there is an electricity supply line out on the main road, and you can link up with it for a small fee.'

We soon discovered that the electricity was almost two kilometres away and a hookup, if it had been allowed, would have cost an arm and a leg. Furthermore, corruption was so rife in the area that ENEL officials gave the current only to their close relatives or to speculators who were willing to pay hefty bribes.

Puddu had other attributes that we found unnerving. He seemed to assume that every miserable piece of land he showed us would be just perfect for our needs. Rather than hang around to explain it all to us, he had a habit of dropping us on the land and then wandering away across fields and ravines to talk to the peasants.

We eventually realized that all this gallivanting across lavender fields and climbing over fences was part of Puddu's operating style. He took advantage of his hours out with clients to look around for more property to control, just as a sparrowhawk circles overhead looking for more sparrows. Some of the peasants greeted Puddu with a certain grudging forbearance, but many more backed away from him as if he were followed by a swarm of hornets.

'Stay away from that lisping Sardinian,' one farmer managed to murmur to me. 'Wherever he goes, everybody but him loses money.'

Another Bracciano resident assured me that Sardinians did not enjoy good reputations in the Lazio area.

'They get free ferry tickets to come over from Sardinia with their sheep in summer because there is nothing to eat on the island but rocks and thistles. The ferry dumps them in Civitavecchia, and from there they spread out into the Maremma like a plague of locusts, and everywhere they go good Christians end up with knives in their livers.' (Originally the term 'Maremma' was used to describe the coastal marshland, but now it refers to a wider inland swath.)

I protested that Puddu didn't look like a cut-throat to me but my friend rolled his eyes.

'You should have seen his father,' he said. 'He came over from Sardinia one day in June with thirty sheep, all of them limping and sick, and by the end of the summer he had sixty healthy sheep, eight pigs and three Maremma horses. He wore an old black suit with a black hat and home-made leggings, and all he carried was a big white umbrella and a sheepskin blanket. He was so ugly that little children would burst into tears when they saw him.'

Whenever Puddu rumbled back from his getting-to-know-you forays in the Lazio campagna, his face was wreathed in a wide false smile.

'All settled?' he would ask us. 'Shall we go back and sign the papers?'

But when we told him that we were not buying the smile would disappear and Puddu would relapse into black despair.

There was really nothing more he could do, he would say, he had shown us the best piece of land in all of Lazio, and we hadn't the grace to appreciate it. There was nothing like it anywhere, even at double the price. It was useless to go on wasting his time and ours, as we clearly did not have a good idea of what we wanted.

That decided us. We had had enough of Puddu. We would go out and find our land without a mediator.

Finding the Land

I T DIDN'T TAKE US LONG TO REALIZE WHY PUDDU TOOK SO
many field trips around Lake Bracciano. The country
people are almost pathologically attached to their *terreno* and
selling it is like giving up a lifetime pension or finding a leak
in a thousand-litre barrel of wine. They are convinced,
possibly with reason, that they will never own anything else as
valuable and if some calamity forces them to sell a piece of
vineyard or an olive grove they try to put off the fatal day as
long as possible.

Pressures upon them to sell are therefore effective only if
accompanied by some special form of arm-twisting, and in this
sphere Puddu was without peer. He pretended at all times that
his main aim was to find a buyer for a poor farmer's land, thus
enriching the seller, but the farmer never lost track of the
subliminal message, that Puddu held a monopoly position as
the only real estate man in the area and no property deals

could take place around Lake Bracciano without his benediction.

Looking for land without an intermediary was therefore quite a hassle, as the locals had a real aversion to naming a price. They reasoned that once the bird was out of the cage they could never get it back in again.

But if, rough foreigner that you were, you insisted on hearing the magic number, the landowner might furtively flash two or three fingers of the right hand, held at pocket level. From this hand language you were given to understand that the land cost anything from two million to two hundred million lire; and even if you spelt it out in writing, you could be quite sure that the final figure would be considerably more than you first understood. If you protested, you would be subjected to a lot of smiling talk about how you did not understand because you, poor fool, were a foreigner. But you would pay the higher amount anyhow.

There was another problem in dealing with the locals – their wives. There are generally two kinds of wives in country villages – the 'I know nothing about anything' type, demure ladies who hide from all responsibility under a cloak of wide-eyed innocence, or the strong-minded women who have opinions on everything and are happy to air them. Most of this second group are better educated than their men and they keep in touch with the property market with a tenacity that is quite intimidating. So when a husband comes home from a long day in the fields and tells his wife that he has asked one million lire for a piece of land, she wastes no time in broadcasting her opposition.

Cursed be the day that she ever married such an idiot – a man who can't sign his own name, much less add up a column of figures! Doesn't he know that with inflation and all the other plagues of the earth, prices in Italy are going up at 30 per cent a year, yes, even 40 per cent?

She then flings on a shawl and hurtles out into the night to see her sister, and her sister's son Baldissero who went to the Scuola Superiore and knows more about land values than any mere dirt farmer. The sister and Baldissero assure the distraught woman that her husband is out of his mind. The sum he quoted was at least 50 per cent too low, and everyone knows that the prices in the Bracciano area are skyrocketing.

Reassured, the lady hurries home to berate her poor mate in a vibrato that would put Callas to shame, and the next time we meet him the husband looks hard at his boots and tells us that we had not understood the price because of our deficient Italian. In truth, the land we fancied costs almost double what we had mistakenly thought.

We ran into the overbearing-wife phenomenon several times. Once we found a piece of land next to Lake Bracciano much to our liking despite the fact that it was partially inundated with water for four winter months; but every time we went to ask about it, the owner raised the price by another million lire. His wife's theory was that anyone who was mad enough to want that particular bit of swampy lakefront would also be mad enough to pay any price.

Another obstacle we encountered was multiple ownership. A father had died long ago in Oriolo leaving the property divided among his six children, two in Australia, three in Italy

and one in Canada, and the one in Canada was not interested
in selling because he had a sentimental attachment to the land
of *povero babbo* (poor daddy). This is known in Italy as the *tre
fratelli, tre castelli* (three brothers, three castles) syndrome.

Eventually, defeated by this wall of silence and contra-
diction, we tucked our chins into our collars and went back to
Puddu, who did not appear surprised to see us. Miraculously,
on our first excursion he took us to a rather pretty piece of hillside outside Canale Monterano, an ancient village which lies
midway between Bracciano and the hill town of Tolfa.

It was a long thin patch of thistly pastureland, thrown like
a straw-coloured scarf across a sweep of open country, leading
from a dirt road in a southerly direction towards the lip of a
rather steep ravine. Vineyards and olive trees and a few
scattered fig trees were all there was to break the monotony of
the open *garrigue* landscape. Only after we looked more
closely did we see that there were many other strips of land
about the same size as ours, all leading to the ravine, and
cut off from each other by spiny hedgerows crowded
with wild pears, prickly hawthorns, medlars, blackberries
and wild roses. It was available. It was cheap. The sun was
shining. We had looked long enough.

We asked Puddu to get us together with the owner as soon
as possible.

'That is not necessary,' he said with his usual crooked smile.
'I am the owner.'

This wasn't altogether accurate. When we met a week later
in a notary's office in Bracciano, Puddu's niece (who had come
to do the signing) handed us the papers which indicated that a

peasant named Pasquale had given Puddu the option to sell his land. So our man was not so much an estate agent as a monopolist who took options on all saleable parcels of land in the zone and permitted a sale only when he stood to make a handsome profit. The peasant got one (low) price and Puddu got whatever (high) price he could extract from the buyer. In this operation he put no cash on the line; it was no wonder that the natives treated him like Typhoid Mary!

We had assumed that Puddu was making a larcenous 10 or 20 per cent profit with his little game, but we had vastly underestimated the man. When we met Pasquale about a year after the deal was done, we found out that while he had received only 650,000 lire for the land, Puddu had rewarded himself with a handsome fee of 850,000 lire. On top of this he had charged a 4 per cent agent's fee. Never underestimate the ability of an illiterate Sardinian.

This tale should end right here, but there was a codicil. While we were signing the documents for the notary public (who billed us another half million for shuffling papers) a final sheet of paper was slipped before us which declared that we had spent only 900,000 lire for the land. We asked him as discreetly as possible if he was sure about that figure. The notary looked at us in a distracted manner and said that for technical reasons the figure was accurate. He muttered something more about a 'discount for foreigners', an arrangement which we found baffling.

Months later, we received a scary grey postcard which summoned us to the office of the Tax Assessor in Prati to 'discuss the matter of the land sale'. After three days of bad dreams and sweaty palms we found ourselves in the tax office anterooms on the Via Cola di Rienzo. It was a typical government office where old men with shiny black suits and calloused hands sat trying to smooth out ancient parchment wills while freelance lawyers hovered around trying to read documents upside down or over people's shoulders.

At last the Tax Assessor himself erupted into the room, a lean fellow with a falcon's gaze and a gold watch by Cartier. His glance swept the crowd with care. Focusing on us, he made a brief nod which meant we were to follow him into his chamber. We were waved into two uncomfortable wooden chairs and a handful of our land papers was flipped in our direction.

'I have seen these papers, and I am not such an idiot as to believe that you spent only 900,000 lire for that piece of land.' His voice was very loud.

We cowered on the other side of the desk, wondering if we could make it to the airport in time.

'You are Cook Roberto, American sculptor with the studio on Via Margutta, are you not? I know all about you.'

We shrank even deeper into our chairs. O Dio! He knew everything about us, the out-of-date Permesso di Soggiorno (residence permit), the missing refuse collection tax, the television tax, the legally inadequate photocopy of the driving licence.

'I like your statues,' he went on, cool as an ice pick. 'For one of your statues I am prepared to forget this unpleasant infringement of the law, punishable by six months in prison.'

It took us a moment to realize that the man was not sending

us to jail but only asking for a bribe. We should have felt outrage, distress and consternation, but I confess our main reaction was cowardly relief. The next morning Robert brought the Tax Assessor two nice bronze statues and suggested he might choose between them.

He didn't even blink.

'I'll take both of them,' he said, and swept the two statues quickly into his big top drawer. Then he raised his voice. (When Italians feel guilty or embarrassed they always raise their voices.)

'What I can't understand is why clever Americans like you ever chose to get stuck in such a God-forsaken corner of Italy. With money like yours, why not go to San Remo or Monte Carlo?'

We didn't bother to explain it to him because we knew he would never understand, but the truth was that we were already smitten with our little chunk of Etruria and were pinching ourselves on our good luck in finding it. In retrospect I shudder to think how little we had informed ourselves about the place that we were about to make our home. We had a vague knowledge that it had once been part of the estate of the Odescalchi papal princes who used it for grazing herds of sheep and longhorn cattle but we did not know how it had come to be divided up into strips for the peasants of Canale.

We also did not know that at the base of the ravine there was a narrow stream surrounded by great poplars, and that crossing the stream there was a splendid Roman bridge with a holm oak growing out of its arch. The bridge was part of an ancient road system that linked the seaport of Cerveteri to other centres in southern Etruria. We were equally unaware that the dark mass of green beyond the ravine was the famous *macchia* (forest) of Manziana, one of the oldest communal forests in Italy, which had once extended all the way from Manziana to Lake Bolsena. Nor did we know about the summer moon that came up from behind the forest, rising like an orange globe from a dark sea, or about the birds that arrived in spring to populate the forest, nightingales and cuckoos, hooded crows and even some crested hoopoes.

We did not know about the winter rains that came down like bullets, or about the lightning and thunder that often accompanied this rain, or about the wind that blew through the rafters and rattled the chimney pots on dark starless nights, while the foxes barked and hoot-owls screeched from deep within the woods. We were ignorant too of the hot sirocco winds from Africa that sometimes brought clouds of red dust from the Sahara. Nor did we know about the cooling winds from the west (the *ponente*) that arose every afternoon in summer when the cicadas were just moving into a higher octave.

We saw the land, it looked possible, and before we knew what was happening, it was ours.

A friend wrote us a prophetic letter from Verona: 'You will love it and treasure it because it is yours, and it will make you all very happy.'

Another thing we didn't realize was that we would be the first modern settlers in this rough and forbidding area. No one had lived in the open countryside below Canale for decades, perhaps even centuries, so amenities such as water, electricity, television, postal services, refuse collection and police protection were absent.

'But why did you decide to settle so far from town?' the local people would ask. 'You, who have so much money, who are friends with the American ambassador and the foreign minister, why did you settle for such a miserable thistle patch?' (This refrain about our money and our high connections was a constant theme.)

We tried to explain that we were not rich, that we had no important connections of any sort; we simply liked peace and solitude. But they stared with their mouths open, refusing to believe us. What would we do about water? We would dig a well. And how would we pump the water? With a hand pump. And how about lights? We would use gas lamps. They just couldn't believe it. They had spent their lives fighting to escape the simple life of the iron stove, the hand pump and the outdoor loo and they could not understand how anyone, especially a rich American family, could opt for such privation by choice.

This eccentricity on our part stimulated much curiosity and the Canalesi began coming down to call on us. The first visitors came in pairs, with the excuse that they wanted to work as carpenters, plumbers and builders. But then gradually we started getting visits from our neighbours, the local farmers, who came down to work every day on their donkeys.

These rough-hewn types tried to be polite as they surveyed our earnest efforts at building and planting but inevitably they could not resist advising us about all the things we were doing wrong. We were facing the house in the wrong direction, planting the wrong trees, and looking for water in the wrong places. Our new olive trees were an inferior variety and would never produce olives, and the plum saplings were too thin and would not last the winter.

'What a pity that Jack is away,' they would say. 'He is visiting his daughter in Viterbo. When he comes back he will help sort out the mess you have made.'

Jack, it turned out, was an old farmer who owned a stretch of vineyard and olive grove just to the east of us, and he would be the perfect guide and monitor for us, having learned to speak our language during his years in a place they called 'Pennis-vannia'. Jack *l'americano*, as he was universally known, would set us straight about our badly pruned olive trees and our lamentable pastureland. He would give us some new cuttings of figs and teach us to graft. Gradually this absent neighbour assumed mythic proportions in our minds combining, we fondly thought, the robust physique of Sylvester Stallone with the Latin savvy of Lieutenant Columbo.

Thus we were more than a bit surprised when the real Jack showed up one warm morning in May. He was a tiny man in worn brown corduroy with thick country boots and a battered black hat and he was leading a donkey on a hemp rope. At first glance he looked rather like a hawk, with a sharp nose and chin, but the minute he spoke this impression was softened by friendly blue eyes and a somewhat toothless smile.

'I wish to salute you,' the new visitor said. 'I am your neighbour, Jack.' (He spoke in Italian and pronounced his name

'Jeck'.) As he said this he led his donkey over to a fig tree and tied him securely, then pulled a flask of pale red wine from a worn saddlebag and put it on the ground next to our picnic basket. 'This is wine from my vineyard,' he announced.

We all took a drink from the flask and gasped. It was like drinking vinegar.

'Wonderful!' we spluttered.

Jack looked blank and we discovered that his knowledge of English was not as extensive as his friends had indicated. In all the years we knew him, he came up with only three English phrases: 'How are you today?', 'That's all right' and 'No problem.'

We switched to Italian.

'*Il vino è una meraviglia.*' (The wine is a marvel.)

He scratched his ear and chortled.

'*E casareccio,*' he said with becoming modesty, '*ma almeno è sincero.*' (It's home-made but at least it's genuine.) We could tell from his look that even he was not convinced he had a Pinot Grigio on his hands. We took another gulp of the dreadful stuff, trying to smile as we did so, and in that precise moment we had entered into a new realm. We were no longer just the strange Americans who were moving into the area, we had become custodians of the great Canale secret – that the local wine was pestiferous.

Membership of the insiders' group brought more rewards than just acid wine. From the moment when good old Jack passed through our brambly hedgerow, we had acquired not only a friend but also a walking history of Canale itself going back not seventy but four hundred years. Like Rip Van

Winkle, Jack's lifetime experience was rooted in customs and habits that went back several centuries. He was born in 1890 into the slow, ox-driven world of the peasant, a vassal of the uncaring Papal States, and all his life he scrabbled a living for his family of eight using a spade to plant his grapes and olives, and a sharp and narrow *zappa* (mattock) – the instrument the Etruscan farmers used back in 500 BC – to keep down the weeds. When he was exhausted in the evening, he drank a litre of sour wine and let his donkey carry him home to bed.

As Jack told us during our long picnics under the cherry tree, he was born at the time when Canale was still struggling to recover from centuries of neglect. His home in the village, which had also been his parents' home, was made of rough local stone and mortar and consisted of a kitchen, where the family gathered around a wood-burning stove (the only heat in the house), and two bedrooms, one for the parents and one for the six children. In the beginning, there was no running water, no electricity and no bathroom, although in the post-war years these amenities began to arrive. Under the main house there was a *cantina*, stoutly locked with chain and padlock, where pigs, chickens and donkey (the family Ford) were kept and where valuable produce such as wood, olive oil and wine were stored. All washing was done at the village fountain, which was a ten-minute walk away, and household water came from the fountain too.

Peasants in those days had few choices as to how to make a living. The proximity of the Manziana forests meant that many of them worked for big landowners either as wood-cutters (*boscaroli*) or as charcoal-burners (*carbonari*). The *boscaroli* cut the wood by hand and loaded it on wagons for the market. The *carbonari* cut the smaller branches in uniform lengths, piled them into neat pyramids, and then covered the pile with a mixture of earth and mortar to make a kind of airless oven. The wood was then burned slowly inside the oven until it became charcoal, which was used as a heating fuel or in foundries. Since the woods and the charcoal industries were on the Vatican land, most of the profits went to the papal nobles. Prince Odescalchi of Bracciano made the biggest profits of all, for in addition to the charcoal he had control of some iron mines on the island of Elba, and the combination of iron ore plus charcoal turned him into an early version of an oil sheikh.

Those who did not work as woodsmen or *carbonari* had few options open to them. They could work as cattlemen (*butteri*) and spend their days on horseback tending large herds of princely cows or horses, or they could join the clan of poor shepherds who trailed endlessly on foot over the *macchia* keeping watch over flocks of sheep or herds of pigs.

The lowliest jobs of all went to those poor farmers who hired themselves out as seasonal labourers to till the prince's fields in the growing season. Jack was one of the pool of young men who reported every spring to the prince's deputies, rough uniformed types known as *caporali* who would assign him some distant fields to cultivate. Jack bought his seed, often barley or corn, at the going price and then rode off on his donkey to tend the fields from Monday morning until late Saturday. He carried with him a loaf of home-baked bread, a few sausages (if available), a small bottle of olive oil and a flask or two of wine. This meagre ration, supplemented by whatever he could scrounge in the countryside, had to last for a week. If the weather was bad, he had to sleep in caves or hastily improvised straw huts.

The rewards for this kind of feudal service were pathetic. Jack had to give back to the prince one fifth of the corn he grew as payment for using the fields, and then he had to sell more corn to acquire money for his family. Unfortunately the only buyer was the prince, and the prince's men paid low prices and some even had a habit of rigging their scales so that 100 kilos weighed in at a meagre 90. Thus in a bad year the prince stood to make money while the peasant came away empty-handed and soon found himself heavily in debt.

This life was so harsh that in 1912 Jack decided to emigrate to the United States. He ended up with an aunt and uncle in Scranton, Pennsylvania, where he got a job working in a local coal mine. Unfortunately the miners were on strike for a good part of Jack's first year and when he finally began to work regularly, the First World War started and he was obliged to return to Italy to serve in the Italian army. At the war's end, he went home to Canale to marry a local girl and take up his life as a struggling farmer. Fortunately for Jack, the prospects for a young farmer had improved somewhat since the war. Some land reform measures had been introduced in Canale and returning veterans were given parcels of land – about 15,000 square metres each – to help them become self-sufficient.

These parcels were no great bargains. They were at least

three kilometres out of town, a trip which had to be made
every day on donkey-back. Also there was no water on the
land (and not enough money to dig a well or build a house) so
the new farmers could grow only crops which needed little
irrigation – olives and grapes, the traditional crops of the
poor. Water for making Bordeaux mixture to spray the
grapes against phylloxera had to be brought in on donkey-
back too.

It was a tough life but somehow Jack, aided by his wife
Nina, managed to feed a family of six children. The secret was
to grow as much food as possible in the warm season and
make it last over the winter. The basic crops were wine
and olive oil which served household needs and could be used
for barter, but Jack also planted as many food-bearing trees
and bushes as he could on his plot, paying special attention to
fruits which would last over the winter such as hard pears and
apples. In addition he planted several varieties of fig, including one which had three crops a year. He dried some of the
September figs in the sun and wrapped them in laurel leaves
so they were still good at Christmas. To add to his Christmas
feast, Jack put in assorted nut trees including two almonds,
two walnuts, and six hazelnut bushes which grow unusually
well in the Viterbo area.

In a patch of land next to his vineyard, Jack also planted
some of the tougher vegetables that can soldier through
summer with very little water: courgettes (*zucchini*, which
gave edible flowers as well), three kinds of tomatoes including
a yellow one that could be uprooted and stored to keep all
winter, and beans of all sorts – slim green beans to be eaten in

July, fatter black beans for August, and tougher *borlotti* beans which could be dried and eaten all year round.

One afternoon Jack brought me a basket of *borlotti* beans which he had just beaten with a stick to release them from their dry shells.

'All this work for a few *pernacchie* (farts),' he chortled.

Other field crops necessary for his family were onions, potatoes and garlic which were planted in winter and harvested in the spring; and green crops such as cabbages, kale, broccoli, spinach and Swiss chard which were planted in late summer to be ready in late autumn.

Jack had also learned in childhood to recognize the edible plants that grew naturally in the fields and hedgerows around the town. In spring he knew where to find the wild asparagus, which was not an asparagus at all but a form of wild grass that came up with a curled bud. He knew all the native mush-rooms too, and in September and October he was down at the edges of the woods hunting for *ovoli* and *porcini* and *galletti*, the delicate little yellow mushrooms that the French call chanterelles and which are as tasty as truffles. He always kept an eye peeled for wild chicory, which made a spicy cooked vegetable, and other strange green plants that grew in the hedgerows and provided mixed salads that scratched the tongue. Wild medlars and blackberries were also picked in season.

Jack knew how to hunt for eels in the stream that ran below our property and, every time it rained in summer, he had a special bag ready to collect the snails which inevitably came out to nibble on the damp growing leaves. Before being steamed, the snails had to be purged for three days on a diet of pure grass.

Nearly all Canale housewives were good at preserving foods too. The biggest job of all was bottling tomatoes in August. An average family would fill two or three hundred bottles, boiling and straining the tomatoes first and then boiling them again when bottled, wrapped in newspapers so that the glass jars wouldn't break in the boiling water.

Canale wives also knew how to dry tomatoes, *melanzane* (aubergine), mushrooms and figs, and how to preserve other crops such as artichoke hearts, peppers, sliced courgettes and wild mushrooms by boiling them and storing them in oil. Bottling food in vinegar was another method of preservation, but oil was more favoured as a preserving medium. The Canalesi left it to the northerners to make pickles.

Some of the more enterprising farmers also managed to augment their food production by keeping a few cows or horses or pigs on their property. Even those who could not afford the bigger animals managed to keep a pig or two in the *cantina*. The home-grown pig was fattened up with tasty scraps from the kitchen for a year and then slaughtered, usually at Christmas, to yield fresh sausages, *strutto* (lard) for cooking, cooked ham, smoked pork, and liver and bacon, essential for making good spaghetti sauce. For some Canale families the pig was the only meat that reached their table all winter, although many housewives managed to keep a few chickens in the *cantina* along with the pig, thus providing fresh eggs and an occasional plump bird for the Sunday pot.

Finally Jack did what all peasants do in an economy where money is scarce. He became proficient at the delicate business of barter – swapping a few litres of extra olive oil and wine for milk, honey or beef. His father had taught him how to make cheese from the local sheep's milk too, so he worked out a deal with Canale shepherds whereby they gave him the sheep's milk and he repaid them with a kind of fresh cheese which became *pecorino* after a long period of drying. He was also given a baby lamb every Easter in return for letting shepherds graze their flocks on his pastureland during the autumn and winter seasons.

An informal labour exchange system existed in the Lazio villages. If Jack needed help getting his roof retiled, he called in a friend or relative and it was understood that he would stand ready to help the relative when his roof blew off. He also had a standing contract with the Canale barber who gave him a weekly shave and a monthly haircut in return for eight eggs a week, and the Canale tailor was ready to make him a corduroy suit in exchange for a fifty-litre demijohn of sour wine.

Jack needed cash for only a few items such as salt, sugar, coffee, soap and shoes and he was usually able to sell enough wine to raise the money. Cooperative management of some of the biggest farm machinery was another system which enabled Canale families to get the services they needed. The olive mill in the town was built by the olive growers themselves, and paid its way by charging grinding fees to non-members. Farmers who grew wheat also had a part interest in a huge old threshing machine known as the *trebbiatrice*, drawn by a tractor which rattled out into the grainfields exuding a great cloud of smoke and straw every June.

The farmers took turns tending the machine, wearing

burlap bags over their heads and shoulders to keep the straw
dust at bay. Their duties involved pitching the fresh-cut stalks
of grain into the machine with pitchforks, lugging bag after
bag of processed grain to the waiting wagons, and stacking
great bundles of straw that had been baled while the wheat
was winnowed. The annual arrival of the machine provided
the excuse for a kind of village fête, and the Canalesi came in
numbers to check on the operation and join their neighbours
for a picnic. By high noon, a time when the machine chose to
have its daily breakdown, there could be upwards of sixty
locals in attendance including the wheat farmers themselves,
who had brought their newly cut grain to be processed, their
wives, who had come down from the village for the picnic,
and numerous children (and their dogs), who showed up on
foot or on bicycles to take part in the fun.

On the first day of the *trebbiatura* I finally met Jack's wife,
La Signora Nina. She was a stocky little woman who wore a
shapeless black dress and a blue apron. She had a blue
bandanna on her head, below which all I could see were a
button nose and a pair of piercing black eyes.

She came straight up to me, reached out a worn hand for a
handshake and screamed, 'I am the wife of your neighbour
Jack and I have brought you lunch.'

I tried to explain to her that we didn't want to disturb her,
but Sora Nina was a woman who did things her way.

'You are the new neighbours, so it is my duty to entertain
you. I have brought everything in my bags here.' She then
began to unpack picnic equipment that seemed more suitable
for an expedition to Everest than a *scampagnata* in the Italian

countryside. The supplies included a nearly full bottle of olive oil, two flasks of sour red wine, two large flat loaves of home-made bread the size of kettledrums, a can of anchovies in oil, six tin plates, an assortment of tin cups that didn't look very clean, two onions, a bottle of coffee, a jar of artichoke hearts in oil, a chunk of home-made bacon, seven tomatoes, sugar wrapped in newspaper, salt wrapped in newspaper, and a half round of pale yellow *pecorino* cheese.

Sora Nina took two country knives from her sack and set out at a fast pace into the field.

'Now I must find some greens for the *panzanella* (squeezed bread),' she trumpeted. I realized then that the trumpet was Sora Nina's normal speaking voice. Just as giraffes developed long necks to reach the tops of trees, so Canale women have, over the centuries, developed voices strong enough to reach their menfolk in the fields.

She came back with the pockets of her apron loaded with chicory and other assorted greens which she rinsed in a shallow pan of water. Then she took out a loaf of old bread, propped it against her chest, and began cutting big slices, pulling the knife dangerously towards her bosom as she did so.

Each piece of bread was doused in water and wine and carefully squeezed by hand. The dampened bread then went on to a tin plate, where it was covered with olive oil, a handful of mixed greens, and a topping of cooked salami, chopped olives and mushrooms in oil – '*panzanella*'!

It was delicious. As we ate the lady circled around us banging dollops on to our plates – a hunk of preserved anchovy, some aubergine in oil, and thin slices of preserved courgette.

'Eat! Eat!' the signora screamed at us. 'Don't be shy! When you eat with Sora Nina, it may be simple but at least it is genuine.'

Then she turned to a group of her friends who were sitting nearby.

'These people could be eating like princes at the American Embassy or with the President of the Republic; instead they have chosen to eat Sora Nina's *panzanella*.'

February

The First Pot

LOOKING BACK, I CAN PINPOINT THE EVENT WHICH would lead to the garden in the country. It was the gift of pale pink geraniums.

About three years before we started thinking of buying land outside the city, we moved into a top floor apartment near the Fontana de Trevi in Rome. Here for the first time we found ourselves the joyful owners of a smallish balcony which looked out on to the imposing Renaissance towers of the Quirinale palace, framed by towering palms and cypresses. The balcony was just wide enough for us to set up a small table and eat meals there and listen to the chimes of the palace clock which rang out the quarter hours.

Our daughter Jenny, who was seven, had been told by the *portiera* (concierge) that when a blue flag was flying from the tower it meant that the President of the Republic was in residence. So every evening when we sat down to supper, she would look for the blue flag, and if it was flying she would call out, '*Buon'appetito, Presidente Gronchi.*'

One of the first visitors to our fourth floor eyrie was a painter from Venice who brought me a pot of pink geraniums, and as I set it out on the balcony wall I saw how much prettier the Quirinale looked with the flowers in the foreground. What I did not fully realize was that this one pot of flowers was to trigger off a recessive gardening gene in me which would eventually extend to a house in the country, a cool greenhouse and an extensive collection of irises and Chinese roses.

But in the beginning I moved slowly. I bought a red geranium and then a white geranium to go with the pink and then I bravely bought a lavender wisteria in full bloom. It was while I was putting out the wisteria that I realized I was not alone in this chimney-pot world; our balcony overlooked a small community of other balconies and rooftops that stretched out across old Rome, and there I discovered Rome's secret army of terrace gardeners. They came out every morning in their pyjamas and dressing gowns and proceeded to potter around among the pots with the kind of care and devotion that you find only in true believers. They would repot a cactus, move a freesia to a more shady spot and whisk away all the dead flowers from their geraniums. They often ate their lunch or supper out on the terrace as we did, rising now and again to adjust a pot or clean up some fallen leaves. The late evening found them out again in their dressing gowns carefully watering their pots, sometimes with buckets of water lugged from the kitchen but usually with hoses or improvised tubes which came from makeshift taps. The hubbub of city living was four floors below.

In some ways pot gardening is the most satisfactory form of gardening there is, and for many city folk it is the only form of flower gardening they will ever know. If you compare results achieved to labour expended it is surprisingly efficient. You can put in only eight or ten pots, let them flower as they will, and if they don't do well you can tuck them into the background. You can move your pots around to get different colour schemes and make completely new effects by adding a flowering bush or even a small statue.

A pot garden can also be gentle on the purse, for most of the flowers that grow best on terraces are easy to propagate or can be acquired for very little money. The most common terrace plant, the geranium, is one of the easiest plants to reproduce. All you do is cut off a growing shoot at any time of the year, and you can be sure of having a flower within a month or two.

Outdoor vegetable markets are good places to buy plants; frequently you will find that the lady who is selling melons also has a few plantlets for sale, pulled headlong out of the earth and wrapped in packages of damp newspapers. She may not know the name of the flower, but she can usually tell you if it needs sun or shade, and how much water it requires.

For many years the wholesale flower market in Rome had the generous custom of opening its doors to ordinary gardeners on Tuesday mornings. This market was located in a series of catacombs across the piazza from the Basilica of Santa Maria Maggiore and it was every bit as exotic as the market in Papeete, Tahiti. It had that heavy damp feel of a tropical rainforest mixed with an almost tangible scent of musk and roses

and violets, and the scent grew heavier as the morning wore
on because there were no windows. There was always a
Dominican friar in brown robe and sandals standing in the
door with his cup in hand, asking for missionary money, and
behind him was a long tunnel bursting with flowering
roses.

If you proceeded down the right-hand tunnel, you would
come to banks of cut carnations, dahlias, asters, peonies,
mimosas and tropical flowers, and at the very end you would
reach a section that had potted flowering plants. There you
could pick up for a few hundred lire pots of nasturtiums,
azaleas, bougainvilleas and plumbagos and in between the
pots were packets of bare-root plants – asters, zinnias,
petunias, violets and larkspurs.

I would watch the Roman housewives shopping and
wonder what mysterious impulse lured them here each
Tuesday morning. They were a mixed group: smart Roman
matrons with well-cut hair and well-cut suits (the scissor is an
essential element in Italian chic) and an even larger group of
solid middle-aged women – the kind who wear the same
winter coat for ten years, and carry large well-worn bags
containing bedroom slippers, bus passes, an extra sweater, a
folding umbrella and two packets of fruit drops for the grand-
children. These women seemed unlikely to succumb to either
frivolity or fantasy, and yet I could see that they came to the
flower market because flowers were important in their lives.
They would tweak a petunia's leaves with a practised hand
and study a plant's root system with care before buying, and
when they went away there was a new hopeful light in

their eyes. They had found something they loved and they could hardly wait to get it home and try it on the terrace.

In time, to my regret, the flower market in the tunnel closed and a new market opened in a sanitary modern building that looked like a hospital in the Trionfale section of Rome under Monte Mario. The romance and smell of the old flower market was gone but the farmers and nurserymen who had switched to Trionfale greeted their faithful customers with a better assortment of flowers than ever. My terrace garden grew from one pot to thirty. I had five kinds of geraniums in bloom plus two lemon trees, a few pots of spring bulbs, and one pot for the Christmas tree which grew from a two-foot baby to a six-foot stringy adolescent in about five years. This tiny garden gave me hours of joy all year long, and in good weather it was not uncommon for me to spend an hour each day potting, repotting, worrying and tidying in the shadow of the presidential palace.

A friend came to lunch one day to find me still pottering when I should have been getting lunch.

'It's all right,' he said. 'Don't apologize, it's therapy.'

In 1959, when our daughter Jenny was seven, Henry was born and we found our flat on the Piazza Scanderbeg was too small for the four of us. We had to move to a larger place. The problem was that, having savoured the joys of a sunny balcony for so long, we could not face life in Rome without a terrace and this was not easy to find in the centre of the city. In the end we found an apartment which suited our needs on the Piazza Borghese near the Spanish Steps. The terrace was a bit larger than the one at Piazza Scanderbeg but it was lower down so

that it did not command such a spacious view; still, it had a
southern exposure, well shielded from the killing northern
winds, and a charming view of the little church of the Divino
Amore which lit up its electric cross every night when the sun
went down.

We had signed a contract with a moving firm but when the
men finally came to move us they took one look at our terrace
and announced, 'No pots.' An exchange of views followed. I
said if they didn't move the pots they couldn't move anything.
They said that potted plants were never included in moving
contracts, and that our demand that they lug lemon trees con-
stituted breach of contract if not outright fraud. We argued
that the smaller pots were no bigger or heavier to move than a
crate of dishes, so they agreed to move some of these. I then
busied myself jemmying the lemon trees out of their pots and
wrapping them, roots, lemons and all, in big plastic bags.
These in turn were tucked into the corners of some of our
larger *armadii* (wardrobes) and the movers lugged them down
the four flights of steps without even realizing what was in
them. The lemons suffered not at all from the drastic root
pruning; indeed they flourished.

A lot of foolish things have been written about the diffi-
culties of pot gardening, but the harbingers of doom are
generally wrong. The best terrace gardener I knew in Rome
was Eugene Walter, our actor, painter and writer friend from
Mobile, Alabama. He was told by a leading iris expert that it
was impossible to grow irises in pots. Eugene smiled his best
Etruscan smile and within a year he was growing huge clumps
of *Iris germanica*, *Iris sibirica* and even *Iris kaempferi* in small

terracotta pots on Piazza del Jesu. The secret, he said, was to use guano fertilizer from Tierra del Fuego.

But Eugene knew that there were limits to what could be done in a few square metres of dirt. So he drew up a set of rules.

The first was not to devote too much energy to any one plant.

'If it doesn't flower in the first year, move it to another place and give it a little more compost. If it doesn't flower in the second, put it out with the garbage. You can't waste time,' he said. The footnote to this rule was that if you are given any plants at Christmas or Easter or Valentine's Day, throw them away as soon as the holidays are over.

'They've been pumped full of monkey juice for the holidays,' Eugene said, 'so they can never live a natural life again.'

His second rule seemed on the face of it to contradict the first – if a plant that you have grown from a seedling suddenly turns sickly, try to find out what is ailing it. Look at the leaves and flowers to see if there are any bugs or diseases. Then look to the roots. My big Chinese wisteria which bloomed for many years on the terrace suddenly one spring started to look peaky. I watched it closely, trying to decide what was wrong and finally discovered that after a heavy rainstorm a puddle of rainwater lingered in its pot for the rest of the day. My wisteria was waterlogged. Eugene came over, and together we pried the plant out of its pot – a job that required a kitchen knife, a screwdriver and a hammer – and then we found that the roots of the wisteria had grown so large that they completely blocked the exit. The roots were stagnant. We gave the plant the root pruning of its life, filling the bottom of the pot with broken pottery and a new layer of fresh soil and for good luck Eugene also gave it two cupfuls of rice pudding, which he said was mother's milk to climbers. By the following spring our plant was blooming not only on our terrace but also on the terrace of the floor above.

Stagnant water may be a no-no, but Eugene found that as long as drainage is assured, you can't give a pot plant too much water in the hot weather. One sizzling hot summer he had to tend his own terrace plus that of his neighbour and fellow cat-saver Anna Magnani across the street. He established a schedule of watering his own terrace first, then he went over to Anna's at noon and did his own again at night. This meant that Anna's terrace got water once a day and his own twice, and his terrace came through the summer much better than Anna's.

His fourth rule was to pay close attention not only to the location of each pot, but also to the size. I had built up a good collection of pink and red geraniums, but I had trouble making the white ones grow. My white geranium, brought from Positano, remained rather feeble until one day a sharp wind from Africa blew the pot over and broke it. I simply scooped up the plant and stuck it into a corner of the wisteria pot, which was the biggest on the terrace and also contained Eugene's rice pudding. The white geranium was so grateful to have this space and special menu that it grew into a one-metre bush and produced close to eighty flowers by midsummer. Several guests mistook it for a hydrangea.

From all this it should be obvious where my first geranium

had taken me. I had moved from a couple of flowers to a whole terrace and I had even learned to grow a wax plant and a delicious night-blooming moon vine.

I knew that I was hooked, an authentic member of the flower clan, when I was struck down with Asian flu. One damp November I had a headache and a fever and I lay thrashing in bed, trying to entertain myself with a detective story. My attention wandered. I was morose.

'Can't I get you something else to read?' Robert asked.

'You know what I'd really like?' I said. 'I'd like the *Garden Encyclopaedia* and the catalogue from Thompson and Morgan.' He fetched them both and I spent a contented evening reading and making lists.

A few days later, the urge had become explicit.

'Honey,' I said, 'a terrace is nice but what we really need is a place in the country.'

Building the House

ONCE WE HAD FOUND OUR PARCEL OF LAND, THE IDEA was to build a simple little house that would fit into the landscape as if it had always been there. It would be a kind of shack really, somewhere we could go for weekends and summers, and we would soldier along without electricity or telephone just as the natives had for hundreds of years. To substitute for electricity we could install a gas refrigerator and gas lighting. Our heat and hot water would come from burning wood. (It took us quite a while to realize that living simply can be extremely complicated.)

But one thing we could not go without was water, and so our first effort was to find out if there was any water on the territory. We asked around and were advised that the only way to locate water was to find a *rabdomante* (water diviner) and several people suggested that we should look up a certain Fra Ubaldo, an elderly Franciscan who had ended up in a small monastery in the Oriolo area. It appeared that although Fra Ubaldo had had quite a good career as a water diviner when he lived in Rome, he had been transferred to the countryside for reasons not clear.

The monastery, when we found it, was an imposing stone building with a bell-tower hidden in a chestnut wood above Oriolo. At first glance it seemed to be uninhabited. Eventually two smallish men in brown robes appeared at the main doorway and the older of the two turned out to be Fra Ubaldo himself. A figure out of a Giotto fresco, he was small and round, with a trim white beard and an expression of deliberate solemnity. He was wearing a Franciscan habit of brown wool, belted by a white cord with a rosary hanging from it. His feet were clad in the traditional Franciscan sandals worn over a pair of thick brown wool socks.

We told him our business and he responded that he would be most happy to come and hunt for water for us, but since he had no transport we would have to fetch him the next day after he had performed his morning chores. He followed us as far as the car, remarking in a somewhat lower voice that whenever he went out dowsing, he made it a habit to ask for a contribution to the missionary fund. We said that would be no problem. He then added, almost as an afterthought, that he would need a forked willow twig to help him find the water, and a bottle of grappa, the rough, brandy-like distillation from the residue of grapes used in wine-making. He was accustomed to take a cup of coffee as it helped him with divining, he explained, but black coffee was so strong that he needed to dilute it slightly with the more mellow flavour of grappa.

We went to fetch him at the arranged time. The children came too as the idea of a Franciscan friar hunting for water with a stick intrigued them mightily. Henry, who was only five, thought it was some kind of game; but Jenny at twelve took a scientific interest and planned to write it up for her science class.

Since we had not yet built our house and were staying with friends in Quadrone we had brought a lunch basket with us, which included some *suppli* (rice balls), ham and cheese sandwiches, a thermos full of hot coffee, and bottles of Coca Cola, wine and grappa. Fra Ubaldo suggested that since it was nearly lunchtime, it might be better to have the picnic first and go about the arduous task of water divining afterwards.

We spread out the lunch next to the almond tree, and handed around sandwiches followed by the drinks in paper cups. Although Fra Ubaldo ate only one sandwich, he came back for wine three times, remarking on the excellence of the vintage. Once lunch was over, we offered him the coffee fortified with grappa, which he accepted with pleasure, and then he explained that he must go and meditate a while before he took on the strenuous business of discovering water. With this he settled himself with his back against the almond, and we realized soon afterwards that he was sound asleep. The first hour passed and he continued to sleep but at about three thirty the children, who had been kicking a football around, managed to kick one ball straight at the sleeping brother. He awoke with a start, expressed surprise at the lateness of the hour and led the children off to hunt for willow sticks.

They reappeared in ten minutes walking Indian file, the

friar in the lead holding a smallish forked stick straight in front of him and Jenny and Henry behind, each brandishing suitable forked sticks. The three walked very slowly, sweeping back and forth across the hillside, and occasionally Fra Ubaldo would hesitate and lower his willow stick so that it pointed more decidedly downwards. Then, after a pause, he would shake his head and resume his walking. After about fifty minutes of this, the three of them had climbed the hill until they were almost on a level with the almond tree again, when all at once Fra Ubaldo let out a low whistle, stopped dead, and the willow twig in his hands began to rotate very fast. Even though I regarded this operation with some scepticism, I was convinced that the twig was revolving of its own volition; and to my surprise Jenny's stick was too. (Fra Ubaldo also did the water divining for some friends of ours in Trevignano, and all three family members swear that the light heartwood *inside* his willow branch rotated so fast that it let out a cloud of white smoke.) At length, when he was sure he had water, he began very solemnly to count aloud: '. . . *venticinque, trenta, trenta-cinque.*' Then he announced, 'You will find water, a great river of water, at thirty-five metres exactly.' He reached into his pocket and pulled out a short pointed wooden stake, which he instructed Robert to pound into the earth, to mark the spot where the well should be drilled.

'Thirty-five metres,' he said. 'The Madonna was with me.'

To celebrate this triumph he suggested another round of grappa. Once this was finished, Robert gave him an envelope containing a generous contribution for the missions and we drove him back to the monastery.

A few days later a well digger from Cesano was contacted, and in time he arrived in his truck bearing the well-digging equipment, which consisted of a big generator for power, three wooden poles like smallish telephone poles which would form a tripod, and a lot of iron pipes, pipe connections, ropes and wires.

The well digger was a tall angular man named Antonio, who immediately made it clear that he did not approve of the fact that we had called in a Franciscan friar to find the water.

'These religious people should keep out of the water business,' he told us somewhat sourly. 'How do they know where the water is? You should have left it up to professionals like me.'

To protect himself from the possibly disastrous results of the friar's intervention, Antonio insisted that we sign a complex contract before he even started drilling. This stipulated that we were obliged to pay him 700,000 lire in advance for drilling our well and he would actually go down forty-five metres – but he would not refund any money if no water was found. In the usual well-digging procedure, when the well digger is also the *rabdomante*, he is prepared to guarantee that there is water where he says there is, and to back up this guarantee he will refund a quarter of the money if the well comes up dry. But if he is not the *rabdomante*, he takes little responsibility for the choice of spot, and if the well comes up dry he does not suffer.

Once the contract was signed, Antonio went to work setting up the wooden tripod which would support the well-drilling equipment. I had an idea he would use some kind of high-speed drill which would burrow down fast to find water – like oil drilling in the movies. Instead Antonio produced a big chunk of cement in the shape of a torpedo which he attached to a chain and rammed into the earth like a battering ram.

There was a metal triangle at the bottom of the torpedo which had a hollow space near the tip, and this apparently filled up with earth every time the battering ram crashed into the ground. It was then pulled to the surface and the hollow triangle – or scooper – was emptied out. It seemed to me that the amount of earth dumped was pitifully small, no more than a shoebox every time. I began to worry that with this system it would take at least six months to dig down the thirty-five metres. It was like trying to bail out an ocean liner with a couple of teacups.

In the event it took Antonio only ten days to smash his way down to thirty-five metres, but the bad news was that all he found was hard rock. No water. Swearing under his breath, Antonio bashed on and on, and the telltale noise of the battering ram resounded hollow over the Canale hills – bang, smash, quiet (while the torpedo was withdrawn) then bang, smash, quiet again. By this time we were going out every day to watch anxiously as our well proceeded, and a few local farmers joined us to remark that they had long feared there was no water in the area. (Their interest was not a form of triumphalism but genuine concern. They knew that if there was no water, the value of their nearby land would drop quickly, whereas if there was water, they would be able to dig their own wells at a far lower price than we had, since the guarantee against failure would no longer be needed.) Well, we went down to forty metres, then forty-two and forty-three, and all

Antonio was getting was hard rock. Antonio glared, and kicked at the torpedo. Tempers became frayed. And then, late one grey afternoon, the torpedo smashed down again and came up unbelievably dripping with water. Not clear water, but brownish water full of gravel. The next time there was more water and less gravel, and every time the torpedo was pulled up it was clearer and colder. It became obvious that there was plenty of water down there at forty-five metres. Antonio declared that he had hit a very deep *falda* (vein).

He began to get out the pipes to line the well, but a funny thing happened when he sent down his measuring rod to see how long the pipes should be. The water level had risen to thirty-five metres! What had happened was that once Antonio had blasted through the rock, the water below, which had been compressed, had risen swiftly to reach its own natural level of thirty-five metres. Pass around the cup in praise of Rabdomante Fra Ubaldo of Oriolo!

Having dispatched the problem of the well in such a seren-dipitous fashion, we tackled the house itself with high spirits. We had originally made an ingenious design for a U-shaped house with the open end facing to the south, like the villas at Herculaneum. The idea was that the central patio, cut off from unfriendly winds on the north and east, would be a perfect place to shelter delicate and tender plants and would also provide a sun-trap for dining out in chilly weather.

But this was not to be. A kindly architect friend reminded us that a low U-shaped house spread out over 250 square metres required a lot more roofing than a compact two-storey house where you can cover the same area with only 175 square metres of roofing. In most countries, roofing is a relatively minor matter, as you can cover a roof with tin or shingles or corrugated iron or even straw, but in Italy the absence of cheap wood means that roofing is the most expensive item in a house. Wood has been scarce in Italy ever since the Romans cut down the forests to build their Mediterranean fleets, so modern Italian builders are forced to dig clay from the ground and make substitute wood planks out of terracotta. The under layer of any roof is made of flat hollow tiles about the size of a thin coffee-table book which are held together by round iron rods pushed through the hollow centres. This makes a terra-cotta equivalent of a wooden board sixty centimetres wide and three metres long – and heavy as lead. On top of this layer of roofing material come the regular roof tiles called *coppe* (cups), which are the traditional humpback tiles (like wine bottles cut in half) and laid out flat. No cement is used to hold the *coppe* down; their weight is enough (theoretically) to hold them in place. It goes without saying that all this terracotta runs into a lot of money, not to mention a lot of weight. (And this great weight may, in fact, explain why so many Italians get smothered when their roofs fall on them during earthquakes.)

Given these problems, we were forced to settle for a compact two-storey rectangular house, eight metres wide and eleven metres across, and with a roof exactly half as big as originally planned. As Robert said, a matchbox with a balcony.

Before we began building the house we had to get permission, and to get permission we had to hire a local *geometra* (draughtsman) who would also serve as *direttore di lavoro* (site

manager). Enter Signor Romano Fiorello, a *geometra* from
Manziana. Signor Fiorello was a tall, good-looking man of
about thirty-eight who had all the necessary attributes. He was
an expert draughtsman; he knew how builders worked, he
knew what made cement crumble (too much sand, not enough
cement), and he had a talent for unblocking bureaucratic
bottlenecks. His technique was to blow a lot of cigarette smoke
in bureaucratic faces and shuffle basketloads of papers on their
already overcrowded desks.

If Signor Fiorello had any defect, it was his occasional
melancholy which was rooted, we soon discovered, in his
unhappy family life. We never knew the details, but it
appeared that his wife was a woman of fierce independence.
She would jog in the Manziana woods for two hours every
morning, starting at 6 a.m., a practice unheard of among
Manziana women in those days. She was also a committed
student of yoga, and she commuted regularly to Rome to sing
contralto in the Santa Cecilia choir. All of this activity left her
with very little time for the family. According to Fiorello, he
was never sure when he went home for lunch if there would
be any lunch prepared. She also did something that was extraordinary for an Italian housewife living in the country – she
sent the family laundry out to be washed and ironed.

Despite this neglect, which left the handsome Fiorello with
sharp trouser creases but unmatching socks and a five-day
growth of beard, he performed all his duties for us admirably.
He produced an excellent set of drawings for our square house
complete with arrows to show which way the doors opened (in
Italy doors always open inwards, to outfox thieves who could

otherwise unscrew door hinges) and he provided a sterling crew of five stonemasons from Tolfa, who promised to build the house in three months and, surprisingly, kept their word.

Their building methods were archaic to say the least. The masons (actually two masons and three *manovali*, mason's helpers) had very basic tools. Each man brought with him a *male-peggio* – literally 'from bad to worse' but actually a sharp stone-cutting implement, half hammer, half axe, which can crack rock into suitable sizes for building. The senior masons also carried in the back pockets of their overalls a flat trowel for slinging mortar, a folding wooden measure which could calculate the size of the stone, a roll of string with a lead weight on the end to use as a plumb line, and a spirit level. The younger men, being less specialized, had to make do with a plastic bucket for carrying mortar and a pair of strong shoulders; and we noted that in almost every building crew there would be one youngster who had the strong profile and muscular legs of a figure on an Etruscan vase.

To provide backup for this crew, a truck from Tolfa used to come by regularly carrying such items as an antiquated petrol-driven cement mixer, which was started by pulling a cord just like an outboard motor. It also carried a selection of wooden boards and planks, heavily spattered with old cement, which could be used for pouring new cement forms or making crude platforms where the workers could climb when building the house. The rough *peperino* rock, grey and brown in colour, was brought in from a quarry near the Mignone river and the truck also carried sizeable loads of *pozzolana*, a grey volcanic sand which was mixed with lime to provide mortar. The boss of the workers, a stocky young man named Vincenzo, had made an estimate of three million lire (roughly £2,000 in 1964) for building the house, and that was the price to the end!

There is little doubt that Robert and I, both thrifty Boston Yankees, saved a lot of money by researching the secrets of building *in economia* (do it yourself) in Italy. Our greatest discovery was a series of demolition yards located along the old Appian Way on the southern outskirts of Rome. There, spread out in the blazing sun, were acre after acre of building materials which had been torn from fine old Roman villas and buildings fifty and even seventy-five years old.

Lined up were rows of chestnut windows and window frames which had once looked down at the city from government buildings, walnut doors from forgotten embassies, small rustic doors from country villas, and even a set of tin-lined doors, with tiny outward-opening windows, which had come from a demolished prison.

There were spiral staircases, baths and showers in all sizes and shapes and miles of copper pipes, great heaps of fine oak panelling for libraries, and collections of used terracotta tiles known as *cotto* shining like ancient leather in the sunlight. There were wrought-iron gates and grilles and terrace railings, roof tiles, garden lamps and fine old stone fireplaces just looking for new houses to illuminate.

We spent two days at the Demolizione Appia yard with tape measures and notebooks trying to calculate what we might need, and finally after some extended haggling with the bristle-chinned junkyard owner, our shipment was ready to go. It had cost us a substantial sum – one tenth of the cost of our house – but the owner was so pleased with the deal he agreed to transport everything to our construction site in his own truck, free.

So the very next day a mixed bag of demolition goods was delivered to our astonished workers in Canale. The consignment included five huge wooden doors, one small prison door for our basement, fifty flat *peperino* tiles for garden paths, six hand-wrought terrace grilles, two wrought-iron garden lamps, two porcelain sinks, a stone birdbath, six wrought-iron candlesticks and fifteen large chestnut windows. The windows were the real gems in the collection, as they were lovely arched casement windows from a more gracious epoch and many of them still had their original glass panes which were hand-made and full of flaws like old bottles. Each of these sets of windows came with their own frames, plus movable inside wooden panels called *contraluci* (against the light) which could be swung shut to keep out the sunlight. In addition they were equipped with beautiful shutters known as *persiane*, narrow strips of wood fitted carefully into frames which could be closed and locked and were guaranteed to repel burglars. (The cost of each of these sets of windows was exactly 10,000 lire and I have been told that now, thirty years later, it would cost one million lire *apiece* for a carpenter to duplicate them. But we have no intention of replacing our beloved fittings; we simply scrape them down and give them a thick coat of paint and yacht varnish whenever we think they need it. And when we are too busy to do the job ourselves, we hire a painter who charges us more than 100,000 lire just to paint each window.)

Once the windows were delivered, the building job became easier; all we did was prop up the doors and windows where we wanted them, and instruct the builders to build around them. Slowly but surely the stones were cut and fitted around the windows and doors and gradually the walls crept higher and higher until we were ready to build the roof, using a combination of heavy chestnut logs and terracotta tiles.

The stone house which resulted from this was in some ways more like a barn than a house. There was no plastering in the interior, which meant that when the wind blew in winter it could blow someone's hat off indoors. Window sills were crude too, made of rough stone, so that if you leaned out of the window you would get sore elbows and the shelves in the bathroom and kitchen were made of rough *peperino* so that pots and bottles tended to fall off. But we were very happy with our rustic paradise. We had wanted something basic and basic was what we got. Now we could get to work on the thing we really cared about the most – the garden.

March

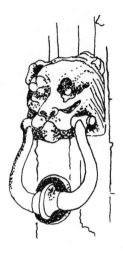

Planning with a Bulldozer

TRYING TO FILL A LARGE CHUNK OF ROUGH ITALIAN hillside with fragrant flowers and bushes that attract butterflies is not as easy as you might think.

For one thing the earth tends to be tough and non-resilient, having been trampled for hundreds of years by herds of grazing sheep. To put in an azalea someone had given me at Christmas, I had to use a heavy pickaxe. Furthermore, the sheep who grazed were surprisingly choosy about what they ate; although they loved everything that was green and tender they were decidedly against plants that prickled. So over the centuries the only crops that grew well were the crops the sheep eschewed, such as monster thistles and spiny blackberries which can rip large gashes in ankles and reduce cotton shirts to shreds.

Everybody we asked had a different idea of how to go about domesticating our soil and turning it into the kind of spongy black flour you read about in composting books. Some Canale farmers told us to plant the whole area with red clover, which would take about six months to mature, and once matured it should then be ploughed back into the earth to make green manure – another six or seven months.

There was a theory that we could soften the soil by covering it with a foot of compost material, but since we didn't have a compost heap (that would come later) this seemed impractical. There was also talk of putting the whole area to alfalfa, which by some mysterious process would fix nitrogen in the soil. But this involved a lot of big machines moving back and forth on the earth, and some of the permaculture people warned us that if we ploughed the soil, or even roto-tilled it a lot, the heavy machines would compact it even more than it was already compacted. There was also an idea of injecting bacteria into the soil, or trying out a special new grain that was revolution-izing farming in Uganda.

I went to the British Council Library in Rome and looked up a pamphlet on 'Soil Types in the Roman Campagna', only to learn that the soil north of Rome is volcanic, potentially fertile but historically overgrazed, holding locked in its stubborn grip any number of rich minerals which need only to be 'gently turned over by hand and freshened with a mixture of manure and green matter'. Oh dear. The article added – apparently in the hope of cheering up the reader – that since our soil was belched up from the earth's hot belly in the form of molten lava and ash, it had a granular texture and no rocks at all. The absence of rocks was wonderful of course, but not really all that important when you considered that the whole territory was one solid rock to begin with.

To keep up my morale, I continued to draw plans on yellow lined paper carefully marking out the areas where the borders and 'island beds' would be. I made wide loops to indicate the flower groups, big circles for the shrubs and squares for the flowering vines.

But there is an old American saying, 'Life is what happens when you are making other plans', and one day as I was sketching some new ideas I realized that my plans would have nothing to do with the way my garden turned out. Events move faster than you expect. That very morning a truck had rumbled in with iron pipes and had beaten down my newly planted lilacs. Several days earlier our neighbour Jack's wife, Sora Nina, had come over when we were away and planted a big clump of Mexican yuccas right on top of my salvia seedlings. (The earth was softer there.)

You realize in the end you are really not in command of anything. What will happen will happen, and it will no doubt be something too dreadful to contemplate. So I tore up all the clippings from *Maison & Jardin*, flicked the switch on to automatic pilot and decided to go with the flow.

A perfect example of the uselessness of planning came when we were suddenly called upon to decide about the driveway which would lead from the main road to the house. Since this was a distance of five hundred metres I had tentatively sketched a U-shaped drive which would permit visitors to enter the property at one point and exit at another, admiring the peonies and fruit trees as they went.

But none of the builders appreciated my graceful circular

approach. It was too ornate; it would ruin too much good land that would be better put to alfalfa. It would complicate the mowing in spring and make the hay baling impossible. It would provide a perfect escape route for motorized thieves or runaway horses.

And then fate intervened again in the form of a very large truck which came lumbering through the rain bearing at least fifty quintals of newly quarried *peperino* stone for our side walls and front terrace. Since the rains had not started when the earlier rocks were delivered, there had been no problem about driving from the road to the house on the hard-packed fields.

But now it had been raining for two days and the fields had gone soggy, making the truck driver nervous. He got out of the vehicle, a stout fellow with a red face wearing a jogging sweater marked 'Massachusetts Institute of Technology', and stamped his boot into the gummy earth. Then very deliberately he began to untie the back flap of his truck, preparatory to unloading the rocks on the still-solid road – an operation which made it clear to the builders that they would have to lug the rocks from the road to the house in wheelbarrows. This threat galvanized their attention and they came tearing across the field yelling to the driver to close the back flap and keep his cool; there was absolutely no danger that he would get *piantato* ('planted') in the field. Vincenzo got there first to assure him that if he chose a high track right across the top of the land, he could make it to the house in less than a minute.

The driver climbed back into his cab, shaking his head with foreboding. Very gingerly he turned the wheel hard right and pointed straight towards the half-built house. The truck inched carefully on to the field and proceeded gradually southward until the wheels began to spin – at which point he frantically threw the gears into reverse, in the hope of getting back on the firm road again. But it was too late; the harder he gunned in reverse, the more the wheels sank, and by the time he had gone forwards and back a few times, he was mired up to the hubcaps, and furious. Scenes of chaos followed. Vincenzo ordered his men to try to create some traction by throwing down boards and lengths of tarpaper (intended for the roof), but this only threw a fine coating of mud over the boards and the sweating workers.

The men then tried pouring sacks of cement on to the ground, in the hope that this would harden a little and sop up some of the moisture to give the wheels something to grab on. But in spite of their efforts the great truck refused to budge.

Beside himself with rage, the driver descended from his cab and stalked over to Vincenzo and for a moment we thought he was going to hit him. But instead he shouted, 'Blast the Madonna and all the Madonna's children. You have planted my truck in this goddamn pig pasture and I will probably be planted here until June when the rain stops.'

Then in a paroxysm of rage he flung himself into the cab again, started the motor, pushed a lever and the back of the truck rose until the rocks began tumbling out over the back flap, strewing about a third of the cargo on to our soggy field. Instant Stonehenge.

His idea was, apparently, that if he dumped enough rocks he would lighten his truck so that he could get himself unstuck, but after repeated attempts he realized he wouldn't get out until he was pulled out. He then commandeered a motorcycle from one of the builders and roared up to Canale in search of Massimo, the mechanic and driver for the Canale cooperative (Università Agraria) which owned the biggest bulldozer in the area. The report came back that Massimo was off cutting a new dirt road through to the Baths at Stigliano, but that he would be sent down to us at seven the next morning.

We all assembled on the hilltop at six forty-five. The rain had mercifully stopped but the mired truck surrounded by mounds of *peperino* stone and dirty-white cement gave our property the look of an old car dump.

Shortly thereafter, we heard a tremendous clanking and banging of metal down the road and the village bulldozer hove into view. It was a huge machine, much larger than the mired truck, and it ran on a set of moving chains like a Mark IV tank. Thus when Massimo came rumbling on to the scene he was accompanied by such a rattling and whistling that he sounded like Rommel's Afrika Korps advancing on Tobruk.

Massimo himself was a big man, easily six feet three, with black hair and ink-black eyes and he was wearing a wide Mexican hat which gave him a look of Pancho Villa. The big man surveyed the scene, glancing with distaste at the truck and the discarded rock heap. There were no salutations, no pleasantries about the weather.

'*Porca Matosca*,' he muttered.

This is a fairly blasphemous expression which takes the

Madonna's name in vain, but which attempts to lighten the blasphemy by mispronouncing it – like using 'darned' for 'damned'.

Without further ado, he threw his machine into first gear and manoeuvred it to the front of the truck, and then he pitched two lengths of iron chains to Vincenzo, ordering him to hitch them to the stuck vehicle. Once they were attached, he inched his way forward until the chains were taut. There was one ghastly moment when it looked as if the chains would break, but then the truck began to shudder as if it had just awakened from a terrible dream, and slowly the wheels started to move. A small cheer went up as the two dinosaurs moved haltingly across the field to the house, bulldozer out front, truck lurching behind it. As soon as the convoy arrived, the truck driver leaped out and cut himself loose from the bulldozer, and then proceeded to dump his cargo close to the back door. The crisis was over.

We offered coffee, fortified with grappa, to the assembled onlookers and it was only as we were pouring out a second victory cup that we realized the bulldozer driver was among those missing.

We soon discovered that Massimo, always a stickler for neatness, had returned to the scene of the disaster to tidy up. He had run his machine back and forth several times from the public road to the house following the line which the truck had taken. When he came to the difficult part, full of fallen rocks and muddy tyre holes, he had simply shoved his blade straight through – like a grandmother cutting the frosting on a birthday cake – and swept all the broken rocks and boards and cement to the sides so they made a modest wall along the newly packed driveway.

'There,' he said, pointing proudly to his handiwork, 'your entrance road is now finished.'

Finished it was indeed. And so was the U-shaped drive bordered by flowering peonies.

Once this job had been done, the big man consented to come in and have a coffee with us. He refused to let us lace it with grappa, explaining that he never accepted spirits until after the sun had passed halfway across the horizon towards Tolfa.

As he stepped on to the terrace he let it be known that if we had been English he would not have come.

'I have never got along with the English,' he told us, taking a long drink of coffee. 'Frankly, when they were here during the war, their officers were very *prepotenti* (stuck up). They wouldn't eat in the same restaurants as the soldiers. The Americans were more democratic, but they wouldn't listen to what we told them either. A lot of Americans are very stupid.'

Further conversation revealed that Massimo was a Communist and although he had been too young to enrol in the Italian army during the Second World War, he had been involved in partisan activities in the last months of hostilities. At a sharp curve on the road to Tolfa he and a gang of Canale youngsters had planted a landmine which had blown up a German staff car, and he had also volunteered to help a group of Australian fliers who had been shot down near Bracciano and were hiding out in the Manziana woods. The young Canalesi took turns guarding the Aussies and bringing them food, and eventually Massimo led several of them south to rejoin the Allied troops just before the final push on Rome.

We felt called upon to produce some wartime exploit which would win us approval in the eyes of this freedom fighter, but nothing appropriate came to mind. To make up for this, Robert offered to show some of the wax statues he had made which he would soon cast in bronze. Massimo was immediately impressed. Here was an American, no doubt a rich American and probably stupid, but he did not spend his time exploiting the workers. He wore dirty blue jeans and worked with his hands and was, as a result, an honorary member of the working classes.

He clapped a large hand on Robert's shoulder.

'OK, comrade,' he said, 'I've got the bulldozer down here for the whole morning. Let's start getting this place cleaned up.'

The two of them went out to claim the bulldozer and for the rest of the morning they worked in surprising harmony to make order out of chaos. Their strategy was simple: Robert walked to a pile of junk that needed moving, and Massimo would roar in with his bulldozer blade and shove it bodily towards an outlying area that they had designated the official dump. Load after load of broken tiles and shattered ceramics, large paper sacks, leftover rolls of tarpaper, empty wine bottles and crumpled cigarette packets were heaped together on the dump on the far edge of the olive grove, and as they came back towards the house Massimo would carefully scrape up all the thistles and briar patches which stood in his way and put them in a pile for burning. It was a joy to watch as he manoeuvred his great hulking machine with the delicacy of an embroiderer doing a hem stitch – a flick of the blade here, a scoop there, and the land was tidy as a tablecloth.

By high noon, the worst of the junk had been consigned to oblivion, but there still remained the three great heaps of earth that had been removed to make the basement.

'There is only one thing to do with all that earth – terrace it,' Massimo said as he joined us for a lunch of spaghetti. 'You wouldn't know, being Americans, but the only way to stop your house from sliding down the hill in a rainstorm is to level the land out into terraces and build walls to support them. You can grow tomatoes on one level, and maybe some fruit trees on another and fig trees below. If you look at any good Italian farm, you will see that they have been making terraces here for a thousand years. Otherwise you will float away with the first storm.'

I started to object that I had already made a pretty garden design. I wanted to put in a long double border leading from the pumphouse to the house; I wanted to set up a laburnum arbour which would turn pure gold in early May, and I wanted some more protected gardens near the house where I could grow clumps of tender agapanthus and plumbago, and possibly even some espaliered lemon trees. I also wanted a large open space near the house where we could have a pool – a small horse-trough pool – which could be fitted with a splashing fountain, visible from our living-room terrace.

Massimo looked at me, and then poured his third tumbler full of red wine. (He had explained that as long as he was eating lunch he could permit himself a glass or two of wine.)

'But Signora Giovanna,' he protested, 'of course you can have a pool. I will dig one for you later. Any place you want. But you cannot build a swimming pool into the side of a steep hill. You need terracing, and walls to hold the terrace. Then we'll think of the pool.' He looked across the table and caught Robert's eye, and it seemed to me that Robert made a very slight nod. He was a man who liked getting things done fast, and he figured that if you had a friendly bulldozer sitting there ready to go to work it would be insanity to send it away.

I saw that I could not prevail against these two, so as soon as the meal was over I drove off to visit Anthea in Pisciarelli. Our friends Anthea and Luigi were at about the same stage in house building as we were. Anthea and I had already exchanged views on the mysteries of converting wild stubble fields into gardens.

When I drove up her woody lane in Pisciarelli, I could see that there were two small tractors working in the field in front of her stylishly modern house.

'We're all having a big day with machines,' said I. 'We have a bulldozer over in Canale, and you have two tractors.'

'I'm not sure about it,' my friend replied in a slightly querulous tone. 'Someone told Luigi that we should plough that field and then plant alfalfa.'

'Why alfalfa?' I asked.

'I don't really know that either,' she said. 'I think it's supposed to enrich the soil.'

'And what will you do when they cut the alfalfa?'

'That's what worries me,' Anthea sighed. 'I'm afraid that,

when the alfalfa is gone, the field may be so enriched that the weeds will grow higher than ever.'

We repaired to her half-finished terrace for a cup of tea, and she brought up the subject of swimming pools. Luigi, a civil engineer, had been making enquiries.

'Luigi thinks they might take a lot of looking after. His friends say that they spend more time cleaning their pools than swimming in them. They always make them white, of course, which means that all the spots show.'

Anthea paused, meaningfully. She was good at meaningful pauses because she was an actress.

'I have something else against swimming pools,' I said. 'I think they are ugly. No matter how hard people try to make them pretty with blue tiles and white travertine, they always end up with that Day-Glo turquoise colour which destroys all the other colours in the garden.'

We both sighed.

'I had a friend in Genoa who got a special landscape architect just to make her a pool of black stone – basalt, I think – to avoid the turquoise effect,' said Anthea.

'And how did that look?' I asked.

'Dreadful, it was so dank I didn't dare put a toe in for fear something would bite.'

I remarked that the only nice country pool I had seen in Italy was an old horse-trough made out of native *peperino* with water lilies in it.

'But if you get a horse-trough, I suppose you should have a horse to go with it,' Anthea mused.

I little realized how prophetic this statement would be.

After a few years of country living, Luigi and Anthea would end up with six horses, four dogs and eighty-three turkeys. Some people go for animals; others go for flowers and fruit trees.

I arrived back on the hillside of Canale just as Massimo was closing down for the day. I found my whole garden laid out in terraces. There was one wide circular terrace by the front door, and two small terraces next to it. Then, ranged below like the lower steps on the Tower of Babel, was one terrace (suitable for dining) with olive trees, and a second for tomatoes and basil. Everything around these terraces was bare, scraped clean like a hard-boiled egg.

'Isn't it wonderful?' Robert said. 'The builders will put up some stone retaining walls to hold the earth, and then you can grow vines on them or anything else you want.'

It was at this point that I noticed a sizeable crater over in the middle of the olive grove where it looked as if a meteor had fallen.

'What's that?' I asked.

'That's the surprise,' said Massimo. 'That's going to be the swimming pool. I have a cousin with a stoneyard over near Trevignano. He can get you some blue tiles to line the pool, and on the outside you can put in a good wide edging of white travertine.'

I must have looked crestfallen because Robert came over and patted my arm.

'Don't worry, honey, it's all going to be beautiful. Next week Massimo is coming back to help plant the trees and fix up the pool. He'll do it partly with the *ruspa* (bulldozer) and partly with dynamite.'

Massimo did indeed come back the following week on the *ruspa*, accompanied by his cousin Spartaco the dynamiter. They were towing a trailer loaded with balled and burlapped cypresses and other conifers.

'I've just been around to the Forestale,' Massimo announced, 'and they gave me all these trees. There are about a hundred cypresses. Half of them should go along your driveway and the other half should go in the windbreak on the north side of the house. The rest are big pines to go down near the woods.'

The two men unhooked the trailer and set off on the *ruspa* towards the lower field. Spartaco was a dynamiter straight out of central casting, a muscular fellow in a pair of khaki camouflage shorts and a sleeveless green undershirt, with a green bandanna on his head. He carried a wooden box with a red hand flag attached to it, containing all his explosive gear.

As soon as the two men had reached the lower field, Massimo detached the bulldozer blade and inserted a huge iron drill which was powered by the tractor motor. He then proceeded to drive in large circles around the field, stopping now and again to lower the drill and dig a hole roughly two metres deep into the earth. Once fifteen holes had been dug, Massimo clanked off to fill in the swimming pool (which I had rejected) leaving Spartaco behind to shove pieces of electric wire, fuses and dynamite into the pre-drilled holes. The red flag was then set into the earth not far from the proposed explosion site, and Spartaco knelt down and lit the fuse. As we all stood on the upper terrace with our hands ready to block our ears, we could see Spartaco walking casually away from the hole. Nothing happened for a moment and we decided the dynamite was a dud, and then there was a low roar from deep inside the earth and a kind of buckling on the earth's surface and a shovelful of dirt came spurting from the hole. Two hooded crows who had been feeding nearby flapped into the air with squawks of alarm.

Spartaco pulled out his wires and popped the first of the pine trees into the new hole like a boy putting a straw into a bottle of Coke. He then picked up his red danger flag and moved on to the next hole, and the dynamiting continued.

Massimo noisily shovelled earth back into the rejected swimming-pool hole, cutting a few chunks out of the olive trunks as he did so, and once the earth was smooth he rumbled north and began digging two long ditches parallel to the entrance drive where the cypresses were going to be planted.

If the truth be known, it was not a restful morning. When Spartaco wasn't setting off his explosives, Massimo was backing and filling in the ditches, and the air resounded with the thunderous booms from the lower field alternating with the steady roar from the bulldozer on the top. Around noon there was an ominous clank from the bulldozer. After inspecting the engine, Massimo announced that a gasket was broken, so he and Spartaco went off to Canale to get new parts.

They resumed operations in the early afternoon, at which point I had dragged a deckchair out under an olive tree hoping to take a nap. The next thing I knew Jenny was pulling at my sleeve.

'Mommy, you must come, the bulldozer has dug up something very very funny.'

We went out behind the house, and there we found the bulldozer stalled at the top of a long curving ditch. Its huge blade had been lifted up, and hanging from it like fish from a giant fishnet were a cluster of awkward sticks and tubes and twists of wire that had clearly come up in the excavation. My first thought was that they were tree roots that had somehow got in the bulldozer's way, or perhaps the blade had dug up some strange Etruscan relics.

'What is it?' I asked. 'It looks like spaghetti.'

'Spaghetti!' thundered Massimo. 'You know what it is, it's water pipes – the water pipes that bring water from the pump to the house. Nobody told me to watch out for water pipes.'

I was speechless.

'You know what, Mommy,' Jenny said, trying to comfort me, 'why don't we send all the machines home and dig our holes by hand from now on.'

The Fine Art of Planting Seeds

AFTER THE TRAUMA OF DYNAMITING HOLES FOR TREES, I looked forward to the gentler pleasures of planting tiny seeds and watching them emerge silently as little green seedlings.

I have always been a compulsive collector of seeds. I am drawn like an addict to seed packets on display at nurseries, supermarkets and flower stores and like all addicts I have drawers full of seeds which have lost their labels and even their envelopes.

I do most of my collecting when I travel, hoping, I suppose, to bring my travels home with me, and every time I return from a trip I unpack with great care because every sock, every glove and every pocket is crammed with hopes and memories. As I unpack, I hear the high voice of a little Indian boy who was taking tea with his mother on the hotel terrace at Brindivan, near Mysore.

'But, Mama, what is that American lady doing crawling under the banana tree?'

I would like to make it clear that I am a responsible seed collector. I take only seeds which are abundant and which nobody else wants – seeds gathered in waste places, forgotten alleyways and abandoned gardens.

Once unpacked, I line my seeds up on the window sill to dry out and wait for the Ides of March, the season when traditionally in central Italy you plant most of your seeds. Just as there are a dozen formulas for rescuing fallen mayonnaise and getting ink spots out of white linen suits, so seedsmen have a dozen ideas about how to turn hard little seed pellets into living and growing green things.

Thompson and Morgan, the British firm where I do much of my mail-order shopping, has a special booklet on sprouting seeds.

'To be successful with many seeds,' the catalogue says, 'particularly the exotic varieties, a seed propagator is imperative.'

The Park seed people from Greenwood, South Carolina, offer a 'bio-grow' seed-starting kit which consists of a collection of thin brown cakes of compressed growing medium about three centimetres across. You poke your seeds into the top of these, wet them, and they blow up like chocolate soufflés, full of their own nutrients. Once the seeds have sprouted in the heart of the soufflé, you plant the whole thing in your garden.

One garden writer who takes a no-nonsense approach to seed planting is Mrs Josephine Nuese from Lakeville, Connecticut. In *The Country Garden* she puts it this way:

For countless years I raised countless annuals in the house each winter, without benefit of any modern luxuries and usually the seedlings turned into magnificent plants, far better than any I could buy. I started the seeds in pie tins (the old-fashioned kind until the foil jobs came along) and my own starting mix, sterilized the seed by shaking up a pinch of Semesan in the seed packet, kept the pans in the guest room with the heat turned low, and hustled the pans into the sunlight whenever and wherever there was sunlight.

Another school of thought insists that seeds sprout best when subjected to constant mist, as at the bottom of Niagara Falls. An English writer, Deenagh Goold-Adams (author of *The Cool Greenhouse Today*), keeps a steady shower of mist blowing on to the soil from the moment she plants seeds until young plants come up. This system, needless to say, requires electrical equipment. You need an electric control box, a solenoid valve which turns the water on and off and an electronic 'leaf element' which regulates the frequency of the misting. If you can handle all this, then you spread out a John Innes seed compost and moisten it down.

Mrs Goold-Adams comments: 'Opinions differ as to whether to give a light watering with a fine rose after seeds are sown or whether to water from below either before or after sowing the seeds. In any case, moist soil and a moist temperature need to be maintained either in a propagating case or by covering the receptacles with glass or plastic until germination takes place.'

My feeling is that seeds should sprout as nature intended,

but even here there are problems. For instance, the role played by birds and animals in the germination of seeds is only just beginning to be understood. Take the case of the sapota tree which used to grow to a great age on the island of Mauritius. All the sapota trees on Mauritius today are elderly, and no young trees are coming along.

Botanists began to study this mystery and discovered that while the sapotas still make edible fruits, none of the local birds or animals seemed to have a taste for them. Acting on a hunch, they tried force-feeding the fruit to turkeys. And guess what happened? Once the seeds had passed through the stomachs of the turkeys, they began to germinate the way they used to two hundred years ago.

The botanists scratched their heads and wondered what large vegetarian, now vanished, had been walking around Mauritius several hundred years ago, eating sapota fruits. It didn't take them long to remember. The dodo!

The sapota tree apparently could not germinate until its seeds passed through the digestive tract of a dodo. When the dodo disappeared the sapota began to die out too. But now with the help of stubborn people and reluctant turkeys, the good old sapota tree may once more flourish on the island.

This at least was the story as I first read it in a wildlife magazine. I have now discovered that the story has a post-script. The biologist Stephen Jay Gould, in his book *The Panda's Thumb*, recounts that after the first revelations were made about this 'mutualism' between tree and dodo, a killjoy biologist in the Mauritian Forestry Service, one Dr Owadally, wrote to *Science* magazine to question the story.

Dr Owadally pointed out that the tree – which turns out to be a tambalacoque and not a sapota – grows in the upland rainforests of the great island, and not on the plains where the dodo used to wander. Further, Dr Owadally suggests that some of these trees on Mauritius may well be only seventy-five to one hundred years old. And the dodo became extinct in 1675.

Mr Gould refuses to make any final judgement. He says that if the Mauritian botanist is correct and there really are trees less than one hundred years old then the dodo thesis collapses. Still, he is rooting for the mutualism theory and so am I. Otherwise, how to explain the failure of this tree to reproduce itself in the twentieth century?

As for my own seed theories, I tend to divide seeds – like Gaul – into three groups.

There are seeds that will come up no matter what you do to them as long as you don't sprinkle them on toast. This includes annual larkspur, annual poppies (formerly known as opium poppies) and such easies as zinnias, snapdragons, marigolds, calendulas and sweet peas.

The snapdragons have two problems: they are so tiny they are in danger of being washed away, and ants have a passion for them. I try to sow them on top of the soil and I put their pot in a bowl of water to discourage ants.

The larkspurs and poppies are absolutely foolproof, providing me with lovely sheets of blue and pink flowers every spring, but I no longer pay any attention to the writers who suggest planting them in early spring. If they are planted in September before the cold sets in, they will make much healthier plants in May.

Then there is a second group of seeds which is trickier –
biennials or perennials, which are often quite slow to
germinate. This is usually because they have a hard coat and
need to be soaked or chipped so that they will let moisture in.
Lupin seeds, for instance, also need nicking and should be
soaked overnight in water. I have learned not to be in too
much of a hurry for perennials of this sort. I put one batch of
seeds in a pot one September and forgot about them. In the
spring when I was cleaning out the pots on my terrace, I
started to empty one when I noticed some little green seedlings
among the weeds. It was the lupins germinating at last. They
had taken six months to come up.

The seed of the passionflower is another tough little object
and should be nipped with a pair of scissors before being sown.
I had one batch of passionflower seeds which began to sprout
in about twenty days but then continued to sprout as the spirit
moved them for the next eight months. The moral of this story
is never to throw out the earth in pots where seeds have been
sown. If need be, plant other seeds in the same pots: but never
take it for granted that just because a pot appears empty it does
not harbour, unsprouted, some little gem for your garden.

Just as teachers love their most difficult students so I confess
I have a weakness for the third category of seeds which is the
most difficult of all. These are the seeds of tropical flowering
trees and I like them best because they make such a magnificent entrance into the world.

The flamboyant tree, or *Delonix regia*, is an operatic production in every way. The seed pod of this scarlet beauty is a
leathery bean about a foot long, and it takes a screwdriver or

a hammer to get it open. The seeds inside are about an inch long and harder to crack than walnuts.

But when this giant decides to germinate you know at once that Something is Happening. First the big green shoulder of the sprout appears in a loop like a miniature Tower Bridge. Then the loop uncoils to bring forth two cotyledons or seed leaves. These open gradually, and soon the delicate feathery leaves of the tree itself spring out from between the seed leaves, and you know you are in business.

I had collected many flamboyant seeds on my travels, but my luck in persuading them to sprout was spotty. I would pop them into my seed box, keep them well watered, and hope. If I got one seedling out of a dozen seeds planted I was doing well. I would then do some judicious digging and in time I found that most of my flamboyant seeds were not germinating because moisture was not penetrating their hard shells.

I consulted the experts. Some said to soak the seeds overnight in hot water. Some said rub them with an emery board. Some recommended cracking the seeds with a nut-cracker to let in the moisture.

This last suggestion seemed the most direct to me, so I developed a system of nipping off the pointed tip of my flamboyant seeds with a pair of sharp garden scissors and then putting them on damp cotton to sprout. An old tin cigar-box or a cough-drop box lined with damp cotton made a good home for sprouting seeds and had the advantage of being portable. I could even keep track of them at dinner parties. Most of my seeds so treated began to show green within about two days, and once I was sure that something was growing, I would hustle them into a pot filled with good damp compost.

The difficulty with this system was that it was artificial and various things could go wrong. The worst was that the seed coat, having been pierced artificially, would open just enough to let the root out, but would keep the growing part of the plant, the cotyledons, clutched in an iron embrace. I often had seedlings which germinated very well, but when they sent up their sprout the seedcase was wrapped hard around the two seed (or top) leaves and strangled them. To avoid this I would try to pull the seedcase off without hurting the plant within. If it wouldn't pull off I would cut it or slit it with a razor, but this was hazardous. I finally developed a technique of slitting my seeds down the sides with a razor before putting them on to cotton.

There is another problem with inducing labour. The seeds which have been nicked and have sprouted sometimes lose their bearings when they are planted in earth and start to grow down. If a seedling has not made an appearance after it has been in the earth for a week I burrow down in the soil and look for it, and if it is heading in the wrong direction I turn it around. Robert complains that all this meddling is doing the seedlings no good, but I reply that I am doing what any good midwife would do.

I use this rather rough technique with all the hard-crusted tropical seeds and I believe that my batting average is pretty good. My problem is not in getting the seeds to sprout but in developing the results into full-grown flowering trees. Getting them through the chilly winters is the most difficult. I have tried them indoors in the sunny dining room. This treatment, however, is far from ideal because the dining room is dry and the plants miss the moist heat they are used to. I am lucky to get through the winter with one quarter of my small exotics. I have had a few successes, I am happy to say. I have brought several *Cassia corymbosas* through and they are now big flowering trees, giving us great swaths of yellow in mid-summer. I have also managed to bring on a couple of unidentified cassias that I got in Sarawak, and a little longan tree from a fruit which I bought in the Yucatan. I don't know if this will ever give me a fruit.

However, I am still working on some of the more glamorous ones. At least five times I have started *Cassia grande*, that glorious pink cassia from Ceylon, and I have had trees that have made it to forty centimetres and then given up. I am also still struggling to get a big poinciana. I babied one along until it was sixty centimetres tall, which was bigger than the poinciana at Kew, but then it mysteriously expired. The closest I have come to it is a beautiful little relative which is somewhat hardier, the *Cassia gilliesi*. This marvel with its feathery leaves and its extraordinary poinciana flowers with yellow petals and aggressive spikes of crimson stamens now adorns a prominent spot on my terrace. It has survived three tough winters so I think we have made it.

My friends tell me that I am too anxious about my seeds, that I should relax and let nature take its course. But I am given courage in my struggles by some old-timers in the plant world who dig up seeds, turn them over, and meddle with them even more than I do.

A man whose expertise I respect is the tropical tree

authority Edwin Menninger, whose book *Flowering Trees of the World* is a bible to tree planters. Menninger, brother of the Menninger psychiatrists, has spent more than thirty years exploring the world of tropical trees, and he has grown from seed and distributed to gardeners all over America more than one hundred thousand trees. His imagination and ingenuity in getting seeds to sprout shows the dedication of a true scientist. He tells, for instance, of his harrowing time trying to get a teak tree to take off:

> Some years ago the author received from Calcutta a package of seeds of the famous timber tree, Teak (*Tectonagrandis*). The seeds are about the size of garden peas, but each one is covered with a thick corky rind, making the whole as big as a marble. The seeds were dry, so were placed in a glass of water to be soaked overnight, but they were so buoyant that the water failed even to wet their surfaces. Another glass jammed into the first, kept the pellets under water, but next morning when released they popped to the top as dry as ever despite the immersion. Out came a knife and file, and a lot of the corky rind was cut away. The seeds were soaked another twenty-four hours, then planted. No germination. Every few days an exploratory dig showed that nothing was happening. Perusal of some Indian books turned up a chapter in Cleghorn on 'How to Grow Teak Trees from Seed'. This sounded pertinent and the eighteen pages were greedily devoured; about all the book said was that germination was difficult. However, a gleam of light emerged from one sentence. Observers had found, the book said, that after the annual brush fires swept

through the teak forests of Burma, an immediate upcropping of seedlings resulted. Oh! Oh! The author went out to the propagating shed, dug up the poor little teak seeds for the umpteenth time, put them in the family popcorn popper, and shook them over a slow fire. Pop! Pop! went the seeds, like so many little firecrackers. Back into the vermiculite they were plunged and 100 per cent germination resulted.

A second Florida authority who had years of experience in introducing tropical plants was a Dr M. Simonson. He wrote about seed development.

My experience with seed germination mostly covers soaking in hot water or filing, or both. I have had fifteen-year-old Acacia seeds germinate after such treatment. The same applies to many legumes. As I sit here writing this I have a beautiful fifty-foot-high *Schizolobium excelsum* outside the window. I got the seed January 29, 1950. I planted it at once and nothing happened; the incident was forgotten. A year later working over some old potting soil I found the familiar hard seed unchanged. I had more time then and I filed a small place on the edge and planted the seed again. In five days it sprouted with this present result. Just last year it began to branch at about forty feet from the ground and now has two beautiful heads with its six-foot-long leaves.

A man after my own heart.

April

Finding the Perfect Helper

ONE OF THE JOYS OF LIVING IN ITALY IS THAT IF YOU CROSS your fingers and breathe softly, you can hang on to autumn so long that it eventually blends into spring. Winter seems to be lost in the scuffle. Or if winter does make an appearance, it is so fleeting that it does not cause much trouble. One day you wake up and it is cold and blowy but two days later you are having lunch out on the sunny terrace, and you are so hot you have to take your sweater off.

In our area we can be picking chrysanthemums and roses right up to Christmas and while they are still in flower we will notice spots of blue coming up beside them. These are the blue Algerian irises (*Iris unguicularis*) which start blooming as early as November, and as the days get gradually warmer more blue appears along the garden paths until it looks as if a chunk of sky had fallen to earth. The flower first looks like a tiny green furled umbrella in the midst of its spiky foliage, and then it opens to reveal lavender blue petals with the yellow sepals in the centre.

The butter-yellow winter jasmine flowers at the same time, and can be combined with the blue iris to make a nice tuzzy-muzzy for your table. To this you can add the soft pink flowers of *Bergenia crassifolia*, which in March poke their heads through the handsome round leaves which cover the ground all year long.

The next serious arrivals are the spring daffodils, dainty maidens in the mist. First come the paper whites which we used to grow indoors on pebbles in Boston, and then come all the golden February daffs. My favourites are the tiny ones with the switched-back petals, known in the trade as 'reflex petals', which remind me of the ears of frightened rabbits or stubborn mules.

Other bulbs which look nice with the daffodils are the early tulips, especially species such as the lady tulip (*Tulipa clusiana*) which shows pink and white stripes in early spring, and the candia tulip (*Tulipa saxatilis*) which is a gentle rose pink. My tulips are fickle; they refuse to come back a second year.

The rest of the garden begins to take heart as March nears its end. Big clumps of bronzy yellow wallflowers live up to their name by clambering up tufa walls or stone steps. Beside them come bunches of yellow calendulas, named after 'calendae', the first day of the Roman month, when interest was paid. This seems to indicate that calendulas bloom every month of the year, which is not strictly true. (It is not true that interest is paid every month either.)

A friend reminded me that the dominant colours in my

early spring garden are yellow and blue – the shades of Easter – but actually there are other colours at this time, the brilliant pink flowers of the almonds and the contrasting cherry blossoms, which look like snow out of season.

As April gains strength, the apple blossoms which look as fresh and pink as peppermint ice come out in the upper field, while down on the lower slope the olives begin to put out their fuzzy grey-green flowers, promising a good crop in the autumn.

Finally it dawns on you that all of this is your responsibility; there is weeding to do, holes to dig and bushes to plant, and you need someone to help you. The resident sculptor, having an affinity with wood, will happily take care of the fruit trees as he likes to cut and prune and graft and pick fruit. But he is not so keen on helping with flowers. In fact, finding the perfect person to help with flowers is a chore in itself.

The owners of large Italian gardens are constantly wailing that there are no trained garden workers any more; and if you want anyone worthwhile to help in the garden you have to train them yourself. The landscape architect in charge of restoring the neglected Boboli Gardens in Florence told me that when he took over the job most of the garden workers he inherited (municipal employees all) refused to handle manure because they claimed it was bad for their health.

Unaware that the problem was even more acute in Lazio, we asked around for anyone who could help in the garden. Within two days we had found Beppe, the father-in-law of Bruno, our garage mechanic. Beppe was a short solid fellow with dark hair, rather hunched shoulders and a permanent scowl, and although he knew all about tending grapevines he was fairly innocent of the more arcane details of flower gardening.

In the beginning I put him to work weeding our newly planted border but it was obvious that he was used to more solid work so we sent him down to dig out the basement. When our builders started work on the house they dug out only half of the basement on the theory that being Americans (and having no pigs or chickens) we didn't need all that much room downstairs. Much later we woke up to the fact that the other half of the basement, the part deepest under the hill, would be an ideal grotto for keeping our wine cool. So we armed Beppe with a pickaxe, shovel and wheelbarrow, and for the next four months he worked steadily digging out the reddish clay, loading it into a wheelbarrow and dumping it in piles below the house.

Once he had emptied out the basement, he went on to attack the semi-abandoned vineyard and it was immediately clear that this was work that warmed Beppe's soul. He used to come every weekday on the bus from Veiano, arriving about eight o'clock, and before he headed for the vineyard he would collect a flask of strong country wine and lean it against a convenient tree trunk so it was available while he worked. Machines run on petrol; Beppe ran on wine.

His standards for keeping up the vineyard were as rigorous as a dedicated mechanic tending a Rolls-Royce. All the vines had to be dug deeply and fertilized heavily. When the first leaves sprouted they had to be trained along their supporting poles and as they continued to grow he spent hours nipping off all the little *nipoti* (nephews) so as to funnel the strength into the grapes themselves. This operation alone took more than two weeks. In addition the vines had to be sprayed against phylloxera whenever it rained or even when there was a heavy morning dew, so Beppe spent a lot of time ranging up and down the vineyard with a copper sprayer on his back full of Bordeaux mix.

Since we generally ate lunch around the same time he did, it seemed unfriendly to leave him under a tree eating his wife's cold pasta from a plastic box, so we invited him to join us for hot spaghetti. Beppe appreciated this invitation, partly because it gave him an opportunity to refresh his wine supply, but also because he could tell us stories about his life on the Russian front in the Second World War. He had arrived in Russia in midwinter having been conscripted by the Germans and after a month of one-sided fighting, he turned his back on the front and started walking home to Italy. The trouble was that Russia was such a big country it took him most of the winter to get to the border, and he had to use his wits to survive, scrounging for tree roots, trapping rabbits and stealing from barns.

The story we heard most often was about a fight he had with a Russian peasant over a sack of potatoes, which resulted in Beppe losing most of his front teeth. This loss, plus the previous loss of back molars, meant that Beppe no longer had a workable set of teeth, and could not even chew his way through a small sausage. We feared that this might give him future health problems, so we gave him some money and told him to spend it on a set of false teeth. A few days later, he arrived at work on a black Lambretta motorcycle. He explained with no show of embarrassment that he needed a motorcycle to get to work more than he needed false teeth. Survivors of the Russian front know how to line up their priorities.

When the grape harvest was ready to be collected, Beppe seemed to acquire a second wind and he threw himself into the wine-making process with unaccustomed gusto, even staying over the first two nights to make sure that the *cappello* (hat) of the fermenting grapes was pushed down so that it would not dry out and turn to vinegar, a word better not mentioned in wine-making circles. When we drew the finished wine out of the *tino* (wooden fermentation vat) and put it into barrels we heaved a collective sigh of relief.

The wine turned out to be peculiar. The first barrel we opened was too sweet. It was drinkable but it did not go well with chicken or fish. To get something more robust, as they say in TV ads, we took all the wine from the second barrel and put it straight into bottles. They looked very professional stacked on their sides in our basement. By the time we got around to opening them, we noticed that they had collected little bubbles around the corks and the corks came off with a resounding *pop*. The wine bubbled as we poured it and we discovered with glee that we had somehow managed to produce a most alluring champagne. Tingling and delicious! I bought six flute-shaped glasses so we could share our champagne with our friends and we had several festive evenings celebrating. Then the weather got very hot and one afternoon in August we heard a series of explosions in our basement. On investigation we found out that three of our champagne bottles had blown up, scattering glass and champagne all over. What had happened, according to Beppe, was that there was so much sugar in the wine that the hot weather had sent it into a second fermentation and the pressure of the fermenting gases was enough to crack open the bottles. We tried putting some of the wine in thicker champagne bottles with champagne corks and wire hats to hold them on, but these blew up too. The explosions continued like the beats from a funeral drum throughout August and then they started slowing down. We found that our marvellous champagne (what was left of it) had turned yellow and tasted like – well – vinegar.

Submerged in gloom, Robert sat down and added up our wine-making expenses including Beppe's salary. With the money we had spent we could have treated ourselves to excellent Sancerre every day of the week. There was only one thing to do: plough up our ageing vineyard and forget the whole thing.

We dreaded breaking the news to Beppe.

'Don't worry about it,' he said, when we finally told him. 'It happens that I have a cousin in Barbarano who wants me to help him run his flour mill. With the motorcycle I can get there in fifteen minutes. I told him that you needed me here to help with your vines but if you plough up the vineyard, you won't be needing me any more.'

Our second 'helper', Gino, lived closer at hand. He was the retired street cleaner of Canale and he was a first-rate hole digger and weeder. He could dig a huge hole for a peony bush in about half an hour using a big round post-hole digger, and he weeded very efficiently with a small hoe which he slid sideways under all the plants to break their roots.

Gino was a shortish man with rather bowed legs which made him walk with a list to starboard. Having swept the streets of Canale for thirty years he knew everything that was happening in the town, and served as an unofficial town crier, psychoanalyst and gossip. People stopped Gino on the streets to ask his advice and he made regular stops along his route to take coffee or munch a bun with old friends and recount who was seen leaving whose house at dawn. Although he no longer swept (when he had reached the age of retirement and a pension, the job of street cleaner had been turned over to a woman, much to Gino's disgust), he still made a circuit of his old route first thing every morning and this meant that his work schedule with us had to be compressed. He would come to work around eight thirty but since he was also sacristan of the church he had to tear off to the village at eleven forty-five so that he could ring the church bell at high noon. If anyone died in the village, that meant two additional trips to ring the bells, first to announce the death and then again for the funeral.

Once he had rung the noontime bells it was only natural for Gino to have lunch with his wife and after this he made a second promenade along the main street; he frequently didn't get back to us until three thirty. He was off again at about five. We realized that although we paid Gino by the day and had contracted for eight hours, we were actually garnering a meagre five and a half. We discussed this problem with our neighbour Jack, but he said there was nothing to be done; Gino had got into these bad habits during his years working for the bureaucracy. No state or local workers ever worked more than five or six hours, Jack said.

We knew from our own experience that government offices in Rome were open only from eight to two, but the workers started streaming out towards their cars well before one. This gave them time to go home for a hot lunch and then report for their second (non-governmental) jobs in the afternoon. Whenever Parliament threatened to force them to work in the afternoon, the bureaucrats went on strike, and traffic experts warned that the added influx of government workers on the streets at regular hours would tie up Rome's traffic into permanent knots.

We tried to enrol some amateurs to help with the garden on a more informal basis. One was a philosophy student, who had come to Rome to do research for his master's degree on Wittgenstein. He told us that all he wanted was a room with a bed and a kitchen to prepare meals in and he would do garden work three hours a day. When we went out to see him after ten days we found the student in deep depression. Our house was too far from the village and he had trouble buying food; he was cold at night and had to spend most of his time cutting wood to make a fire, so he had no time for the garden. He was also very lonely.

'What I really need is someone to talk to about ideas. I can't function without intellectual stimulation and human inter-action,' he said looking at us accusingly. We told him he would be better off in Rome.

Our second (and last) amateur helper was a handsome young actor and Zen enthusiast who came originally from Cuba. He wanted to stay at our house two or three days a week 'to meditate' and he would do some garden work on the side. It turned out, however, that his main interest was in getting a good suntan so the only garden work he did was to weed the terrace where he could get sunburned at the same time. He used a kitchen fork for the weeding, but all the weeds came back within a day or two. His chief talents lay in another direction. He could put together an excellent shrimp gumbo, Cuban style, and memorable frozen daiquiris. We told him to skip the gardening and come for lunch any time.

Now, many years later, we have solved most of our early settling-in problems. We have had the house 'winterized', which means plaster walls, good hot water and a fairly efficient heating system. So although we divide our time between Canale, Rome, London and points east I think we basically regard Canale as 'home'. What's more, we appear to have succeeded in our search for perfect helpers. I, for one, have found my best garden worker yet. His name is Piero and he is actually employed as a maintenance man for the Italian railways, which means that he commutes to Rome by car – a hundred kilometres of driving each day. But he is paid so badly that he has to take outside jobs as a gardener to make ends meet.

Piero is a whiz as a weeder; he can go up and down a garden row in less than an hour and extirpate every weed in the place using only a two-sided mason's tool. With his short stocky frame and strong shoulders he can also dig deep holes very fast.

But Piero has another talent which pleases me even more. He is a first-rate social critic and there is nothing he loves to talk about more than the frauds and forgeries, the ruses and shenanigans of the Italian ruling classes. Among his chief *bêtes noires* are politicians, but he is equally disgruntled with union leaders, heads of banks, the mayors of big cities and small towns, television commentators, beauty queens, garbage collectors, traffic police, the Swiss Guards and the Pope himself. He has also acquired, in passing, an inside knowledge of the political shenanigans of Canale, a town which keeps abreast of the latest political currents in Rome while electing the same mayor in each election. The mayor somehow manages to switch his allegiance when the vote is counted, so that he is perpetually a member of the party in power. The roads leading from Rome to Canale are always in excellent shape.

One would imagine that a perennial malcontent like Piero would be a Communist but he was never even tempted by the gritty lure of Karl Marx and his ilk. He prefers to remain above the fray, a man without a party or banner – an anti-establishment critic to the core – but a stimulating companion to have at your side when you're trying to get out the black-berry roots or overpower the oxalis. Conversations at dinner parties are hardly ever so much fun.

Since Robert is a sculptor, always on the lookout for able metalworkers or repairers of power tools, we have gradually built up a list of talented helpers and friends whom we could summon if we needed specialized assistance.

The cinema has given the world a wholly mistaken view of

the Italian male. As seen on the silver screen he is invariably a fast-talking high-living womanizer, rotten to the core, who reads only sports papers and comics, evades taxes at all times, and scrounges from his wife's inheritance to buy cellular phones for his new Alfa Romeo.

What the movies rarely tell us is that there is a whole other world of Italian men out in the country, who drive old cars, wear scruffy clothes, pay taxes and are passionately devoted to the work they do, whether this involves carpentry or electronics or philosophy. Many of them have chosen to live in the country because it is a place where they won't waste too much time on non-essentials, and where they can do their thing without having to explain too much to snoopy bureaucrats or demanding women.

Armando is a typical example. He lives in Canale, but he commutes to Rome every day where he works driving a bus. This job feeds his family but to Armando it is important mainly because it gives him time to do original thinking.

'My driver's seat is my laboratory,' Armando says. 'I set myself a problem when I start out at the Termini every day, and I usually have it solved when I finish in Trastevere.'

Armando's real business is metalworking and he has built himself a metal shop in Canale which is one of the wonders of Lazio. In this shop he has machines which will cut strips of iron an inch thick and a yard wide and he has other machines to cut metal circles, triangles and squares. Many of these are of his own design.

He has invented a new kind of ecological heating system, an iron box where hot water is heated under the glowing embers of an ordinary fireplace, and then circulated through regular pipes. He has made eight hundred of these heaters in his spare time, so when he gets through with bus driving and building heating systems, he has only about eight hours left to eat, sleep and commute to Rome. He has also built a weather vane which predicts weather trends and an automatic watering system which goes into action when the thermometer rises above seventy degrees.

Because of his hectic schedule, it comes as no surprise that Armando has a difficult relationship with women. When first married he decided that he would have the biggest house in Canale, so he drew up plans for a rustic palazzo which would include sixteen rooms, a ballroom, an Olympic swimming pool and a sauna. After thirty years of marriage he has managed to complete the living room, kitchen and two bedrooms. The rest of the house, reserved for his two daughters, has been abandoned because Armando does not approve of the young men whom his daughters wish to marry. His wife Immaculata was so angry at his stubbornness that she stopped speaking to him for two months but now peace has returned and in his extra hours Armando writes poetry and paints watercolours of birds in shades of metallic green and blue.

Mario is another of our local enthusiasts. He is a tall, rumpled woodworker, who can turn a hunk of olive root into a salad bowl in about two hours. To support himself, Mario commutes to Rome each evening to work as a night watchman in the Villa Ada, a Roman villa once occupied by the king of Egypt. Thieves came over the wall not long ago to steal some Roman antiquities and shot Mario in the kneecaps, so that he still has to walk with a cane. Despite his injuries and his all-night schedule, Mario works full time as a woodturner.

He has turned out ten flat wooden plates (for serving artichokes or asparagus) and five salad bowls for us, and he supplies the whole Bracciano area with home-made wooden ladders and wooden gates. Mario keeps six cows and a dozen sheep, and has invented an ingenious system of movable wooden gates which permit the sheep to pass while holding back the cows.

Our camera repair man, Buzzi, first appeared on the scene when he came to attend to our vacuum cleaner, and since then Buzzi has repaired our furnace, our cameras, our washing machine, our sewing machine and our computer. Buzzi can take apart any camera and put it together any way we like, and he has made several motorcycles from scratch, using junk and spare parts. Buzzi lives alone in a wooden shack he made for himself in the *macchia* above Sasso, and he entertains himself by watching TV and collecting pictures of old-time film actresses. He has rigged up his TV set so that he can only turn it on after he has put 50 lire into a box, and the proceeds from this pay his TV tax every year. Like all the others, Buzzi is very reluctant to submit a bill. He prefers to be paid in cherries or plums or, better yet, old pictures of Irene Dunn and Jean Arthur.

Our friend Paolo came round whenever our radios or TV broke down. Actually he began his career as a radio technician during the war. He was a member of a group of young Socialists in the central Lazio area who volunteered to help locate British and American airmen who had been shot down over German territory. His job was to take them back to the Allied lines.

He made three or four trips escorting British and American fliers to safety, and on one trip he ended up in an American camp near Salerno, where the captain in charge was having trouble with his radio transmitters. Paolo, who had studied radio engineering at school, offered to have a look. As soon as the Americans found that this handsome kid was good at repairing radio transmitters, they hired him to become the head of the outfit's radio repair and communication unit.

'This was a big surprise to me,' Paolo said. 'In Italy we could only get ahead if we knew someone, or if our parents had a connection. But Americans didn't care who you knew; they cared what you knew. I liked that very much.'

Paolo continued to work for Americans in the years after the war, first in recording studios and afterwards as a sound engineer in films. He became interested in the mechanics of sound and built a machine which could synthesize artificial sounds. American composers came to Italy to order these new sound machines from Paolo, and several large US music companies offered him his own laboratory with an unlimited budget if he would come to America.

He decided to stay in Italy.

'I was happy working in my own workshop at Bracciano at my own pace,' Paolo said. 'Money wasn't so very important.'

Soon after this the American companies went ahead and produced their own commercial synthesizers, lining their pockets with gold.

Paolo continued to work on perfecting his synthesizer. Then he became interested in an invention which could create a new kind of 'wraparound sound'. This machine looked somewhat like an American football helmet, bristling with wires and sprockets, and some experts said that it was the biggest entertainment invention since wide-screen cinema. His work may indeed have been a forerunner of today's 'virtual reality'.

But by now Paolo has gone on to other projects. Like many true inventors, he is interested only in the idea, the conception; he has no interest in seeing it developed for commercial use. He now has a plan to help solve the energy crisis by taking the hydrogen out of sea water and converting it (by a process far too complicated for me to understand) into an energy source, using sunlight to trigger the reaction.

Bees and Beeswax

ROBERT NEVER DREAMED WHEN WE BUILT OUR HOUSE AT Canale that the country would one day provide him with a rich source of new materials for making sculpture. A sculptor carries the tools of his trade with him, like a locksmith or a crocodile, and no matter how vast his collection, he is always on the lookout for more.

He is thinking always in terms of tough stuff that will resist the ravages of time – iron or stone, ebony or bronze, alabaster or copper – and like Vulcan or Praxiteles he rejoices in hammering the metals together so that they will still be around, sharp and significant, two thousand years hence.

But to get to the bronze stage, the sculptor usually has to go through more steps than a chef making bouillabaisse. If he starts with a clay statue, he goes on to make a plaster mould on the clay, then a plaster cast inside the plaster mould, and from this a flexible mould. OK so far? Then he puts together the flexible mould and sloshes hot wax around in it for a while, and lets the wax cool enough to form a thin layer. The thin wax statue is then taken out of the flexible mould, and surrounded inside and out by a fireproof mould which is cooked in a hot oven. The wax flows out and the bronze flows in. This is an ancient system known as the lost-wax process and it was used both by the Chinese and the Greeks, people of infinite patience. But Robert Cook, the sculptor in a hurry, decided to skip the first steps involving the clay, plaster and flexible moulds in order to save time and cut foundry costs in half. He worked out a system of modelling the wax in long ribbony sheets with a hot tool and then spreading the moulded wax over an armature of bamboo which has been bent with heat and held together with copper wires. (He learned the system of bamboo bending from an instruction book when making a Japanese kite for Henry.)

Eventually he was making statues nine metres long with this method. Robert spent hours looking for the perfect blend of wax which would be stiff and yet pliant, drip-free but sturdy enough to stand up to the rigours of ninety-degree heat or hot modelling tools. Early on he rejected synthetic wax because it was too soft, had an unpleasant smell and was said to be dangerous to work. He chose instead a combination of virgin beeswax, which has natural flexibility and body, plus paraffin for strength, and a daub of resin which makes it malleable.

It goes without saying that the moment Robert discovered there were bee-keepers in the Canale area he was tooling around the countryside contacting all the bee men, who were only too happy to sell their used *pizze* (circular forms) of beeswax which they made from boiling down old honey-combs. Simultaneously, he spread the word among church employees that he was in the market for leftover candles, which are almost pure paraffin.

The road to our house was rapidly filled with bee-keepers on bicycles, church sextants on tractors, and even children with old household candles who were anxious to sell, and soon Robert had accumulated in our basement some two hundred kilos of beeswax from hives as far away as Tolfa and Cerveteri, and a supply of ex-votive candles which filled two large buckets. At a certain moment this heap of material reached a psychological flashpoint and Robert decided the day had come to make his modelling wax.

This urge came in the period before he had built his studio so our kitchen was made to serve as a temporary wax-factory. Unfortunately I was absent at the time. When I got back to the house at the end of the day I discovered that Robert had collected all the spaghetti pots, casseroles and saucepans he could find and put them to work melting down the candles and the beeswax. Once these had liquefied, he strained the whole mess through our sieves, which became encrusted with hardened candle wicks and dead bees. He then poured the boiling liquid out on to our white travertine counter, which made a perfect mould for great sheets of brown wax.

My kitchen looked like the workshop at Madame Tussaud's after an election. There was wax and paraffin spread all over the room, on the floor, on the ceiling and naturally on the stove, many of whose gas jets were blocked. There was wax on our wooden spoons and forks; and there was wax on the fridge and wax gumming up the electric fittings.

But this was only the beginning. The sudden accumulation of all this boiling wax which contained a lot of sweet-smelling honey had sent out a signal to all the bees of central Lazio (who happened to be swarming at this time of year), and they headed in a beeline (to coin a phrase) for the Cooks in Canale Monterano. If there was any lost wax around, they were going to find it.

So there they were in their hundreds, if not in their thousands, crawling over our stove and all the places where the old beeswax and honey had been cooked. We tried various strategies to get rid of them. We cleaned the kitchen and threw away all the wax remains. Our neighbour Jack brought in his cousin, a bee-keeper, who produced a real live queen bee which he kept in a matchbox, and which he hoped would lure the bees away. But the bees were not tempted – perhaps the queen had lost her looks or perhaps the matchbox had given her a smell of sulphur. We took to eating our meals cold on the terrace.

After two days the honey bees decided they had had enough of our kitchen and took off for parts unknown; but they must have sent out a cryptic message to the insect world because almost as soon as they had gone, we were inundated by a much more ferocious creature known in the Canale area as the *ammazza somaro* (donkey killer). These are very large wasps built on the lines of the feared yellow-jackets from my Cape Cod childhood, but twice as big and full of poison. I was stung on the elbow soon after they began to buzz around us – they make a singularly ominous buzz whenever they fly – and my forearm blew up to the size of a melon. But fortunately the killer wasps didn't seem to be too interested in stinging anyone else; their attention was concentrated on the wax and on the outside walls of our house, where they were looking for holes in which to build nests for the summer.

We had a good number of supper guests during the Summer of the Wasps, but I cannot pretend that our suppers were a raving success because the moment we served up the antipasto, the wasps started careening around the table with angry buzzes – wasps adore *prosciutto crudo* – and the guests became nervous. Nearly all of them, with few exceptions, swore that they were hyper-allergic to wasp stings, and if stung they would go into an immediate state of shock and be dead within an hour. So it little availed us to explain that these wasps were more interested in *prosciutto* and finding a home than in stinging our guests. One woman got up from the table, locked herself in the bathroom and refused to come out. Eventually we had to move our suppers from the lovely cool terrace into a stuffy dining room with all the doors closed and the temperature hovering in the high nineties.

The wasp population seemed to be dying off early in September so we joyfully moved our dining table out on to the terrace again. By October it began to get chilly and we decided to dine by the open fire indoors. The fire was started quickly enough but, oh calamity! Instead of the smoke going up the chimney, it poured into the living room and in the midst of it we could see a great number of smoking *ammazza somari*. Some had been roasted alive and dropped like bullets but many more had singed wings and zigzagged drunkenly around the room like kamikaze fighters looking for a place to light and take their revenge. We realized that the killer wasps had built their hive in our chimney.

We sent out word that we needed a chimney sweep to clean out our chimney, neglecting to mention that the obstruction was caused by killer wasps. The word came back that there were no longer any chimney sweeps working in the area, and so in the middle of November Robert wrapped himself in several lengths of blue plastic cheesecloth – the kind used for drying tomatoes – and went up the outside of the house on a very long ladder with a pole to dislodge the obstructing wasps.

When he reached the top, he steadied himself on the teetering ladder and began to poke the pole into the chimney. A few angry wasps came out and circled around his head, but he maintained an admirable calm and kept on poking. At length he announced that the wasp nest completely filled the chimney, and that the pole would not go through.

There were about six of us assembled on the ground, all screaming up words of advice, caution, sympathy, terror and encouragement to our wasp vanquisher, and we hurried to the basement to find some heavier equipment. We found a big chunk of iron – it may have been a hub from an old wagon wheel – attached to a rope and this was rushed to Robert. He dropped the weight down the chimney, like a fisherman dropping a heavy lure into a lake.

A scream came from Henry, who had been stationed as watchman at the fireplace.

'They're coming! They're coming! Millions of them.' And with that Henry came bolting out of the front door followed by a V formation of angry killer wasps. Robert kept banging away with his wasp-buster and he eventually dislodged the wasp nest, which landed bang in the middle of our living-room fireplace. Someone, it may have been Henry, had the wit to strike a match and start a fire in the chimney, and as more wasps and wasp housing fell down they were incinerated on the spot.

I am sorry to say that this scenario had to be replayed the next year too. At the end of the second summer the job of wasp-buster was taken over by a young house-painter who said he was used to working on the tops of ladders and was not afraid of wasps. We all watched as he climbed the ladder and slowly lowered the big iron weight into the top of the chimney. Immediately there was a flutter in the chimney, and an enormous white bird flew out as silently as a homesick ghost.

'*Barbagianni, barbagianni*,' yelled the neighbours who had assembled.

'What's a *barbagianni*?'

Somebody looked it up in the bird book.

'A *barbagianni* is a barn owl.'

'Oh wow.'

My first impulse was to stop the destruction in the chimney so the bird could return to its nest.

But I was overruled. The chimney needed cleaning, everybody said. The barn owl could find another place to settle at night.

Almost as soon as Robert had made his first batch of wax,

he decided that he needed a studio, and three days later he had confected a model for the studio in the new wax. It looked like those chocolate houses they display in Roman pastry shops before Christmas. The studio went up in less than three months, and by autumn he was building a huge camel and a steeplechase for the Mayor of Jeddah in Saudi Arabia. The only problem with working in wax on such a large scale was that the slightest increase in temperature tended to make it more pliant, and shapes could become distorted in the blink of an eye. If by chance some child or foolish adult bumped into the form while it was being cut up to go to the foundry, the bronze might come out seriously askew, and forcing bronze back into shape with blowtorches and welding irons is a terrible chore. Thus Robert never worked wax in very warm weather, and extraneous visitors to the studio were firmly discouraged.

None the less, the best laid plans of men can often go astray, and one autumn the weather played such tricks on us that it made mincemeat of that venerable philosopher Sir Isaac Newton. Robert had been given a commission to do a big statue for an industrial park named The Woodlands near Houston. The corporation wanted a statue which paid tribute to research and enterprise and all the other industrial virtues.

Robert came up with the idea of building a statue based on the famous apophthegm of Sir Isaac: 'If I have seen further it is by standing on the shoulders of giants.'

The statue would show a huge giant striding forward with his weight on one leg, and on his shoulder there would be a small figure of Isaac Newton, also striding forward. A model was sent to the corporation, and the idea was approved.

Work began on the statue in October when the danger of a heatwave was past, and within weeks the massive figure of the giant, four and a half metres tall, arose in the studio. It was a hell of a giant. Work then started on the much smaller figure of the man we began to call 'Isaac' but, right in the middle of the operation, an unexpected spell of hot weather blew across from the Sahara and central Italy was exposed to the hottest October in a hundred years.

The giant gradually began to droop. Isaac on his shoulder began to droop too. In fact, Isaac fell off the shoulder and smashed into pieces. Robert was being assisted at this point by a young Roman dentist named Guido Gori (future art historians will note the surprising number of dentists who work part-time as sculptors). Aided by Guido, Robert put a lot more bamboo slivers into the reconstituted Isaac to make him stand up. He also emptied out our refrigerator, and Isaac was put there to cool.

But overnight a terrible thing happened to the giant. He simply slid down on his stainless steel supporting rod, as if somebody had squashed him, and he ended up a sagging figure with his chest down where his umbilicus should be.

Chaos and confusion. Gori telephoned his wife and told her to cancel all his appointments for the week and Robert, heartened by an act of such solidarity, called in his friend the metalworking bus driver Armando. Heroes come in all shapes and sizes but if they were giving out Nobel prizes for heroism in the art world that week, they would have given them to a Roman dentist and a Canale welder.

Together, working all day and late into the night, the three men saved the statue. With Guido on a ladder clutching the top part and Armando on the ground, holding the legs, Robert gently and skilfully cut the statue in half. Armando then welded three new steel supports to go up the giant's spine, with a piece extending to support Isaac. While he was doing this, Robert and Guido fashioned a whole new midriff for the giant out of specially stiffened wax. Gradually the mid-section was heated and reattached to the torso, and finally the legs were put back where they belonged. The giant strode once more.

Transporting the statue to the foundry in Pietrasanta in Tuscany presented a nightmarish problem but the Pietrasanta foundry workers saved the day. They sent down a butcher's truck equipped with refrigeration, plus two experienced wax workers who chopped the statue into thirty large sections, surrounded them with steel braces and rushed them straight into the cool interior of the butcher's truck. Instead of being set on the floor where they might be jolted, the sections were hung from the meat hooks that lined the interior so they travelled to Pietrasanta just like thirty carcasses of beef. After they were safely cast in bronze they fitted together as neatly as the pieces in a puzzle.

Several months later there was an inauguration in the leafy industrial park, and a permanent sign bearing the Isaac Newton aphorism was displayed at the base. But, as Robert commented, a more realistic sign would have said: 'If I am standing on the shoulders of a giant, it is because I hung from a meat hook all the way from Canale Monterano to Pietrasanta.'

Occasionally, when working in wax became too stressful, Robert would decide to put it aside for a while and work in wood, a good solid material that would neither melt nor stretch. But here again the problem was finding some really excellent hardwoods. Our holidays in Asia and Africa offered Robert an opportunity to visit timber yards and junk shops, and there was a moment on every trip when he would come back to our hotel room lugging a sack with some priceless piece of ebony or rosewood or ironwood.

He clung to a theory, usually implanted by taxi drivers or hotel clerks, that it might be illegal to export precious wood from the country of origin, and although very few woods are actually on the protected list, there was often confusion as to the identity of his finds. Time and again my soft canvas suitcase was emptied on to the bed while Robert tried to fit in his trophies. The idea was that if the wood fitted into the bag, it became personal luggage and therefore above suspicion, and I was obliged to go out and find a duffel bag for my clothes.

My worst setback came in Burma, where Robert found a handsome piece of ebony in a store devoted to paints and cleaning powders. The ebony, we were told on good authority, was ground up and used by the Burmese to clean their teeth. He also found in a nearby store an enormous bronze hammer which he said would be useful in the studio.

The exit from Burma was full of tension as we had to go through currency checks to make sure that we had changed our money legally (who, us?) and there was also the possibility that the ebony and the antique Burmese hammer were on some export control list. So when we came up to the customs desk Robert was in a smiling and conciliatory mood. The customs man, who was young and sporty, took a quick look at our bags and his eye rested on my tennis racket which was protruding from my hand luggage.

The man pointed to the racket.

'Is that one of the new fibreglass models?'

Robert seized the racket and handed it to him.

'You like the racket? Take it. She's got lots more at home.'

So we were waved through the customs with no more questions. As we walked across the tarmac to the waiting plane Robert patted me on the shoulder.

'Sorry about the racket, honey, but it's hard to get good Burmese ebony any more. Wait till you see what I'll do with it when I get it back to the studio.'

'I understand about the ebony,' I said, 'but what was the point of the giant hammer?'

'Oh that,' came the reply, 'that will be perfect for knocking the wasp nests out of the chimney next fall. It's heavier than that iron ball and I can also put a big rope through the handle – scare the damn wasps right out of their nests.'

It's always nice to have something good to look forward to when you come home from a long trip.

May

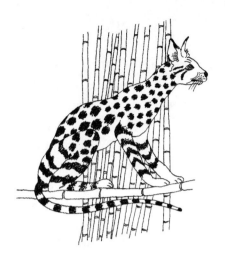

Birds and Cats

WHEN WE MOVED TO CANALE, WE BROUGHT WITH US A bird feeder which we hoped would attract small birds to our front garden, for the books on Italian natural history all reported that our area on the fringe of the Maremma was an ideal environment for birds. Even large raptors frequented this zone, the books said, because the rough terrain around us attracted all kinds of small animals, from hares to lizards and snakes, which made a perfect lunch for airborne carnivores.

We were disappointed from the first; for although we put out the bird feeder on a low olive branch near the house no bird came near it for three months. Then one bright morning we woke up to see a brave sparrow pecking at the seeds.

We realized that this behaviour pattern reflected the general attitude towards birds in our area. Birds were regarded as antipasto for Sunday lunch, preferably grilled with rosemary and good olive oil, and the birds were quite aware of this and kept out of sight during the hunting season. In our early days the hunters used to barrel out from Rome every Sunday morning armed with bee-bee guns and rifles to shoot at everything they saw, from birds to cats to TV antennae. It didn't matter if you fenced off your property; the hunters carried wire clippers with them and invaded the garden anyhow, along with their long-eared hunting dogs who rooted around in the compost heap. On Sunday mornings bullets clattered on the tile roof like hailstones.

But gradually, as time went by, we and the birds began to get the upper hand. For one thing a few nature-loving Romans started building second homes in Canale too, so there were more houses and more fences for the hunters to clip, and instead of one angry family screaming at them to go away, there were three or four, including one headed by a general of the Carabinieri. In addition, we all started to plant fruit and nut trees which offered figs, plums and all kinds of seeds for birds, and we also planted Monterey pines which provided safe and stylish nesting space as well. Our biggest contribution to bird well-being was a stand of bamboo (originally planted to provide armatures for sculpture), which seems to be irresistible to small birds such as finches and sparrows who enjoy roosting in groups in summer. This more hospitable attitude towards birds, plus the forced retreat of the hunters, has created a new bird-friendly environment in Canale Monterano, and many local people say birds are now coming back that have not been seen around for fifty years.

In the early days we had to satisfy ourselves with mostly resident birds: the magpie, a handsome but noisy bird who makes untidy nests, the blackbird, who has a lovely liquid call but who some consider slightly bossy, and the local hooded crow, who has a dry, cynical rasp that reminds me of Fred Allen, an American radio comic of the Fifties and Sixties.

We are getting more variety too, especially among the migrators. The bird year now starts early in April when we hear the first strained note of the cuckoo. Its voice is rather remote and uncertain at first, as if the long trip from Africa has given it jet lag, but gradually it gets its wind and soon two or three cuckoos are calling out with great confidence from the gully below our olive orchard.

The cuckoo is, of course, a parasite who saves itself the trouble of building a nest by laying eggs in other birds' nests and then letting the adoptive mother take care of the chick. Baby cuckoos come equipped with needle-sharp elbows which help them to shove legitimate chicks out of their nest. Thus the intruders get all the parental attention, and quite often you find a small bird such as a finch feeding a baby cuckoo who is twice her size.

Then right after the cuckoos come the swifts and swallows. We may be pruning olives or weeding the roses when we look up into the southern sky and there, dipping and swooping over the horizon, are the early swifts – scouts checking out the area before the whole clan arrives. These scouts come and go for several days, tumbling and leaping in the sky like kids on skateboards, and then after a day or two the rest of the gang come soaring in from Africa. By evening they are filling the country air (and also the air of Rome) with the shrill high-pitched cry which remains our traditional evening bird call until they depart in late August.

After the swifts come their cousins the swallows and the house martins, and among these charming birds were three little barn swallows who managed to fly into Robert's studio one hot afternoon in mid-April, and built a nest in the rafters. We never could figure out the relationship between this trio, but we guessed it must be husband and wife, plus perhaps a maiden aunt who had come along to look after the nestlings. Robert left a window open for the first two seasons so they could come and go even when he wasn't there, but by the third April he had decided that he had had enough of the chatting and chirping so he closed the doors and windows to prevent another round of nest building. The rejected swallows gathered on the telephone line outside the studio for several days, chattering angrily and trying to rush into their old home every time the studio door was opened, but at last they realized that they were not wanted any more and went off to build a nest elsewhere. As soon as they had gone, Robert began to miss them, and so he took to leaving the door open to entice them back, but they never returned. Having been rebuffed once, they decided not to trust him again.

The next two birds to return are not seen so much as heard. The first are the nightingales with the pretty Italian name of *usignolo*, and we start to hear them singing in the olive trees late in April. They are sulky birds who stay hidden in the underbrush but we can hear them singing all summer without ever seeing them.

Another sound in the spring is the shrill fluting whistle of the European oriole, a pigeon-sized yellow bird with black markings on the head and shoulders. I wish I could speak with affection of this golden beauty but he is actually a pest. A compulsive fruit eater – especially partial to cherries and figs – he sees it as his job in life to tell all the other birds when our fruit is ripe and the time has come to attack our trees. Another very loud caller in this season is the green-headed woodpecker. We rarely see him but we are electrified each season by his maniac laugh from the woods which sounds like the hysterics of a tree-climbing banshee.

Other spring arrivals include the stunning hoopoe who calls out 'hoop hoop hoop' from nearby bushes, and numerous finches, including the melodious greenfinch and the pretty little goldfinches who twitter all summer and use our stately cypress trees as a condominium. In summer we are also enchanted by the soft noontime call of the turtle dove and the night-time cries from our resident owl, the great white *barbagianni* who makes a sound like a long sad sigh. Less appreciated is the call from another owl known as the *civetta* (little owl) whose terrifying shrieks at midnight have convinced farmers that he is an evil spirit returning from hell to haunt them.

Then came the memorable summer morning when I was driving back from the market and looked up to see a big red-brown hawk-like bird with a forked tail flying right over Mastro-Orazio's chicken coop. The bird was a lovely vermilion colour with dark stripes and it had an air of silent majesty as it banked and turned, skilfully adjusting its wing angles to get a better look at the chickens. This beauty turned out to be, as I suspected, the red kite (*Milvus milvus*) known in Italy as the *nibbio reale*.

Red kites usually hunt in open fields on the edges of woods but they can also zero in on farms and chicken yards, often hovering motionless in mid-air when prey is sighted. One poet has likened the red kite to a 'brilliantly glowing giant swallow'.

Energized by this close encounter, I went off on a few bird walks in the wild Tolfa hills with a group of enthusiasts from Manziana. After hiking for an hour or so, they pointed up above the trees to a large reddish-brown raptor with cold yellow eyes whom they identified as the *falco pecchiaolo* (honey buzzard). It swooped and dived in a graceful flight pattern above us. The *pecchiaolo*, I was told, goes mad for both bees and honey, and has a weak spot for the paper combs which wasps make in the forest trees. The bird pulls off pieces of these larva-filled combs which it feeds to its young in treetop nests. Every year at migration time, flocks of honey buzzards pass over the Straits of Messina on their way to Africa, and even though it is illegal dozens of Italian hunters gather on the shores to shoot them.

While we were watching the honey buzzard near Tolfa, we were surprised to see an even bigger raptor who swooped down towards us in a menacing way. This turned out to be *il biancone* (big white bird), a huge pale brown and white eagle with a wing span of up to 180 centimetres. The *biancone* feeds on snakes and is known world-wide as a snake eagle or the short-toed eagle because its toes are short and its ankles are covered with scales, a perfect protection from snakebite.

One would assume that the return of the birds has been a

bonus for the wild cats who lurk throughout the Canale territory. But actually the cats do not seem to be doing at all well in the war against their ancient enemies.

When some friends of ours moved from Rome to their new summer house in Canale, their city-bred cat Fifi was so frightened she lost her ability even to say 'meow'. It was three months before she had the courage to leave the safety of their outdoor dining terrace.

Fifi was right to be frightened because there are a lot of creatures roaming around in the Canale pastures who are ready to give trouble to cats. There are the hunters, who can't distinguish cats from birds. Then there are dogs, foxes, porcupines and deadly carnivores such as *donnole* (weasels) and *puzzole* (polecats) who have been known to gobble up turkeys. And even the little birds who used to be regular items on the cat menu seem to have developed a cat-alarm system that works well. The chief sentinel in the anti-cat brigade is the Sardinian warbler, a tiny brown bird with a shiny black cap and bright red eyes, who leaps into action whenever a cat wanders into his territory. Instead of running away, the warbler flies straight into the bush or tree that is nearest the cat, and lets go with an uninterrupted scolding chatter that tells all the world to watch out. The cats naturally resent this harassment, although they try to appear cool, but as the cats move away the birds move along next to them, hopping from bush to bush, until the cats finally abandon the territory. The warbler is known as *capo-nero* (black cap) to Italians, or more picturesquely as *occhiocotto* which means 'cooked eye'.

Even though I am very fond of cats, I have always tried to

avoid a close relationship with the Canale cats because they are nearly all wild. They were either born in the countryside or they were dumped in the fields when their city owners went off for their summer holidays. My fear was that if the cats became dependent on the food we part-timers gave them, they would be in trouble when we went away.

The chief protector of the cats in our area is La Signora Iolanda, the wife of Jack's son Luigi. The signora never undertakes to supply a full diet for the local felines; instead she gives them a supplemental meal of leftover bread or spaghetti or beans at midday, thus encouraging the animals to spend the rest of the day hunting for fieldmice and lizards in the countryside.

Many of the Iolanda cats used to call at our back porch whenever we were in residence, and the one who made the most impression on us was a female whom we named Hyena. She was a slender cat with a coat like a spotted hyena; it was as if some small child had painted her all over with big irregular spots of brown, orange and yellow. Her face started off brown, and then went orange around the eyes with a big yellow smudge on her nose. Her body was a mixture of orange and brown and her tail was striped half brown and half yellow.

The contrast of colours was unusual and cat experts told us it was the result of an odd genetic mix which occurred only in female cats. But despite her funny colouring Hyena was not lacking in class; whenever she watched us as we ate lunch, she sat very erect, with her tail curled around her paws like an elegant Egyptian cat of the fifth century BC. She was so sculptural, in fact, that Robert, the anti-cat man, began to take an interest in her, and even gave her chicken bones from the table. Hyena accepted all of these handouts with enthusiasm, but she had a rule which she never broke: she would not let us touch her. She would come up to the table to ask for food but she refused to take it from our hands – she would wait until we dropped it. By the same token she would never come into the house until two doors were open, and if she saw us closing one, she would streak for the other exit. This extreme wariness, I think, explained how Hyena managed to survive so long in the hostile countryside.

Because I had long been interested in animal behaviour, I spent an odd hour every now and then following Hyena about and keeping notes on her daily activities. I eventually came to realize that Hyena was not only an extraordinarily good mother – as indeed are most felines – but she was also a very clever cat.

She had at least one litter of kittens every year, and on each occasion she repeated the same behaviour pattern. She chose to have the kittens on the top level of our covered greenhouse (under a thick bush of plumbago) so that she could keep watch for trouble coming up from the greenhouse and also from the garden.

She usually kept the kittens in the greenhouse for a week and then she would move them around from one hideout to the next, always near the house – and the moment she realized that some person or animal had discovered her nest, she would move them again. As the kittens grew older it was fascinating to watch how carefully she taught them all the survival tricks which she too had learned in her time.

Hyena was such a good mother that most of her litters came through unscathed, but in the end there was a tragedy when she lost her four kittens in one fell swoop. It was an evening in July, as I recall, and I had gone to check on the kittens in the nest she had built for them under a plumbago bush at the corner of the greenhouse, and found that they were all thriving. Several hours later we were awakened by the frightening noise of a cat screaming – a noise so full of terror and anguish that we were sure something dreadful had happened. The screaming went on and on, accompanied by some confused noises of animals thrashing around, and then all was silence. Not willing to face the trouble in the dead of night, we went back to sleep, but in the morning we discovered the worst. Hyena was gone, and in the nest there was only one tiny black kitten left and it was dead; possibly its neck was broken. The other three kittens had vanished. I spent an hour looking for them, but they were in none of the usual hideaways, and early in the afternoon Hyena came back alone, looking worn and pathetic, to take up the vigil beside the dead kitten. The next day the poor cat took the dead kitten away and soon afterwards she came back to the greenhouse, took one last look at the empty nest, and then crouched on the balcony across from the nest and began a kind of low keening noise. It sounded a bit like the soft little chirp which she used to call her kittens, only infinitely sadder. She came back, always alone, and repeated this ritual for the next few days, and I noticed on two occasions that the big tiger cat, whom I assumed had been the father, was lurking in the bushes near the door.

This, of course, put me on a false trail. I had seen all the films of African lions where it was reported that when a new male lion took control of a territory, driving out the old dominant male, he killed all the other male's cubs so that he could establish his new bloodline in the pride. Influenced by this, I decided that it was probably the male cat who had killed Hyena's babies.

I now think I was wrong. Only a few days after the kittens were killed, we went off for a visit to Tuscany and our friends Brian and Evie moved into our house. Brian, who was a painter, liked to do landscape drawings from the *altana* (top floor) and he was up there the first evening drawing the view from the southern windows which looked out over the greenhouse. Dusk had already come and all the birds were quiet, having finished their evening concert in the bamboo patch. Then all at once Brian heard the flap of wings coming over the roof, and three very large, very pale-coloured birds swooped right in front of him and headed down to the greenhouse where they circled and then alighted, briefly, on the ledge right next to the plumbago bush. Then, finding nothing, they flew away.

Brian was certain that these three raptors had killed the kittens only a few days earlier. Although the light was dim, he described the birds as large and white, with a wingspan as wide as his extended arms (about 145 centimetres). It was his impression that it was our old friend the *barbagianni* (barn owl) who had come back with two more of his kind for an evening meal of newborn kitten.

'I really didn't see them very well,' he said. 'First I heard the beating of their wings, and then I saw them zooming straight down to the greenhouse.'

Some birders objected that owls are unique in the bird world in that they fly almost silently. However, Brian was very close to the birds and the night was so quiet that it is possible he did hear the wings rustle as the big raptors flew past him, looking and listening for more kittens. The cats in Canale, far from being the aggressors in the war with birds, now seem to have become the terrified victims.

The Joys of High Spring

APRIL HAS BEEN CALLED THE CRUELLEST MONTH BUT I think the same thing could be said of May, which promises the flowers I love the most – the peony and the iris – but then ends with their banishment, leaving me bereft.

It takes several years before these flowers really get established in the garden, but as their roots grow stronger, they become the true stars of the spring. They make preliminary appearances in April, but it is only in May that the flowers achieve their true potential. The first peony that greets us in the spring is the tree peony, *Paeonia suffruticosa* (Moutan), that has been around the Mediterranean so long that it is considered a native. Actually this stalwart originated in Asia like other tree peonies, and if there were no hybrids to compare it to, it would walk off with the prizes. It is sturdy as a thistle, with rather finely divided blue-green metallic leaves, and the flowers begin forming almost as soon as the leaves drop in the autumn. They show their first colour late in March – great pink crêpe de Chine cabbages with a deep carmine blotch in the centre. They hold their heads up bravely as long as the weather is kind, but a single driving rain can bring all the flowers to the ground in a matter of minutes, and from then on they must be carefully staked. Despite this top-heaviness they are sturdy and disease free, and if you really want a nice big armload of pink in March and early April, you can't go wrong with the Moutan peony. We were given our first roots of this plant by a neighbour and we had a little trouble settling them in. They were not happy in the open border and were equally discontented near the fig tree, but when we finally put them in the lower garden right up next to the tufa wall, facing north, they decided that this was where they belonged. Our peony bush has now grown high and wide so that it is the size of a small bicycle and its offspring flower all along our tufa wall and in the gardens of numerous friends.

Since this original tree peony has been so generous with us it may sound unfeeling to celebrate the greater charms of its descendants, the hybrid tree peonies – but one must be objective. The hybrids, developed by horticultural geniuses at Saunders in America and Kelways in England, bear about the same relation to Moutan peonies as grey Beluga caviar does to the eggs of lumpfish. How can one capture in mere words the wonders of these flowers? It is like trying to get the essence of dragonflies' wings in watercolour. Indeed the dragonfly wing is not a bad simile at all because there is something silky and evanescent about the wing, just as there is in the petal of the peony. Let us contemplate for a moment three of the great suffruticosa cultivars created by Kelways: 'Duchess of Marlborough', 'Countess of Crewe' and the matchless 'Lord Selborne'. The first of these nobles to bloom is the 'Duchess', who appears in early May with petals of deep rose pink fading to a much paler pink at the edges. The impression one gets is of shimmering pink moiré. The 'Countess' comes next, a proud semi-double creature of a lovely shell pink like a taffeta shawl, crumpled slightly, but eternally elegant. And finally around mid-May comes 'Lord Selborne', an enormous semi-double beauty resplendent in the softest tones of pale salmon. When it is fully open this peony looks like a starched petticoat that has been made of silk shantung by the finest silk weavers in imperial China. When fifteen of these priceless flowers open more or less simultaneously and the colours radiate out into the sunshine, there is nothing to do but draw up a chair and contemplate. In the gardens of Suchow, China, special patios are set aside just so that visitors may contemplate peonies in full flower.

We have other peonies which do not have quite such distinguished pedigrees but which are natural aristocrats all the same. Three came from a small flower shop near the Piazza Navona. I was buying tulip bulbs there one day and noticed a little wooden box which contained some dry roots tied together with bits of red string. A small card marked with Japanese writing was attached to each clump. I asked the sales assistant what it was all about and she replied that she thought they were tree peony roots which were being sold off cheap at one thousand lire a clump because nobody could identify them. I seized the orphan peonies and even to this day I cannot resist a chuckle when they flower in mid-May. One has very deep single red petals so dark they appear at times to be almost black. Another is an intense carmine colour with lighter splashes on the outer petals; it looks like fine-cut velvet. The third is a deep pinkish red which reminds me of raspberry sherbet.

But grand though these may be, I have still another Japanese peony that is almost but not quite in the class of the incomparable 'Lord Selborne'. I call it the 'Princess of Kyoto'. I found it when I was wandering through a farmers' market in Kyoto in 1985 and noticed near the vegetable benches an elderly farmer sitting on the ground with some rootlike bulbs which made me think of peonies. I couldn't talk to him nor he to me but I managed to convey to him that I wanted to buy the bulbs and wished to know the price.

Laboriously he wrote out the figures on the back of an envelope. It was five dollars – a large sum for a small bundle of roots. Judging, perhaps ingenuously, that they must be special if they cost so much, I bought them. Now, years later, they have developed into a substantial five-branched tree peony that produces armloads of glistening white peonies every May. Their whiteness is of a purity that is hard to describe, with a faint pink shadow barely visible around the edges, and the crisp taffeta petals are bunched in a most delicate way around golden stamens. I have to stop and stare every time I go near the bush when it is in flower and always when I do this, my mind wings back to that Kyoto market and the nameless Japanese farmer who knew a good peony when he saw one.

The culture of the tree peony presents no problem, as it loves cold winters and also appreciates heat in summer. However, it can be a bit choosy about where it is planted, and it is likely to rebel if planted too close to tree roots or in a hole which it regards as inadequate.

When I got my first tree peony roots from the Roman florist I was in a hurry and I tucked them into rather small holes under a cherry tree. They produced only a few meagre leaves and no flowers; so after two years I found a new spot for them under the terrace wall, and dug three very sizeable holes which I filled with a basketload of compost and some well-rotted cow manure. The foundling peonies responded by doubling in size and now in spring each plant rewards me with from ten to twenty irresistible blossoms.

Herbaceous *Paeonia lactiflora* starts blooming almost as soon as the tree peonies finish in mid-May, and it is my impression that it smells sweeter than all the others – a scent of roses mixed with a fugitive dash of vanilla. I have only to walk past a group of them and I find myself whisked back to the peony bed outside the dining-room window in my childhood home in Newton Center. The herbaceous peonies I ordered from Kelways came from their 'Scented Collection' and they include a double red, a double white and four double pinks which seem to be the sweetest smelling of all. The white, which has a huge bushy flower, is called *P. Lactiflora* 'Shirley Temple'. One of the best pinks is 'Gypsy Girl', with dark outer petals, and inner petals which are a mixture of rose and cream.

All this talk of peonies should not obscure the fact that there is another major adornment in my May garden which must rank as the second most wonderful flower in the world – the bearded iris. The story of the development of the iris is one of the most exciting in botanical history. The original wild irises were rather modest, a few simple flag flowers in basic shades of white, pale blue, dark lavender and yellow. Starting with these four tones, hybridizers slowly developed a treasure trove of iris colours that would make a maharajah weep. There is no need to enumerate the colour combinations but I am told that more than five thousand varieties are available in catalogues. Perhaps a couple of hundred of these are listed under one name in one country and another in a second. An exuberant plicata or pleated iris named 'Golden Ripple' in Seattle has been introduced as 'Summer Sun' in Fiesole and there are many more duplications, but this still leaves us with more than four thousand varieties to choose from. There are some iris lovers, and I am one of them, who feel the hybridizers may have gone too far with the plicatas and the polka dots but if some people like them I see no reason to have them struck from the scene. The dachshund, after all, is an artificial product, and no one I know wants to eliminate this friendly little quadruped.

Gradually, as I worked out my colour schemes, I decided to skip the fancier irises and concentrate on the ones whose company I most enjoyed – the simple flags in the softest shades of pale blue, yellow and violet. The main border, running from the pumphouse to the house, would get all the best yellows. A second bed, which would be created along the path in the lower garden, would be reserved for all the most agreeable pastels, with an accent on the blues. The third long border, somewhat off the beaten path, would be a low maintenance or holding garden for all the other irises.

Actually the hot dry conditions of central Italy seem to suit the bearded iris. None of my irises has ever suffered from the root-rot that affects irises in damper climates, and I see little evidence that an iris which is watered regularly in summer does better than one which is not. The leaves of both come down with a certain amount of brown-spot every summer, but these can be cut away with little trouble.

This is not to say, however, that irises will flourish on total neglect. In the first few years after we had created the long bed, we were rather cavalier about the weeding, and we soon realized that we were beginning to lose plants. We now make a habit of weeding the long bed quite thoroughly twice a year, and it has regained its old vigour. Weeding iris is a tiresome chore as there is a danger of cutting off the tender young spears as they emerge in the spring. Hand work is the only answer. Later in the year, when the flowers are taller, it is possible to go in and weed with a hoe or a sharp instrument but there is still the danger of chopping the rhizomes to pieces.

It is helpful to remember that iris rhizomes generally arrange themselves in a circle, like children sitting on the beach with their feet together. The rhizomes, like the legs of the children, usually point into the centre of the circle; so the place to weed is along the rounded backs of the plants where there are fewer roots. A spade or a hoe can go in quite safely at this point, and if possible the earth should be moved away from the rhizome to expose it to the sun. If the centre of the rhizome has become large and overgrown, it is always a good idea to pull it up and discard it after blooming. I have also found that a small handful of mixed fertilizer on each clump from time to time brings good results.

All this is not to give the impression that the high spring garden is made up exclusively of beautiful peonies and rainbow-coloured iris because in between these gems are sprinklings of salmon, grey blue and mossy green which lend a certain tartness to the overall picture.

Coming into the garden from the pumphouse, the first colour that strikes the visitor is the pale pink of the floribunda climbing rose 'Clair Matin'® which blooms repeatedly. This is a sturdy plant with bunches of shell-pink flowers which emerge from tight crimson buds and it looks exceedingly pretty climbing up the rough stone wall of the pumphouse. On the southern wall of the house, a pale milky blue plumbago bush sprawls upwards towards the roof: and across from this in the border there is another quite different blue, the misty grey-blue of the *Ceanothus* × *delileanus* 'Gloire de Versailles'.

Beyond the ceanothus there is a low clump of the French lavender, *Lavandula stoechas*, its darkish violet flowers contrasting nicely with some yellow irises and clumps of yellow calendulas. Behind them is a big abelia bush which is just beginning to put out a few pink flowers and in the foreground a mass of purple and blue acanthus with handsome leaves reminiscent of Greek columns. Many Italians regard the acanthus as a weed and complain about its thorns, but I like its sturdy architectural look, and the fact that it is such an easy grower. Next to this there is a ripple of pink iris, which makes way for a large stand of ground-hugging white osteospermum flowers, the kind with the dark blue centres and blue on the underside of the petals. These recent imports from South Africa are surprisingly hardy and have come through several winters a bit daunted but not destroyed. The border ends with a splash of mustard yellow from the big Jerusalem sage, *Phlomis fruticosa*, and this colour is echoed in the early copper-yellow blossoms of the 'Mermaid' rose which arches across a corner of the house.

The small terraced garden close by the front door is devoted to herbaceous peonies interplanted with pale blue iris and blue catnip. Our dining terrace overlooks this peony bed and the wide stone terrace wall is covered with terracotta pots of blue plumbago and pink and crimson Lady Washington (or regal) pelargoniums. The most arresting of these is 'Carisbrooke' which looks like pink sorbet with darker spots towards the centre. This plant has now grown into a smallish shrub, and last May it gave us twenty or thirty clumps of gorgeous bloom. Many visitors mistake it for a flowering azalea. It is odd that I, who generally spurn azaleas, am quite smitten by a geranium whose main claim to fame is that it looks like an azalea. I also have a wonderful dark red pelargonium called 'Black Prince'. Unfortunately 'Carisbrooke' blooms only once, but 'Black Prince' shows signs of blooming again in August.

As the gardener wanders from the upper border to the lower terrace there is a sense of drifting through a mist of diffuse and impressionistic colours like saffron and cerulean blue and peach, but no matter how great the satisfaction, there is a nagging awareness that time is marching on and that all this beauty will shortly disappear.

I remember taking a last walk around my garden one glorious evening in May, and sitting down beside the fig tree to write in my diary:

> After May
> It's downhill
> All
> The
> Way.

I must confess that when I wrote this I was reckoning without roses; for I had long been of the opinion that roses really won't grow well in Mediterranean climates. I am not sure where I picked up this idea; it may have been from Edith Wharton's book on Italian villas, which suggests that for the summer months it is best to abandon flowers altogether, or it may have come from articles in British garden magazines complaining that roses are never really happy in the heat. Obediently I crossed roses off my list and looked elsewhere for summer colour.

But there came a time when I started visiting the new Italian gardens in central Italy, and I realized that I had been somewhat premature in my judgement about roses. There is a vast diversity among roses, I discovered, and some of the best of them – especially old-fashioned varieties such as China roses, Noisettes and Moss roses, and ancient climbers – are much more suitable for Italy than their rich cousins, the elegant Hybrid Teas.

This new enthusiasm for old roses is visible everywhere you turn. Several nurseries which specialize in old roses have opened branches in Rome to cope with the increased demand. British growers of antique roses, taking advantage of the newly relaxed European Union rules, are shipping barrow-loads of bare root English roses to Italian gardeners. Even the directors of the Boboli Gardens in Florence, the stronghold of Renaissance formalism, are replanting their famous island beds with hundreds of antique French roses.

The question immediately arises: what has caused this dramatic return to the roses of yesterday? There are several answers. For one thing many gardeners, finding help un-available, have woken up to the fact that the Hybrid Teas, though beautiful, require a lot of extra care and are far too exclusive to prosper in do-it-yourself gardens.

Dissatisfaction with these hybrid roses is nothing new. Back in 1942 America's foremost authority on hot-weather garden-ing, Elizabeth Lawrence, blamed commercial growers for letting priceless stocks of heritage roses disappear while they concentrated on the synthetic charms of the Hybrid Teas, which were more profitable in the cut-flower trade. Mrs Lawrence complained in her book *A Southern Garden* that the new hybrids were not at all suitable for her North Carolina garden. 'A great wail is going up for the lost tea roses, the Moss roses, the China and the Bourbons,' she wrote. 'In addition to their peculiar grace and wonderful fragrance they are particu-larly well suited to our climate, more so than many of the modern roses.'

Two generations years later another expert on hot climate gardens, the Marchesa Lavinia Taverna in Italy, was even more outspoken in her distaste for the Hybrid Teas. In her book *Un Giardino Mediterraneo*, published in 1982, she made a distinction between what she called the 'true roses' (or old roses) and the Hybrid Teas, which she declared were not only 'vulgar and decadent' but were also lacking in a proper modesty – not really roses at all. Real roses, she wrote, were the older natural roses, the kind that made loose bushes full of sweet-smelling flowers, required little care and ended the year with a flush of bright rose-hips.

Until her outburst many Italian gardeners were convinced, as I was, that Italy was not rose friendly. The Marchesa Taverna, however, was not one to accept this defeatist view, and she hunted around in old gardens and nursery catalogues to try to locate some of the simple roses she remembered from her childhood. One group which attracted her curiosity were the China roses which had first appeared in Europe around 1800 and had the advantage of blooming almost continuously from April to December, the only rose to show such pluck.

To show her faith in the China roses she bravely planted 350 bushes of *R.* × *odorata* 'Mutabilis' (changeable Chinese) on the hillside of her new garden at La Landriana near Anzio. This rose is nowhere near as flashy as the Hybrid Teas but it is ever-blooming. Seen singly the roses are not all that impressive, but when you encounter 350 large 'Mutabilis' bushes covered with thousands of multicoloured flowers in the middle of December, it is a scene that remains imprinted on the memory.

Since the Marchesa and a few other rosarians started their search, informal cottage gardens full of heirloom roses have sprung up (almost in secret). The Mediterranean climate wasn't hostile to roses after all, it turned out; it was just that the roses that grow best in Italy had been forgotten.

The history of the old roses – and of their subsequent eclipse – could be set to music (harp and flute) or recited by an epic poet. First there were the wild roses, the simple pink and white dog roses, the sweetbriar rose and others. In the early days the wild roses were crossed to make some charming mixtures such as the Albas, which bloom in early summer, or the Centifolias which were growing in the sixteenth century, or the Gallicas beloved of the Empress Josephine. A breakthrough came in the late eighteenth century when the very first China roses were shipped to Europe from China. These little bushes which produced their flowers in modest bunches were an immediate sensation because of their ever-blooming fortitude. In fact, one of the first of the China roses was called *semperflorens* 'Slater's Crimson China' in honour of Gilbert Slater, a director of the East India Company, who first spotted the rose in 1790 and sent it home. As soon as the bushes arrived from China, the Europeans started marrying the new arrivals to European roses, and to this day any continuous flowering rose is bound to have a Chinese rose as its ancestor.

Two of the most popular hybrids produced by crossing were the Tea rose (not to be confused with the Hybrid Teas) and the Noisette. The original Tea roses had simple soft-coloured flowers and they were called 'Tea' roses because they were sent with tea on ships from China and, some said, they smelled of tea – whereas in truth they smelled more of fruit or new wine.

The China rose produced a second important offspring, the Noisette, which was destined to become one of the most vigorous and beautiful climbers of all time. The first Noisettes, hybridized by an American named Philippe Noisette, are warm-climate climbers which range upwards from two to ten metres, and are especially good for Italy where they achieve their best flowering in the autumn, a time when Italy undergoes a second spring. Favourite Noisettes are the pale pink 'Mme Alfred Carrière' and the egg-yellow 'Maréchal Niel'.

The specialist dealer Walter Bianchi, who has one of the biggest collections of old roses in the country, wrote in his catalogue: 'The antique roses seem to be superbly adapted for Italy. In a Mediterranean climate, roses that bloom only once can be disappointing because, if the heat arrives too soon, their flowering period can be very brief. Old roses instead flower abundantly until winter, and occasionally into some of the coldest months; they are not too disturbed by the cold because during the hot summer, there was time for their wood to harden.' Bianchi added that these beauties 'grow well in all of the Italian territory and they grow magnificently wherever there are olive trees or fields of grain'.

Having joined the ranks of old rose growers rather late I am hurrying to catch up. An opportunity to try my hand presented itself last winter when Robert announced that he was tired of pruning some of the smaller olive trees around the house and was thinking of cutting them down.

'Those trees will never give us any olive oil,' he said. 'They were damaged in the frost of 1981, and they will never amount to a row of beans; better to cut them down and start with something new.'

'Don't do it,' I said. 'I'll grow climbing roses up them.' And before he had a chance to object, I had ordered a dozen bare-root climbers from Peter Beales and a month later we were planting them out, being careful to keep them a metre away from the tree trunks, so they wouldn't be bothered by olive roots. I had stayed up nights compiling lists of the roses I wanted, but I can only hope that I chose well. Near the house we put in 'Complicata', an ancient single rose from the Gallica family. It blooms only once, in June, which is a pity, but to make up for this it has masses of pink flowers with paler centres which are vigorous enough to fill an olive tree and cover a pergola too. The rest of the ramblers will swarm up the previously unloved olive trees making a nice combination of pink and crimson with the green-grey leaves of the olives. These include 'Awakening', which is a double quartered form of 'New Dawn' recently discovered in Czechoslovakia, and 'Aloha', whose flowers will have sixty or so rose-pink petals. I have also planted a vigorous climber with the enticing name of 'Parkdirektor Riggers'® which will give us clusters of single crimson flowers near the blackbird's nest; 'Laura Louise', which will be mild pink to salmon; 'Galway Bay', which will be salmon and free-flowing too, and a *Rosa banksiae* 'Lutea' which has already produced a flush of pale yellow flowers climbing the olive tree in the lower terrace.

The experts warn that growing rambling roses requires patience; that it may take three years for them really to hit their stride. But who cares? We know they are there, biding their time while their roots enlarge and their buds grow and ripen, and they give us something to look forward to. Growing roses teaches the value of patience and of contemplation, virtues in short supply in this harassed world.

June

Country Weddings

JUNE IS SURELY THE MONTH FOR ROSES; BUT PERHAPS MORE important, it is the month of weddings. And there are almost as many varieties of wedding as there are roses.

In the early days, the unspoken reason for many country marriages tended to be solid practicality; how much did the bridegroom earn in a month and how big a dowry could the bride muster? How well connected were the parents? Love was incidental. This strictly businesslike approach yielded eventually to something that was a little more romantic – weddings for love, weddings for affection, weddings for a nice honeymoon in southern Spain. But country weddings have taken a very peculiar turn of late and what we have now are weddings as spectaculars or managed commercial events. The bride and groom have become simple actors in a show that is put on by people who make money from it – caterers, hairdressers, make-up artists, musicians, cooks and the countesses who rent out their castles to provide a tasteful background for hundreds of photos which can be saved for posterity in white leatherette photo albums and full-length video features. We have moved from wedding as straightforward commerce to wedding as show business in less than two generations.

We learned much about the first kind of wedding from an early *tuttofare* ('maid of all work') called Lucia, who hailed from the village of Blera, which is only about fifteen miles as the (hooded) crow flies from Canale.

It was actually because of the Blera connection that we hired Lucia. We thought she would not be averse to accompanying us from Rome to the country when the summer holidays began, as she could get to visit her family at least once a week. Only after she had been working for us a while did we discover what a practical girl Lucia was. Her story was in fact typical of a whole generation of village girls who were driven to seek work in the big cities after the deprivations of the Second World War. Having spent the war years grinding acorns to make coffee and carrying water from the village well for both cooking and washing, Lucia had been willing to take almost any post-war job which would assure her three meals a day and a warm bed. Her first job as a *tuttofare* was for a Roman lawyer's family and her daily stint involved preparing and serving meals for six people, cleaning a large apartment and waxing all the floors. She was also required to do the family wash, and this meant carrying the laundry on her head to the roof and washing it by hand in a cold water fountain.

She began work at six in the morning and was rarely

finished before ten at night. She had to work on all holidays, was given three hours off on Sunday afternoons (but she had to return home to cook the Sunday supper) and her pay was eight thousand lire a month which in those days was roughly five pounds.

Lucia's living conditions were equally Spartan. There was no maid's room in the apartment, so she had to unfold a cot in the kitchen every night after the dishes were done. Her sleep was not infrequently disturbed by visits from the lawyer's oldest son who came ostensibly in search of mineral water.

The food supply was also restricted. The lawyer's wife kept the refrigerator and cupboard padlocked and while members of the family enjoyed meat and butter every night, Lucia usually had to content herself with eggs and margarine.

Gradually, as she moved from job to job, Lucia gained courage and began to make certain small demands. She dared to tell her fourth employer that she was accustomed to eat meat twice a week and that she would be unable to wash clothes unless she had a good detergent (not a bar of yellow soap) and hot water. Somewhat to her surprise her employer agreed. Later she was lucky enough to find a family who possessed a semi-automatic washing machine.

She was helped substantially in her upward climb by the Italian Parliament. During the early Fifties a group of Communist deputies sponsored a series of reforms aimed at ending the exploitation of domestic help, and the centre parties went along with them in hopes of forestalling other more menacing reforms. Maids suddenly found themselves blessed with social security, health insurance, an extra month's pay at Christmas and time off on all religious and national holidays.

By the time she came to work for us, Lucia was thirty-seven and sitting pretty. She no longer had to contend with a semi-automatic washer but had one that was fully automatic; all she needed to do was to pop the clothes into the machine's hungry mouth and the family washing was done.

Lucia was also delighted to find we did not keep the refrigerator locked, and so she was able to eat beef steaks and roast lamb with comforting regularity. She also had free access to the cheese and wine, not to mention shampoo and aspirin. The improvement in her condition showed. She acquired twenty extra kilos, an accumulation which, far from regarding as a disaster, she tended to look upon as a prudent investment against some future famine. Not for nothing do the Italians speak approvingly of buxom females as *tosta* (solid) or *bella piena* (pleasingly plump) while shaking their heads sadly over women who have lost weight, complaining that they are either *secca* (dry and withered) or *sciupata* (wasted, spoiled or damaged).

In all the twenty years in Rome Lucia had acquired only one thing which she sometimes regretted – a daughter. This acquisition, a result of the son's midnight visits to the kitchen, had been embarrassing, and to make things worse the lawyer fired her the moment her condition became obvious. Lucia was by no means the first working woman to be faced with this disaster, but she was one of the few who accepted her fate with good grace, sending the child to a convent of Sardinian nuns rather than abandoning her on the steps of a Roman church, as was the more common practice.

Seventeen years after the unfortunate event, Lucia was quite reconciled to it. In a year or two her daughter would be out of the convent, fully educated, and she and Lucia, earning two salaries, would be able to set themselves up in a small apartment complete with TV and a washing machine of their own.

One would say, looking in from the outside, that Lucia had coped with her misfortune nobly and could now take satisfaction in her position in life. And yet to say this would be to squint at the true picture, for in Lucia's heart, as in the hearts of most Italian domestics, there lurked a desire for a *sistemazione*. According to the dictionary *sistemazione* means a 'regularization' or a 'trimming, as of a ship's hold', but to *tuttofari* in Italy it means only one thing – marriage. The word appears to have very little of a romantic connotation to it, as I have said, because it is only in wealthy nations or very sentimental ones that a girl can afford to get married for love. In rural Italy *sistemazione* means just that, a trimming of the hold, a stocking of the larder, and the less said about love the better.

Lucia kept her secret well hidden, but it was there all the same. What else would explain the hope chest under her bed with the two dozen hand-hemmed sheets and the three dozen pillowcases? If anyone had asked, Lucia would have explained that the sheets were for her daughter, but the initials on them were hers. Her daughter would be married in good time, Lucia knew, but she was also convinced that she herself, with a growing nest-egg in the bank, stood a fine chance of landing a husband – better perhaps than she had had twenty years ago.

An opportunity, not perfect but plausible, presented itself when we moved out to the country to spend three summer months. Being a country girl, Lucia was very pleased with the move and soon began to make friends in the village. Her best friends were our neighbours Jack and Sora Nina who lived in a small clump of houses near the outskirts of the village. Jack spent much of his spare time in the Circolo dei Anziani (club for elders) playing *scopone* but Signora Nina conducted her social life at home, and if one can speak of a salon in a village of three hundred souls it was certainly Signora Nina who ran it. On any Saturday or Sunday afternoon her kitchen was likely to house anywhere from five to eight chatting friends. Lucia got into the habit of going to visit Signora Nina on Sundays, when she didn't go to Blera, and one afternoon she found the signora taking care of two little boys. Nina explained to her that they were the children of her sister's son Giuseppe, whose wife had died in childbirth eight months earlier. A hard-working mason, Giuseppe had no one to watch over his boys and Nina had secretly taken it upon herself to find a new wife for him as soon as possible. This was not an easy task, as there were surprisingly few marriageable girls in the village and most of the younger ones were not at all interested in a widower with two small children.

As she recounted the story to me Lucia showed an astonishing familiarity with Giuseppe's situation.

'The piccolo boy no longer wets his bed and the older one is a well-behaved child. They both go to school all day where they wear black smocks so there will not be a big laundry problem. Then there is Giuseppe's mother,' Lucia told me.

'She is seventy-nine and lives alone near the Signora Nina. She does most of the work for herself.'

I expressed certain reservations about the mother.

'No, no, it is all right. She is already old for her family,' Lucia assured me. 'Most of them were dead at sixty-five.'

'And how about Giuseppe?' I asked.

'Oh, Giuseppe,' Lucia replied. 'He earns six thousand lire a day as a mason. He has three vineyards and over two hundred olive trees which give him a quintal and a half of olive oil a year. He has five pigs and two dozen chickens in his yard right now and he owns his own house with electricity and a television.'

Lucia looked over at me and smiled. It is impossible in the course of any human encounter to decide the exact moment when an idea is born but at that instant I realized that Lucia had decided she would become Giuseppe's second wife.

Lucia had seen the young widower only once; he had been leaving Nina's kitchen one evening when she went to call. He was a presentable man with clean hands and a clean white shirt and he did not have that frowzy red-faced look most feared by country women – the look of a wife-beater and a drunkard. The marriage, it seemed obvious, would have much to offer on all sides. It would give the little boys a mother, it would give Giuseppe a housekeeper and it would give Lucia the *sistemazione* she had always yearned for.

There were drawbacks, to be sure, but they seemed almost to balance out. Lucia had the regrettable daughter, but she also had the money in the bank. Giuseppe had the mother and the very young children, but he also had his own house, his own land and a good reputation as a sober wage earner.

The Signora Nina had promised to get Giuseppe's reaction to the matter and the following weekend the preliminary vote was in. Giuseppe, who had observed Lucia only fleetingly, had found her not disagreeable although she was undeniably older than he was. Lucia for her part had one final request; she would like to see Giuseppe's house before making up her mind. She had always made it a point to check on the houses where she went to work, so why not check out the house where she might spend the rest of her life?

Nina apparently understood her point and obtained the keys to the house from Giuseppe's mother. As Lucia told me later, the house lay on a little hillock just a short distance from Nina's, and once the two women had assured themselves that the master was not at home, they crossed the artichoke patch in front of it and opened the gate. Nina went first – small and sprightly as a sparrow – and Lucia followed. Her first view of the house pleased her. It was a modern construction, recently built of tufa blocks and then plastered.

'It was new,' Lucia told me with satisfaction. 'That means cement dust of course but new houses do not have insects. Giuseppe made this with his own hands, so he is not your ordinary village loafer.'

She found the house bright and fresh, if untidy, inside. One entered directly into the kitchen which had a large table in the centre, a white stove, a refrigerator and a TV set. A door from the kitchen led to the master's bedroom which contained all the standard bedroom items, a matrimonial bed, an *armadio* (wardrobe) in pale fake mahogany, a dresser and three large crystal mirrors, one over the dresser, one on the *armadio* door and one on the wall. A small picture of the Madonna hung over the bed. In an alcove off this room was another smaller bedroom for the children.

Around the back, down an outside staircase, there was a small *cantina* for storing wine, cheese, chestnuts, pork, dried grapes and other provisions. Lucia was greatly satisfied with the larder. 'He kills two pigs in the winter,' she told me. 'He also has dried apples and plenty of good green olive oil. I suppose he needs a woman to help him put up tomato preserve and dried figs. I myself am very partial to cherries in alcohol, the sour cherries of course.'

There was only one drawback as far as Lucia was concerned and that was the bathroom. It was downstairs too, next to the *cantina*. And instead of a bath, there was only a shower. Lucia had spent the first twenty years of her life on a farm which had no running water but her experience in Rome had led her to expect better things.

'It is a sacrifice, getting along without a bath,' she sighed, 'and it is even more of a sacrifice that you have to go outside to get there.'

Lucia stared at a pot of geraniums on our window sill, her small round face a picture of misery. Then she shuddered as if trying to throw off the whole dreary picture.

'No,' she said at last, 'I could get along without a hot bath which is so nice for the kidneys. But to go out in the cold on a wet December night, no, I cannot do that again.'

The word was relayed back to Giuseppe who had no comment to make, and to his mother who expressed regret. But amid all the talk there was no one who criticized Lucia. She was a *brava donna* and if she now felt that she could not manage without an indoor bathroom, then no one should blame her.

The affair was thus closed with no rancour and no scenes. Lucia put her sheets and pillowcases back in the trunk under her bed. Giuseppe went on working as a mason, and his female relatives took care of his little boys.

And then one day in the middle of summer Nina came down with Jack's lunch and some surprising news for Lucia. 'Do you want to know what Giuseppe is doing today?' she screamed in triumph. 'He is starting to build a new bathroom off the kitchen inside the house.'

Lucia made no attempt to hide her satisfaction.

'Ah, so he has finally understood,' she said. 'He is a man who can be reasoned with.'

It would be a small room attached to his house, still without a bath, said Signora Nina, but there would be a bidet and a hot shower.

Lucia seemed hardly to have heard her.

'Ah well, it is indoors none the less. That is the important thing.'

From that day on Lucia's life, like a barge freed from a sandbar, took on a new purpose. She got out her sheets and began to air them all over again. She started going through her wardrobe, throwing out old dresses and buying new ones. She took to spending her days off in shops that sold fabrics, and she began to buy towelling and table linens.

Giuseppe for his part went stalwartly ahead building the bathroom after his regular working hours. He did not seek any further acquaintance with Lucia and Lucia did not seem to feel that this was necessary. The bargain had been struck, Nina was the witness, and Lucia was sure that she would have ample time to get to know Giuseppe after they were married.

She kept a careful watch on the progress of the building and everything about it pleased her. She saw the walls going up, straight and tidy against the fig trees, then the small window and the roof. Then one Monday afternoon in early September Nina burst into our kitchen.

'I have something terrible to tell you, Lucia,' she said, her voice unnaturally low.

'What is it?'

'He is getting married.'

Lucia stopped peeling potatoes.

'Giuseppe?'

'Yes, and there is nothing we can do. He will be a married man in ten days. I should never have put any trust in him.'

Lucia's small, round face seemed on the verge of crumpling up like a piece of wadded newspaper.

'But who is he marrying?' she wailed. 'I thought he was marrying me.'

'He was,' Nina went on sorrowfully, 'but something went wrong. And it is partly my fault. The girl is a girl from the village. She is the daughter of a niece of mine. She is only twenty years old and very flighty. But it is my fault. I asked her to come up to help me hunt for mushrooms.'

'And what happened?'

'She saw the new bathroom,' Nina mourned, 'just before he put on the roof.'

A spark of understanding came into Lucia's eyes.

'So then what happened?' she asked.

'She managed to hang around until Giuseppe came home from work. I should have known it,' Nina said, 'a widower with two children and an old mother is one thing, but a widower with two children and an old mother and a brand new bathroom with hot water is something else again.'

Soon after this blow, Lucia abandoned us and got a job with an engineer's family in Rome. One day I ran into her by chance when crossing the Piazza del Popolo and was impressed by her air of prosperity. She was wearing a suit of excellent wool and although her girth had undoubtedly increased, the eye was drawn to her gold lapel pin and her wide gold wedding ring.

I remarked on her evident good fortune and she beamed.

'Oh Signora, I have been extremely lucky,' she said. 'My daughter Patrizia was married to an air force captain, and now lives in a very nice villa in Checchignola. They travel to Florida every year for holidays. And I was married too about a year after Patrizia.'

I asked for details and they were proudly produced. Lucia had met a prosperous *tappezziere* (upholsterer) who came to work regularly in the household where she was employed. He was about fifteen years older than she was, but he owned a paid-up apartment with two bedrooms in an excellent district of Monte Mario and had a pension from his days making parachutes for the army. The *tappezziere*, poor man, had a daughter whom Lucia described as *infelice* (unhappy) – I got the impression that she was mentally disturbed – and so before the marriage Lucia and her husband-to-be signed an agreement whereby, upon the death of the husband, Lucia became the sole proprietor of the apartment while agreeing to take care of the daughter as long as she lived.

Lucia said it had been a very successful marriage. Her husband had unfortunately died five years ago and soon after this the daughter had become unmanageable and had to be institutionalized in a state-supported *manicomio* (psychiatric hospital). Lucia now lived the life of a lady of leisure. She grew geraniums on her little terrace which looked out towards Frascati, she invited Patrizia and her husband to supper once a week, and once a month in the good weather she went to visit the step-daughter in the state *manicomio*.

'I don't think she recognizes me any more,' Lucia said to me, 'but I go anyway. I am a woman with a very tender heart.'

Massimo

ONE OF THE PLEASURES OF SUMMER IN THE COUNTRY IS that the heat gives everyone an excuse to relax and spend more time hanging out with their friends. Massimo the bulldozer driver cut his work schedule in the hot weather, spending more time on road-repairing in the overgrown *macchia*, and since he was not allowed to take his bulldozer out on to the macadam roads because of the damage caused by its heavy iron chains he fell into the habit of parking it with us at night.

He usually came down to us in the morning on his motor-cycle to fetch his machine and in the late afternoons, after parking it next to the studio, he often joined us for a glass of wine.

It is impossible to relate all the things we talked about during those early summer evenings but we approached the subject of politics with some care. Massimo was a blind admirer of everything Russian and even kept a big flag with a hammer and sickle in his wardrobe at home. He had in fact taken several tours organized by the Italian Communist party to Moscow, and he was very proud that he had been included in a group of Italian dignitaries who had been received by Leonid Brezhnev at the Kremlin. Whenever our arguments got too heated he would shake a fist at us and repeat an old Communist warning: '*Ha da venir Baffone.*' (Watch out, the man with the big moustaches [Stalin] is bound to come.) The warning was given in much the same tone that mothers used to warn their children that they'd better behave or the bad witch would get them.

The more we got to know him, the more we realized what a tempestuous fellow Massimo really was. He hated the local priest, a rather pompous man who walked up and down the main street of Canale with his hands behind his back like a penguin, and he detested the priest's sister, an ample red-haired martinet who grew gigantic dahlias in her front garden and exercised a firm control over Canale social life.

'If a woman like that is the flower of Christianity, then I am La Madonna di Pompeii,' Massimo muttered darkly.

He was also involved in local politics, though we could never make out what his official position was. One morning he came down to fetch his bulldozer looking blacker than usual.

'I'm in a terrible fix,' he confessed to Robert. 'I drank too much wine at the bar last night, and I got into an argument with the Mayor [who was also a Communist] and I knocked him down. They say he may send the Carabinieri after me.'

But the Carabinieri never came and when we asked Jack about it, he chuckled.

'Don't you worry, the Carabinieri will never come after Massimo,' Jack said.

Oddly enough, women did not seem to play a very important part in Massimo's life but suddenly during our third summer, when he was turning forty-eight, he surprised us by announcing that he had just married a local woman named Henrietta, who had been widowed a year before and had two young daughters. We had not been invited to the wedding because Massimo wouldn't suffer a church service. The knot was tied by the Mayor (who seemed to have forgiven the bar-room episode) during a brief ceremony in the town hall, a most unusual procedure for Canale.

Massimo's life didn't change a particle because of his altered status. He still went home at night when it suited him, parking his big motorcycle in the front hall, and Henrietta obediently kept his meal waiting. After supper he still went out to the local winery where he played cards, drank litres of frightful wine, and got into political fights with his friends and neighbours.

At length, again to our surprise, Massimo announced casually that Henrietta was expecting a baby, and soon Henrietta gave birth to a little girl whom they called Giuseppina. Massimo put on his Mexican hat and carried the baby all over Canale so that his friends could admire her, a tiny creature done up in white ribbons and lace, and he put her in a basket and brought her down on his motorcycle to show us.

But when the time came for the baptism, he was adamant.

'Those women are not going to get me into the church,' he said. 'I would rather drink a glass of ammonia than go in and shake hands with that priest.'

So Henrietta and her friends contacted the priest, stitched an organza baby dress and went to the church to have the baby baptized, while Massimo waited outside on the church steps, dark and scowling. He had put on a clean shirt for the occasion, but there was no necktie and no suit jacket for this champion of the proletariat. After the baptism Massimo permitted himself to be dragged to a luncheon which Henrietta had organized at a local trattoria, but he refused to sit at the head of the table and insisted to everyone that he had only come because of his affection for his little girl.

Among his many accomplishments Massimo had one of which he was unusually proud. He was the *braccio di ferro* (arm-wrestling) champion of Canale. Night after night he sat in his bar on the main street and took on all challengers, and no one ever wrestled his hand to the table.

We decided to give him a surprise. Robert's sculptor friend, Don Saco, had phoned us to say that he would be coming through Italy in a week and would like to visit us in the country. Don was a slim fellow with curly blond hair, and in sporty jeans and a loose-fitting jacket he did not look a muscular type. But appearances were misleading as Don was actually a physical fitness buff and had been a *braccio di ferro* champion in the US Marine Corps. He didn't smoke and he didn't drink and he was a member of a prestigious athletic club in New York, where he kept in trim doing push-ups and weight-lifting and serious muscle-building exercises three times a week. With the jacket on, he was just another commuter to the Upper West Side. With the jacket off, he revealed a torso and a pair of biceps that made susceptible ladies faint.

When Don arrived we found out where Massimo would be holding forth that night and at nine o'clock we went round to the bar to have a glass of wine. Robert introduced his friend to Massimo, and then suggested, as if it was a new thought, that Don would like to challenge him to a *braccio di ferro* contest. Massimo agreed to do it just to please us. I remember his smile when he looked over our slim friend. Here was a brash American giving himself airs about his athletic ability, he was obviously thinking. Nothing to worry about.

The two sat down at a wooden table and nearly everyone in the bar gathered round. The two men clenched hands and Massimo gave an immediate tug to pull Don's arm down to the table. The arm refused to budge. Massimo looked confused and gave another, even bigger pull to his hand. To his astonishment, Don started moving Massimo's hand to the table.

The audience became deathly silent.

Massimo looked around in surprise and confusion, and then he moved his rear end rapidly to left and right, sending Robert, sitting next to him, to the far end of the bench. He spread his feet wider apart to get a better purchase on his seat.

I would like to report that Don Saco brought the giant down, but that was not the case. The truth was that after readjusting his seat and concentrating his efforts, Massimo managed to get his hand back in a neutral position, and after a jaw-clenching battle that lasted more than ten minutes the two wrestled almost to a draw. By this time Massimo's face was dark red and drops of sweat stood out on his forehead. But eventually, after a Herculean effort, he gave a heave from his shoulder and pulled Saco's hand to the table. It was a brilliant demonstration of strength, and Saco had to admit that he had found his master.

About six years after this historic confrontation, Massimo was collecting grapes during the October *vendemmia* (grape harvest) and walking back to the vines after a heavy lunch he suddenly toppled to the ground. It took four men to manoeuvre his great hulk into a little Fiat 600, but when they got to the hospital he was already dead. He had had a massive heart attack.

Henrietta let it be known that the funeral service would be in the church two days later, and nearly everybody from Canale came to bid farewell to their comrade and tractor-driver. The crowds were so large that people overflowed on to the streets. Banked next to the church doors were five funeral wreaths as big as wagon wheels made up of bright red carnations and bearing ribbons that said PCI (Partito Comunista Italiano) and PCI Sezione Bracciano. Standing near these wreaths, but a little apart from the crowd, stood a group of men in dark suits wearing red carnations in their buttonholes and I noticed several long black cars, clearly official limousines from Rome, parked near the kerb.

The greatly distrusted Canale parish priest had been tactfully banished from the proceedings – he wasn't even present in the back row – and the very brief service was led by a young priest who had a faintly military look about him. Question: does the party have a special group of young priests whom they keep on tap just to officiate at the funerals of departing Communists? We filed out of the church after the service, stopping on the steps to commiserate with some of Massimo's old drinking pals and some of the farmers whose land he had ploughed. As I surveyed the scene, it seemed to me that I could see a burly man with a Mexican hat standing by the kerb looking over towards us with a frown of derision and even scorn.

'Churches, priests,' I could hear him mutter. 'They'll never get me into a church, never.' But they did, *caro* Massimo, they did.

After the church service, Henrietta invited us to her house to have a cup of tea and meet some of Massimo's relatives from Rome. He had never mentioned any relatives to us, but there in Henrietta's crowded parlour sat Massimo's sisters, three distinguished matrons with well-cut grey hair, real pearls and excellent brooches on their expensive dark silk dresses. It seemed impossible that these ladies could be related to Massimo in any way! And it seemed even more impossible when we met their husbands, discreet, well-dressed gentlemen who could have been accountants or notaries public, or even deputy directors of personnel in the Department of Posts and Telecommunications. Gentlemen of standing and position and dignity; exactly the kind of successful bureaucrats whom Massimo most despised.

I tried to figure it out. How had it all come about? Were the three sisters *vere signore* (true gentlewomen) as my Roman friends would have put it? They looked genuine to me. Or were they simply rural girls who had polished off the rough edges and married above their station to achieve a place as middle-class matrons in Rome? That would have required a stunning effort in social levitation.

The former possibility seemed the more credible to me, which meant that our Massimo was the one who changed. He had decided to give up the pretensions of his bourgeois family and climb off the ladder which led to middle-class respectability, throwing in his lot with dirt farmers, woodcutters and barrel makers – his true brothers and comrades. But if this was so, how was it possible for him to have so completely thrown off all signs of his earlier identity?

I am quite sure that this explanation is too simplistic. The truth, if it should ever come out, could be stranger than anything I have imagined.

July

A Paeon in Praise of Chicory
and a Hurrah for Herbs

WHEN JULY ARRIVES AFTER THE HEADLONG RUSH OF
spring, the pace of country life tends to slow down.
The hay has been gathered and baled, the wheat has been
winnowed, the wine is maturing in the *cantina*, and a few
brave flowers are trying to hold the line against the mercury.
The hollyhocks make a strong display of pinks, scarlets and
carmines and an exciting new discovery, *Lavatera* 'Barnsley',
spreads its pretty flower up and down the paths. This friendly
shrub, a perennial member of the mallow family, was re-
discovered only a few years ago in a forgotten garden in
Barnsley, in the north of England. Unlike most lavateras,
which run to muddy mauves and magentas, 'Barnsley' is a soft
rose doré.

But by the middle of the month most of the flowers are
beginning to give out, except for some stray wild daisies and
one little blue flower that keeps blooming faithfully every

morning – the flower of the chicory plant. Whenever I see this little patch of blue I am filled with wonder because I know of no plant in the vegetable kingdom – not even the bamboo – which has such extraordinary usefulness and variety. You can grind up chicory root and drink it as coffee; you can cook its leaves like spinach, and you can eat its flower buds raw, chopped up with oil and anchovies. As a fresh salad it has become a stylish item for chefs of the nouvelle cuisine and you can savour red chicory salad from Treviso, pink and white salad from Verona, and a delicious white sprout from Belgium which is crisp and tender as a snowdrop.

I first came to know the little chicory when it grew at the bottom of Shipyard Lane in Duxbury, Massachusetts, where we spent our summers. We children used to go down to the shipyard when the tide was out to play hide-and-seek and I remember how delighted I was with the cobalt daisy which popped up every morning between the cradled sailboats. I didn't know that this was a chicory flower but my Quaker grandmother called it the 'blue sailor' and said it bloomed only in the morning.

Time passed and then one day in early July I was weeding the vegetable garden in Canale, a thousand miles from Duxbury, when I spotted a familiar blue flower. It seemed as if some kind of fate had given me back a piece of my child-hood. I carefully staked off the area where the little plant was growing, determined that when I had more time I would try to identify it and save its seeds. The time never came, of course, but in the autumn our neighbour Sora Nina asked me if she could hunt for *la cicoria* in our fields. *La cicoria* is a wild green not unlike a dandelion green which Italians cook with garlic and olive oil. It has a reputation for being good for the blood circulation and the liver. After hunting around our fields, Nina found her biggest clumps right where I had staked off my blue flowers. I realized for the first time that my 'blue sailor' was part of the chicory family. Signora Nina told me that there were other kinds of chicory growing in our fields, especially one called *puntarelle* (little tips) which are the ripening tips of the chicory plant before they bloom. These would-be flower heads look like asparagus but Signora Nina doesn't wait for the flowers to appear; she simply cuts the stalks, then takes a sharp knife and peels back the tougher parts and soaks them in water until they curl up into little green spirals. These are then drained and dressed with a very thick sauce of olive oil, chopped garlic and anchovy.

'You can't have too much anchovy or garlic,' said la Signora. As a late summer salad *puntarelle* is one of the glories of the Roman menu, and I always make it for friends who come to visit.

My curiosity about the varieties of chicory was whetted by these discoveries so I consulted my garden dictionary. I found that chicory, far from being a minor member of the salad family in Italy, is in fact the patriarch of them all. In the section describing vegetables, the dictionary devotes four full pages to the marvels of chicory, while it gives only a single page to all the other salad greens put together.

Perhaps my most surprising discovery was that chicory is not an annual, as I had always thought, but a perennial. This means that a good gardener who is clever with his planting can be boiling or eating fresh chicory most of the year. For commercial purposes it is generally divided into two groups – bread-leafed chicories which make tender salad leaves, and the root chicories which come in winter and are a combination of the white roots and some of the tenderer leaves. None of these various leaves looks much like any other; the only way you can see the family resemblance is to peer down close to the ground where the plants first send their green sprouts and you will spot 'a basal rosette of runcinate leaves' (deeply incised lobes like dandelions).

There are a number of quite different salad leaves which emerge from this runcinate rosette. One, called *escarole* in Italy, is rather like an iceberg lettuce which has been twirled around so that it looks like a seashell. Another chicory leaf looks like an electric-shock hairdo, all curly and kinky, and Henry calls it 'crab salad'.

But if you want to get into the deluxe salad chicories, you have to shell out lots of lire for the pink and red plants called *radicchio tardivo* which come from special growers in the Veneto and are generally sold in winter. These long tubular clumps are classed along with the root chicories because when you buy them there is always a bit of the root attached. This can be included when you are making a salad, as it is the tenderest part of the plant – like the heart of an artichoke. The red root chicory or radicchio actually comes in three varieties. There is the bright red one which comes in a small plump rosette; there is a variegated one which is white speckled with wine-red spots; and there is a third which is long and tapered and red and has a twisted tail and lends itself not only to salads, but to baking or grilling with olive oil. From a nutritional point of view all of these red chicories are loaded with Vitamin C and very good for you. They are said to be somewhat diuretic.

Actually the long, tapered radicchio named 'Variegato di Castelfranco – tardivo' is considered by salad buffs as the champagne of salads and costs double because it takes twice as much work. The special seeds are planted like any regular salad seeds in the spring, and the greens are ready to pick in the autumn. But instead of being harvested, the plants are left out in the cold, and the leaves turn a kind of purple-red. Once they begin to droop they are dug up, roots and all, and heeled into damp earth for several weeks. When the thermometer starts to rise, they are transferred into long basins of fresh water, with only their roots touching the water, so that the new sprouts near the stem will grow again, redder than ever. The colour is achieved by covering the basins with black plastic to eliminate the daylight, and in this cool dark atmosphere the final bright red and white leaves emerge long and curling. The farmers then wash the new plants and shorten their roots, and they are ready for the market.

The various kinds of red radicchio – which are all crisp and slightly bitter – can be eaten in many ways. They can be served as antipasto with sweet raw *prosciutto* which is almost exactly the same colour of pinkish red. They can also be spread out on salad plates, in a design of red stars, and covered with hard-boiled eggs, diced apples, celery and walnuts and black olives. One menu calls for them to be spread out on a plate with hot bean soup poured over them, while another requires them to be served as a sauce for cooked duck; in this case, tiny slices of radicchio are heated along with pomegranate seeds to make a rich hot sauce. And finally they can be grilled and served with good olive oil, a process that has lately become very stylish indeed.

In the Benelux countries farmers have for generations been blanching another member of the chicory family so that it becomes pale, like a white pinecone, and is sold as either 'witloff chicory' or 'Belgian endive'. Reports have it that it was actually the Dutch who came upon this blanched salad delight by pure accident. They had harvested a crop of regular chicory salad leaves in a Dutch greenhouse, and in the late autumn they dug up the chicory roots and dumped them out next to the greenhouse near a manure pile. The roots became partly covered with sand and manure and in a month or two the nursery workers noticed that the old abandoned roots had thrown up some little white sprouts which were actually tightly rolled-up chicory leaves. Delicious! The Dutch made careful note of this, and the next autumn instead of pitching the chicory roots out to make way for their spring bulbs, they carefully planted the roots in a greenhouse under a thick layer of fresh manure and sandy soil. The manure at once began to heat up the old roots and in fifteen or twenty days they had a whole new crop of tender 'Belgian endive' sprouting off the roots. A new luxury green was born.

But now a scholarly Italian friend has advised me that the Dutch are taking too much credit for discovering blanched chicory. She showed me a clipping from a book called *The Fruit and Vegetables of Rome*, in which Giacomo Castelveltro wrote in 1614: 'At the beginning of this dismal season, we use the green leaves of chicory in salads; the tenderest leaves are chopped finely with garlic, which we always eat with chicory ... at the same time we have the shoots of the chicory plant ... buried in sand to make them crisp and white.'

I tried to grow a batch one winter in my cellar. I put my little endive roots into a box of sand and manure right next to our wine barrels, and watered the whole thing. Some time around Christmas I looked down and saw this forgotten box of sand sprouting pale green shoots. I dug down to investigate, and found that just below the surface there was a whole army of small shoots that were fatter and whiter than any salad leaves I had grown before. They made an exotic addition to our Christmas dinner.

I was reciting the marvels of chicory to my daughter Jenny one day as we sat shelling peas in the garden.

'This chicory is really far out,' Jenny commented. 'Next thing you know it will be playing a harp and telling you the correct time.'

'How did you know?' I asked.

I had just read that chicory flowers open and close with such clocklike regularity on summer mornings that Linnaeus used the chicory flower in his floral clock. He used to joke that his clock was so accurate it would put all Swedish watchmakers out of work.

In addition to the chicory flowers and Queen Anne's lace (the common wild carrot), the main ornaments in our pumphouse garden in high summer are an assortment of plants, ranging from rosemary and sage to lavender and various forms of artemisia, which I grow mainly for their grey and glaucous leaves.

The problem in the Mediterranean climates is that there are so many grey-leaved herbs dominating the *macchia* landscape that it seems almost superfluous to bring them into the garden at all. And even if one does try to grow them for display, many quickly become too big to fit the space available.

Accordingly, the only category of cooking herbs that I keep close to the house are the tender little salad herbs – parsley, basil, chive and tarragon – that often get lost in larger vegetable gardens. We now grow all of our herbs in large containers right on the front terrace where they get plenty of water and where we can lean down and pick them while we are eating lunch.

Parsley is not as easy to grow as most herbs, and in fact the Italians have a saying that whenever you plant a parsley seed, it goes down to hell and back before it is edible. We plant the Italian kind of broad-leafed parsley because we think it has the most flavour. It is supposed to be a biennial, growing up one year and continuing to produce in the second year; but we have found that it gets tall and leggy in the second year and you end up eating parsley seeds rather than green leaves, so we tend to cut it down after its first year. My practice is to replant new seeds as soon as the old plants are discarded, no matter what the season, although I think it does best when planted in early spring or early autumn.

The basils, which are annuals, are probably the most useful of the herbs because they are very easy to grow and can be used in a dozen ways in cooking. They are delicious cut up fresh on tomatoes or mozzarella, and can also be used in pesto or spaghetti sauces. We generally buy the basil seedlings that are sold in the spring in plastic boxes in the market, but I am also keen on the basil plants with tiny spicy leaves that come from Sicily.

Chive is not so well known in Italy as it is in northern Europe or in America, but it is quite possible to buy chive plants in nurseries. Cut-up chives are excellent in scrambled eggs or any other dish where a fresh onion taste is needed. The plants disappear in winter like many perennial herbs, but reappear faithfully in the spring.

The artemisias are handsome shrubs for hot weather gardens and the one that is most handy in the kitchen is *Artemisia estragon*, tarragon, known as *dragoncello* in Italian. Since this plant frequently gets swallowed up in the open garden, I grow it in a big pot on the terrace where it is handy when I want a good anise flavour for a roast. It is a perennial and if well treated it will go on for years, although it dies down in winter. In much of Europe they try to sell you Russian tarragon for cooking instead of the far stronger smelling French tarragon. Do not be deceived; insist on the French herb every time.

Another artemisia which is handy to plant, even in the flower garden, is the pretty feathery southernwood, *Artemisia abrotanum*. This makes a foaming bush of finely divided leaves which smell of camphor and can be put in cupboards to ward off moths.

Many of the other cooking herbs are simply too big to fit

into regular gardens. The bay leaf, botanically known as *Laurus nobilis*, grows into a big tree in central Italy, and I keep one near the kitchen door so I can reach for a leaf or two when I am cooking fish.

It is also fun to plant a few very small bay trees in pots when they have only two or three shoots so that they can be braided together while they are still slim and supple. If these braided stems are trimmed rigorously so that no green appears and the greenery on top is cut into a ball, you end up with some nice mop-head bay trees with stiff braided stems which look very stylish around a front door.

Another cooking herb that gets out of hand is the standard rosemary. We removed it from our flower garden long ago, as it grew large and woody and took up all the space, but we took cuttings and poked them along our entrance drive, and now they have grown into sizeable bushes which swing out like petticoats from the line of towering cypresses. In midwinter these rolling waves of rosemary are covered with pale blue flowers, so that driving towards the house is like ploughing through waves breaking on a beach. For the garden itself, I much prefer the manageable little prostrate rosemary which flowers nicely in winter, and can be kept as low as a ground-cover.

The sage *Salvia officinalis*, used in cooking, is a better border plant as it usually grows to only fifteen inches high and in May it can be counted on to produce bunches of deep blue flowers. The only drawback with this plant is that the older parts tend to die back at the end of summer. Sage leaves are good with roast chicken, and also can be crushed into melted butter to make a light sauce for rigatoni.

Several of my friends have a salvia that looks almost exactly like the *officinalis* except that it is twice as big and has leaves that are even more flannelly. No one can tell me what its name is so I can only assume that it is a close relative of the cooking sage; for those who want a more shrub-like plant this is the one to watch out for.

The thyme available to us in Italy is a small ground-creeper called *Thymus serpyllium* which appears spontaneously in our fields. This is too low and mat-like to be much use in the border, but I have transplanted chunks of it into the lawn of the lower garden and there it makes a glorious mauve carpet throughout May and June. The leaves are very good in cooking lamb.

Common lavender, known as *Lavandula officinalis* and much loved by makers of sweet-smelling cachets, really won't do in many gardens because it can grow as big as a rhododendron in a year or two and, like rosemary, it has the bad habit of growing woody and falling over on its side, allowing noxious weeds to flourish underneath. I have therefore shifted to some of the smaller lavenders, and my favourite is the little *Lavandula dentata*, a bushy plant which is easy to handle and has the advantage of producing nice lavender flowers all year long – a trait not shared by the bigger *Lavandula officinalis*. The only trouble with the *dentata* is that it is not altogether hardy and I have twice lost my plants to winter frosts.

A partial answer to this problem is to try still another member of the family, the French lavender, known as *Lavandula stoechas*. This shrub has narrow, fringed grey leaves, and its flowers are dark purple and shaped like small thimbles. From this dark bundle the plant sends out pale purple bracts which contrast nicely with the darker flower heads. The *stoechas* blooms earlier than the *officinalis*, some time in early May, and instead of growing big and woody it tends to grow out horizontally to form a wide purple mat. With its mauve bracts shining in the sun it can look quite lovely with blue and yellow irises blooming around it.

The English have managed to produce some hybrid lavender plants which are smaller and more manageable than the Italian varieties, but I have never had much luck with the 'Munstead Dwarf' or the 'Hidcote' varieties. They never seem very happy with me, and they lack the more exuberant perfume of the Italian plants. I am convinced that this often happens with the plants which Roman soldiers took with them to England. When they left Italy the plants were big and bright, bursting with Mediterranean vigour, but when they come back to Italy two thousand years later they seem smaller and somehow throttled down by the grey skies of the north. (I have noticed this with the passionflower vine. The flower the Romans took with them was a big round flower with a deep blue corolla and vivid yellow stamens. But if you see a passiflora vine in England today you will find that it is smaller and paler than its Italian ancestors, indeed nearly colourless.)

Although I enjoy each of these herbs individually, I am usually unimpressed by the standard herb gardens. When herbs are planted routinely in neat little squares they can be surprisingly dull, especially since their flowers are so tiny. The herb garden at Sissinghurst, for instance, is not a garden that I consider memorable. Just because a group of plants taste good in a soup is no guarantee that they will look well together in a garden.

However, there are two kinds of herb gardens in the Mediterranean area which I find pleasing. My particular favourites are the ancient herb gardens, which were usually called *giardini dei semplici* (gardens of medicinal plants) and were built near monasteries in the Middle Ages. The oldest of them all, and to my mind the most evocative, is the Orto Botanico at Padua, built in 1545 and attached to the school of botany at the university. This picturesque garden, which has changed very little since the sixteenth century, is surrounded by a circular wall, and the medicinal plants are laid out in beds which resemble slices in a pie with a fountain in the centre. No matter where you walk in the garden, you can always see the glorious onion domes and pointed towers of the Basilica di San Antonio which hovers nearby.

As for private gardens, it is my impression that some of the cooking herbs can be used to best effect if they are mixed with other flowers and shrubs chosen for leaf, colour and size rather than for taste. The best garden of this kind I know is the Giardino dei Semplici designed by one of England's foremost landscape architects, Russell Page, at the San Liberato garden on the north shore of Lake Bracciano.

This was the first project Page tackled when he went to San Liberato, and it is located right next to a venerable Romanesque chapel which had to be restored when the Count and Countess Sanminiatelli started building their summer home there. Page decided that the area around the chapel – which lies slightly below the modern villa – was the key to San

Liberato's setting, so he cross-terraced a medium-sized plot, putting in low walls and paths to break the area into a series of smaller beds. Here he and the Countess Maria Sanminiatelli created an original Giardino dei Semplici, which starts with some silvery olive trees and a summer-flowering lagerstroemia and then narrows down to clumps of grey-leaved and bluish plants which spill over the paths. Here are grey-white clumps of *Senecio cineraria* with their flannel leaves along with salvias and prostrate rosemarys, and old roses have been planted to climb up the olive trees. Everywhere among the herbs grow clumps of soft pink valerian, *Centranthus ruber*, which seeds itself in all the flower beds, and even on the walls and stairways. Many English gardeners avoid valerian because it was the plant which grew most vigorously in London bomb sites after the Second World War, and was regarded as a weed. Page, with his keen eye for colour, chose valerian despite this because of its luminous pink which blends in perfectly with roses of all shades.

Once the job was finished Page looked back on his work at San Liberato with satisfaction: 'I know of no other garden more magical than this ... so strong is the atmosphere of tranquillity ... even the details of the gardening sections have come together in silent harmony.'

A Garden Strikes Back

I NEVER DID SUBSCRIBE TO THE IDEA THAT IF YOU TALK lovingly to flowers, they will love you back. But I do believe that for a garden to succeed, it needs one special person to love and care for it. I am not just talking about a person who keeps the hedges trim and turns on the watering system twice a week; I mean a person who gets up at six in the morning and goes out to survey the garden in their dressing gown and slippers; a person who keeps all the latest seed catalogues on their bedside table and reads them every night before turning out the light.

Where would Hidcote be, for instance, without the inspiration of Lawrence Johnston or Sissinghurst without Vita Sackville-West or, for that matter, Monticello without Thomas Jefferson?

But if truth be known there are plenty of unloved gardens in the world whose owners spend vast sums on exotic plants just so they can intimidate the guests they invite for Saturday evening drinks. An example of this kind of conspicuous consumption is a garden that clings to an island cliff overlooking the Tyrrhenian Sea only a short helicopter hop from Rome or Canale. The public figure who owns this dramatic site threw a lot of money at it. Italian reporters are a bit suspicious of where the money came from.

For reasons that should be clear, I prefer not to reveal the name of the eminent person because the charges against him, ranging from theft of public money to conspiracy to bribe judges, have not yet been tried in a court of law. He may be found guilty or he may be acquitted. But the garden itself decided not to wait for the final verdict, and proceeded to self-destruct to pay him back for his indifference. I know of no garden anywhere that has managed to generate so many disasters in such a short span of time.

But first, let us sketch (with suitable cosmetic alterations) an Identikit of the public figure who owns the garden. The Hon. X (as I shall call him) is one of those well-dressed Roman types who wears silk shirts from Ferragamo (with his initials and a small crest on the breast) and has a special cellular phone which is so high-tech he doesn't have to dial the numbers; he just talks into it and the Presidential Palace answers. He is good at any deal which involves favours for funds (mainly US dollars in offshore banks) and he has a special knack for smelling out prime real estate when it becomes involved in litigation. Sure enough his fast footwork, coupled with excellent government connections, has brought him at friendly prices a top floor penthouse in Rome with fifteen lemon trees and a view of St Peter's as well as a country villa in Chianti with thirty hectares of vineyards and a stable full of high-strung Arab horses. He has also acquired a flat way up on top of the Trump Tower in Manhattan full of Andy Warhol paintings, and another large duplex overlooking the Croisette in Cannes where he entertains film stars. He has bank accounts in Liechtenstein and Luxembourg, in the Comoros and the Caymans. He has gold cards issued by Cartier and Bulgari with which he buys gold necklaces and diamond rings for the wives of leading judges, lawyers, journalists and communications tycoons at Christmas. His second wife (thirty years his junior) dresses exclusively with Armani and wears so many gold chains she has to have two bodyguards when she walks the dog in Parioli.

In a sense, his acquisition of the rugged precipice on the Tuscan island is a perfect example of the age-old attitude of Italy's ruling classes, that if they know the right people and have big enough bank accounts they are above the law. Since the advent of the Mani Pulite ('clean hands') campaign there has been a certain amount of pulling back, a certain tucking in of diamond cuff links, but the Hon. X apparently remains a big spender, and now that the investigators are closing in, it is beginning to be whispered abroad that his acquisition of the Tyrrhenian cliff may have been the final act of hubris that brought on his downfall. His Waterloo, to put it bluntly.

The history of this small island property is, as these things often are, clouded in mystery. It is believed that it was part of a strip that belonged in the public domain, controlled by the Ministry of the Marina, and scheduled to remain a public nature reserve for all eternity. Some say that the highest cliff with its whitewashed tower was actually a military surveillance post, built to keep a careful eye on all the ships sailing back and forth from the mainland to Sardinia and Corsica and Elba. But at a certain point, it is said, the ministry decided it no longer needed the strategic lookout post, and the property became privatized. Details of the privatization decree were never made public, for reasons of security naturally, but at a certain point (during the Ferragosto holiday in August when everyone was relaxing in Sardinia and newspaper offices were closed) the property slipped silently into the hands of the Hon. X.

Subsequent searches by journalists indicate that the Hon. X was not the only lucky guy to get himself a big slice of coastland on this once protected waterfront. In fact great sections of the island have gradually been siphoned into private hands and it has become a kind of rich insider's secret paradise, kept deliberately inaccessible by people who want total privacy and direct access to their yachts.

Wild and picturesque it certainly is and the best feature of the Hon. X's rocky peak is its wraparound 360-degree view – sea and towering cliffs on three sides and rugged island scenery on the fourth. If Napoleon had been Italian instead of French this is the place he would have chosen for his last-stand fortress, and in doing so he might even have avoided Elba.

When he acquired the place, the Hon. X discovered that the road into his headland was impassable even for the off-track vehicle he kept there, so he looked up influential friends who loaned him two bulldozers which spent the whole of one summer clawing an all-weather road out of the dense *macchia*. The Army Corps of Engineers then came in to construct a chain fence around the perimeter of the land plus a sizeable guardhouse to accommodate the team of Carabinieri who invariably accompanied the Hon. X when he came to visit his property. For a golden period during his early residency, he and his family commuted regularly from Rome in a helicopter. It was a hideaway that even Aristotle Onassis or J. Paul Getty would have cherished.

When the Hon. X had finished with the heavy roadwork he began to concentrate on the landscaping itself. First he imported engineers to dynamite enough rock out of the hilltop to create a hole for a swimming pool. But when the Hon. X saw the hole he decided that it was not big enough – he needed a pool of Olympic proportions – so the obedient engineers went to work to cantilever the pool out over the edge of the headland, buttressing its seaside corner with a steel-reinforced cement balcony hanging a hundred metres above the glittering azure sea. (Swimmers given to vertigo were warned to stay away from the far edge lest they be struck with dizziness.) Another special feature of the hanging pool was that some of the live rock from the blasted hillside was left projecting through the floor of the pool so that a diver, preparing a swan-dive into the blue-green waters, had a momentary fear that he might break his neck on submerged boulders. Actually the rocks had been smoothed so that they were virtually on a level with the pool floor, so the danger was more imagined than real. Salt water was then laboriously pumped up from the sea to fill this great hanging tub, so the Hon. X and his wife and two young children could enjoy the pleasures of sea bathing without having to stub their toes on the rocky beach below.

While they were at it, the engineers also built a long low building at the bottom of the watchtower so as to make room for a spacious *salotto* (living room) with sliding glass doors overlooking the pool plus a dining room and kitchen with outside terraces and a large bedroom with bath. Another bedroom and a playroom for the children was built into the tower.

However, it soon became obvious to the Hon. X's wife that their sleeping accommodation was not adequate. They needed at least two more rooms with baths for weekend guests, and they also needed a small independent wing for their Polish butler and his wife, who would keep the house running and the pool clean when they were away.

Under ordinary circumstances, the Hon. X would have gone ahead and built a separate guesthouse and servants' quarters next to the tower, but the local island authorities – who resented all the new arrivals from Rome – refused to grant permission for any new building. As a result, the Hon. X was advised by his architects to build all additional quarters underground. The bulldozers were brought in again to excavate two very large underground wings, complete with self-contained apartments for both guests and servants. As soon as these were finished, truckloads of loam were brought up to cover the roofs of the new apartments; then long strips of pre-grown grass were laid on top of the loam terrace, and two hundred pots of roses were imported to create an instant rose garden. Only a few sharp-eyed visitors noticed a row of small windows which were cut into the stone wall *under* the rose garden.

But one rose garden was not enough for the Hon. X. He wanted a dramatic garden, not the usual assortment of succulents and cistus, and so he called in a leading Milanese landscaping firm (for whom he had previously procured tasteful contracts in Milan, Brescia and Turin). This grateful company sent six workers who toiled steadily for more than six months to landscape the hilltop.

Being Milanese, the designer had not had much experience with the scorching suns and harsh winters of the Mediterranean islands, and so he started with an avenue of hibiscus bushes leading all the way from the guardhouse to the front door. Flamboyant trees and frangipanis were also clustered around the entrance, and people who visited this garden during its first phase said it had the lush tropical look of a garden in Bora Bora. As they sat sipping their Taittinger champagne in crystal glasses, they not only turned pink from the sun but also green from envy.

One feature which intrigued the guests was a huge old howitzer – which the Hon. X had scrounged from an army warehouse – and set out on a special plot of grass near the house. The big gun faced directly towards Rome, as if to warn any opponents that here was a man not to be tampered with, but his friends said if he had been really clever he would have turned it due north to face the offices of the Mani Pulite prosecutors in Milan.

For the first six months all went well in the old watchtower above the sea, but as the evenings grew shorter one could hear

the rustle of many wings flapping in the brisk night air. It was
the sound of little chickens coming home to roost. First, stories
started circulating in the press, then whispers began to reach
government attorneys. Finally, the garden itself began to take
its revenge. By late autumn a record frost had rolled in from
the direction of Elba, freezing everything it touched and
forming icicles on the tower. Most of the hibiscus and all of the
exotic vines and flowers died – festooning the driveway and
gardens with great lumps of frozen grey vegetation, silent
cemeteries marking the death of dreams.

But instead of going away as most cold spells do in Italy, this
one went on and on. Gradually the freeze got a solid grip on
the water pipes which carried water up from the sea and in the
dead of night just before Christmas all the pipes in the pool's
recycling system broke, flooding a large section of the garden
including the two hundred rose bushes with tons of salt water.
Once the water had soaked through the roses, it broke
through the cement roof of the basement apartments below
and the Polish butler and his wife woke in the night to find
themselves sleeping in puddles of freezing salt. A drenching
thunderstorm developed the next day, sending new floods of
water into the basement – ripping off the wallpaper, destroying furniture and buckling walls and tearing up the mahogany
flooring.

The butler, worried about more ice damage, got up in the
morning to let all the rest of the water out of the pool but he
made the mistake of putting the plug back in. The rain continued to fall and the pool gradually collected fresh rainwater
which seeped into the fissures in the badly made cement and

then froze and cracked. By mid-afternoon a large triangle of the swimming pool had broken off from the main body and crashed to the sea below, taking with it several tons of cement and sand and buckling the steel. The authorities complained that if there had been any picnickers on the rocks, they would all have been killed.

By the time the Hon. X reached his seaside paradise, the list of damage was awesome. Nearly all of the imported garden soil had been saturated by salt so it had to be scraped off to a depth of at least a foot, packed in thick vinyl bags and carted away. The ruined guest wing had to be almost completely rebuilt. The roof had to be removed, the wallpaper scraped off and rehung and the floors replaced with new ones. Once this was done the roof had to be remade with good cement (not cut with cheap sand) and then covered with a whole new stratum of thick bitumen for waterproofing. Fresh earth brought from a nursery on the mainland had to be unloaded on the hilltop and spread around so that new flowers could be planted.

Architects reckoned that all this repair work would take perhaps a year to complete, and the bill would run into millions. The Hon. X realized that he would have trouble raising these large sums; for as the number of indictments against him grew, the number of his friends shrank; judges who had previously accepted his hospitality could no longer receive his phone calls, and although he called his friends the engineers repeatedly, they told him that all their bulldozers had been sent to Albania.

Thus cut adrift and facing a dubious future, the Hon. X decided to make only the most necessary repairs, such as replacing the salty soil and buttressing the swimming pool. He hired a rental agency which was given the job of renting out whatever sections of the house could be lived in so that the estate could produce some money in a hurry, and the agency engaged a prominent landscapist from Santa Margherita, Mario Minghetti, to come over and supervise the new planting.

Since I was an old friend of Minghetti's, I accompanied him on his second trip to the island to see how the reconstruction work was coming on, and it was immediately clear to me that the garden had at last found a sympathetic designer. This time there was no attempt to create another Bora Bora; the verges along the road were planted with clumps of dry-climate trees and bushes – olives, holm oaks and cistus. Under these were planted mixed grey herbs which required little or no water. It was all quiet and restful.

The view from the top was riveting. The sea and sky appeared to be omnipresent, with only a few picturesque trees, a windblown umbrella pine and two razor-slim cypresses jutting up above the horizon while seagulls swooped and shrieked. White, pale blue and lavender flowers were clustered next to the tower, and a warty old olive tree, spared from the salt water invasion, threw a protective arm over the outdoor dining terrace aided by two smallish fig trees. A few of the surviving hibiscus plants were still blooming bravely by the front door, and the new rose garden over the buried guest wing was enhanced by the addition of blue-flowering lavender bushes.

Over on the seaside edge, not far from the big cannon, I

could see two clusters of rocks shielding terracotta pots filled with cyclamen-pink geraniums, and beyond them was a streak of cerulean blue which seemed lighter than the ultramarine of the Mediterranean.

'What's that?'

'That's the swimming pool,' said Minghetti.

'Oh well,' I said, 'that's not so bad. You hardly notice it.'

The only place on the property which had not been struck with bad luck was a favourite project, the tennis court, which had been carved out of the rock well below the villa. The Hon. X had actually wanted to build a standard Italian court out of red clay which is efficient and relatively easy to keep up but once again the powers that be on the island refused permission. Only slightly daunted, the Hon. X decided to truck in tons of topsoil and put in a swath of fine green grass where the clay should have been, and this would eventually be provided with a net and white lines for tennis *all'inglese*. Even as he went off to fight his court battles, the Hon. X left special orders to keep the grass watered, no matter what else was neglected.

The woodsy setting around this proto-court is fresh and delightful and Mario has put in some *Magnolia stellata* and flowering quince and almond to add colour in the spring. The grass will naturally require a lot of upkeep – but the word around town is that the Hon. X is still practising his backhand with his coach once a week and if Italian justice proceeds down its increasingly bumpy road, full of wrong turns and surprising about-faces, the Hon. X stands a 50 per cent chance of winning a presidential amnesty some time in the new millennium.

Then he will buy himself the latest thing in tennis rackets, a half dozen Lacoste tennis shirts and ten cans of Day-Glo yellow tennis balls and head for the woods.

Tennis, anyone?

August

Cooling Off in the Greenhouse

'WHAT YOU REALLY NEED IS A GREENHOUSE,' SAID
Anthea with the detachment of a Tiffany sales
assistant suggesting a necklace of matched star rubies.

She had seen me struggling to preserve two little datura
plants which had stubbornly refused to bloom outdoors after
three years. Instead of blooming, the poor things came
through each winter by the pumphouse wall looking outraged
and exhausted.

She was right of course. I had reached the point where I
needed to branch out and try some of the rarer plants which
bloomed just a little further south. Sometimes it was a
question of only a degree or two of heat. The datura, for
instance, had been blooming in Amalfi in a huge oil can on the
road to Agerola and a painter friend of ours grew a stunning
pink bignonia vine in his courtyard in Positano. I figured that
with just a bit more shelter I could grow them in Canale too.

There were dozens of other plants which hankered for more intensive heat, and I came to realize that the only way I could accommodate them was to put up some kind of glass enclosure attached to the house. My idea was to glass in either our southern terrace or the patio at the west side of the house and fill the space with hanging hibiscus, tropical moon flowers, jade vines and palms.

I wanted the kind of jungle garden that Henri Rousseau had painted in his studio in Paris. Although Rousseau never travelled to the tropics, he spent his days off from his job at the Customs Office copying exotic flowers at the Jardin des Plantes, and he made jungle scenes that have never been equalled by any other artist. If he could make such wonderful jungles in Paris, why couldn't I make one in the cosier climate of Canale?

I went to the American Academy library in Rome to study the history of greenhouses and discovered that there are more kinds of greenhouses in heaven and earth than I had dreamed.

The most common kind, especially in Britain, are what they call 'working greenhouses'. These are little prefab houses, artificially heated, where you can start seedlings, root cuttings and keep special plants alive over the winter. You can even grow tomatoes and cucumbers in winter but who wants to grow cucumbers in November? You can upgrade the working greenhouse a bit by putting in more heat and a fancier wrought-iron door, and calling it a hothouse or stove, and then you can grow Rothschild orchids or prize gloxinias or African violets. But these houses require thermostats and automatic timers and drip water systems, and you hardly dare leave the premises for fear of a power failure which would leave the place in ruins.

The books also point to the tricky problem of keeping hothouses cool enough in summer. Hothouses in very cold climates make sense, but hothouses in hot climates make no sense at all. We have had several friends who ordered free-standing greenhouses for their gardens near Bracciano. These looked pretty in winter when pots of daffodils and amaryllis bloomed sweetly and seedlings were started for the summer garden, but as soon as spring came, the little houses turned into micro-ovens and everything inside them sizzled like shrimps in a wok. The friends tried whitewashing the roofs; they put up special green awnings to keep out the sun's rays and they installed air conditioning at great expense; but nothing availed and in the end these greenhouses were abandoned as bad jobs.

Even more instructive was the attempt of the Roman nursery Sgaravatti to remodel itself along the lines of an American 'self-service Garden Center'. In this ill-advised and regrettable move the Sgaravatti management abandoned their old-fashioned potting sheds and sent away all the knowledgeable and friendly gardeners who were so full of valuable advice for customers. Half of the gardening area was transformed into a cement parking lot and the other half was made into a glasshouse filled with flat benches. Every Friday a trailer truck arrived from Pistoia and unloaded large flats of potted plants and flowers. These were lined up on the glasshouse shelves like so many cabbages and the only workers left were two men who watered and a stony-faced lady who presided over the cash register.

I suspected that something was amiss when I first went in late April to buy geraniums. The spring sun beat down mercilessly on to the glass roof which acted as a magnet and, as I stepped into the greenhouse, a wave of oven air overwhelmed me. The two men, wearing Garden Center overalls, were valiantly trying to attach strips of awning to the glass roof, but were losing the battle as the plants inside drooped listlessly.

By mid-May the game was up. The temperature in the futuristic new supermarket was close to a hundred degrees. Nearly all the plants inside were dead and the two perspiring workers were rushing all the survivors outside to the shade of the abandoned potting sheds. The lady cashier, her smile frostier than ever, had moved into a potting shed and her register was propped up on a broken pot.

The moral of the story was clear. People who live in hot climates should concentrate on cool greenhouses which are unheated but which offer enough shelter in a cold winter so that the plants don't freeze – in other words, modern versions of the old lemon houses that used to grace Italian villas. If we built anything in Canale it was going to be a cool greenhouse.

The literature on cool greenhouses is sparse and much that is written is unhelpful. The writers have endless advice about gadgets to ensure perfect ventilation and machines that blow in cool mist or damp air, and there is much talk about Venetian blinds and painting the glass white in summer. But amid all the technical chatter there is very little about flowers. Indeed these books end up, as too many garden books do, with the usual boring list of 'Plants which are good for a cool conservatory'. Lists like these often appear to be compiled by the author's typist who seems to crib them from a garden encyclopaedia. What I suspect happens next is that the typist, to save time, puts five standard sets of growing instructions into her computer. When she gets to each plant, all she has to do is punch the key for 'Instructions for shade lovers' or 'Instructions for winter flowering plants' and you get the same instructions, word for word, over and over again for 150 pages. What a reader really wants to know is more specific: why do gardenias always turn brown in greenhouses, how do you keep passionflower vines from strangling everything in sight, and how do you really cope when a big black scaly insect takes over your lemon trees?

So I returned the cool greenhouse books to their shelves, went to the index and punched out a call for 'gardens in Ancient Rome'. Why hadn't somebody told me? While modern writers are lost among useless lists, the Romans long ago were coping with exactly the problems that still prevail in hot climates: how to keep a space warm enough in winter so that you can grow exotics, but cool enough in summer so that they don't give up. The answers, according to the clever Romans, were not so much horticultural as architectural. You had to build your porticoes and garden walls to encourage the sun in winter, and to deflect its sizzling rays in summer.

The architect Varro, in a letter written to Palladius in 36 BC, spelled it out clearly. The ideal Roman villa, he said, should be built on the top of a hillside that faces south and east. There should be flowering porticoes and arcades attached to the villa, but they should have high arches and overhanging roofs. Thus when the sun was low in winter, its rays would come in under the arches and warm up the patio plus all the flowers under the arches. But when the sun was high in summer the sturdy porticoes would create shade for the house and its occupants while letting the cooling breezes through. Varro's colleagues also suggested building these porticoes around fountains, for the Persians had taught them that the splatter of water on cooling tiles can do more for a hot garden than an army of slaves pulling overhead fans.

I learned many lessons from Varro. One was that no matter how the conservatory is built, the roof should not be entirely open to the sky. Some crossbeams and overhangs of solid roofing material must deflect the sun's rays. I also noted that Varro made no mention anywhere of ventilation systems or artificial shading. His idea for a garden portico was simplicity itself. Handle the sun as best you can, creating shade when you need it (in summer) and encouraging the sun to come indoors when you need it (in winter), and the flowers will take care of themselves.

In the end I got my conservatory and it took no arguments or tears. I just hung in there collecting ideas and making sketches until we decided to build a new bedroom on the ground-floor level, and suddenly we had a space between the new bedroom and the dining room.

What we did, essentially, was to fill in the empty rectangular space by building two more walls, one on the east side which had a large glass window, and one on the south side made by sliding glass doors. On top of this was a peaked roof which had sections of glass panels set in among rows of roof tiles.

The construction was done in a local stone so the walls were more than a half metre thick and threw wide shadows in summer, and the garden room thus created was two full storeys high with a balcony that ran between the dining room and the bedroom. From here, wide travertine steps led down to the ground level where we had a tufa floor on which pots could be placed; and banked up against the east wall were two raised beds of earth set into the bare ground so that the trees and vines we planted there could send roots down to China. The ventilation took care of itself. The windows and doors did not fit too snugly so there was always a flow of healthy air moving in from the outside.

My only disappointment was that the builder refused to consider a fountain.

'Look,' Robert said, 'there's not room enough for a fountain in this space and if you put one in, the whole place will get damp and mouldy in winter and smelly in summer. You'd be cleaning it all the time.' So instead of an indoor fountain, I settled for an oval pool outside.

In the first months I was worried that my greenhouse might be too shady. When I planned it, I had hoped to keep flowering lemon trees loaded with golden fruit in the back row, but it soon became obvious that they were not happy there; they needed more sun, and had to be planted outside against a southern wall. None the less the jasmine did well there, as did the passionflowers, and the daturas gave up their spindly aspect and started reaching for the stars.

Still the worry persisted. Perhaps I needed more glass in the roof? Perhaps I should open it up more? But then one hot day in August as I was having iced tea in the *serra* (greenhouse) I realized how surprisingly cool it was. Outside the cicadas were zinging, the dogs were panting in the heat, and the roses were turning to ash on their vines. Inside all was green and leafy and fresh. We had built a tropical rainforest, or what Varro might have called a 'nympheum' except that a real nympheum would have more moss and dripping papyrus and fewer flowers. Whatever it was, the results were refreshing. I wish I could have invited Varro and Rousseau round for a glass of lemonade.

I am not a person who enjoys extended shopping trips – a half hour in a big department store tends to make me dizzy – but shopping for plants for the new greenhouse was altogether different. I hunted up and down Lazio for out-of-the-way greenhouses and country markets, and in time I found a number of plants that were happy in jungle conditions. After all, most tropical vines begin their lives on the dark floors of dense jungles and have to curl and twist their way slowly upwards towards the sunlight. Some of my most prized finds were clivia bulbs, members of the amaryllis clan from South Africa which resent too much sun. These striking vermilion lilies begin to bloom in March and are still flowering their heads off in May. The Jacobina, a pretty bush with pink flowers, lights up dull corners in midsummer and again in the autumn. It contrasts with the waxy white flowers of the Mandevilla vine and the vivid bloom of the bougainvillaea, which produces softer lavender flowers (much prettier than the usual fiery magenta) when it is not out in the dazzling sun.

Thus as we sit at our dining table in all seasons of the year imbibing iced tea or rum punch, we can look straight into a mystical garden which reminds us of the islands of the South Pacific. Hanging above the balcony is a Moroccan birdcage whose inhabitant is an embalmed hoopoe who flew into the *serra* and couldn't find his way out, and broke his neck. Lined below him are constantly changing pots of pale geraniums which provide a flowery screen through which all the other flowers must be viewed. Our resident sculptor keeps promising to provide a plaster tiger for the background but other chores intervene. Until he got too big Henry used to pose for photographs as a greenhouse monkey, but he has now moved a continent away.

Oddly enough our most faithful bloomers, present in nearly every season, are the flowers that started the whole thing – the datura plants from Amalfi. I planted these in the shadiest corner of our new *serra* and they now dominate the garden, filling the air with their overwhelming musky scent.

One winter evening after a day of pruning olives, Robert surveyed the new indoor garden with great satisfaction.

'You know,' he said, 'this *serra* is the best thing we've done. Why didn't we think of it before?'

The Racing Horsemen
of the Maremma

BY AUGUST THE GARDENING CHORES COME TO A HALT AND there is little to do but go to the races – for the noble sport of horse racing boasts a long and illustrious history in southern Etruria.

Close to three thousand years ago, when many of the people of Europe were still painting themselves blue and shoving giant stones around the countryside, the settled citizens of Etruria were flocking to their well-built stadiums to enjoy the chariot races, just as today's citizens flock to the football matches.

Paintings uncovered at Tarquinia show that even in the Early Iron Age the pleasure-loving citizens of Etruria had developed a variety of ways to enjoy their arenas. The bleachers up on top were for horse-racing enthusiasts who really wanted to watch horses running around oval racks, but down under the bleachers, divans looking like Pullman berths were laid on for citizens who wished to relax or indulge in other forms of human commerce. The Romans, not always angels themselves, claimed to be shocked by this hedonistic lifestyle, grumbling that the Etruscans were fat, materialistic and over-sexed.

The minute they had conquered Etruria, however, the Romans began to indulge in the sport of kings themselves and there is strong evidence that it was the Etruscans rather than the Greeks who passed on the passion for chariot racing to the Romans. After all, the Circus Maximus in Rome, one of the earliest and most sumptuous equestrian racetracks in the world, was sited and planned by Etruscan kings.

No one is quite sure when this passion for horses first developed, but archaeologists have found bits of bridles and other horse equipment dating from about 1600 BC in Switzerland and Romania. The first domesticated horses were used for pulling ploughs and in time some braver Etruscans started climbing on to the horses' backs instead of stumbling along behind them. The next thing anyone knew, they were organizing horse races.

Reliefs dating from 600 BC show eager Etruscan riders galloping bareback across the countryside. Following an archaic convention the riders are shown to be very small in comparison to the horses, but by 520 BC the horsemen have grown until they loom ponderously above horses that look too small to support them. One marvellous series of four bronzes at the British Museum shows riders sliding off the sides of their racing horses to finish the final lap of the race on foot, a gymkhana event which was very popular among Etruscan horse buffs. The torch of equestrian events was picked up swiftly by the Romans who staged great chariot races at the Circus Maximus, but as time went on the sporting quality of the chariot races declined. Spurs and knives were placed on chariot wheels to make the races more dangerous, and other bloodthirsty sports involving lions and Christian gladiators were introduced to keep the crowds happy. Eventually the barbarian hordes swept into the city, and the curtain came down on all the wine and circuses.

By the time of the Renaissance, the clatter of horses' hooves was once more heard on the streets of Rome. The Via del Corso, which cuts Rome from north to south, became a favourite horse-racing site. The fantastic Corsa dei Barbari (race of riderless horses) was held on the Corso during the Carnival period every winter and the Via del Vantaggio (advantage), located near the north end of the Corso, was so named because that was the place where younger or less experienced horses were allowed to get a head start.

It wasn't until I moved to the Maremma and went through my first summer racing season that I realized how the people of southern Etruria are besotted by horses and *buttero* (cowboy) lore. Even more than the Camargue region in France, which has built a thriving tourist industry around its wild white horses, the Maremma area of central Italy is imbued with an equestrian tradition that goes back beyond Cicero to the dawn of history.

An astonishing number of the local inhabitants keep horses. You see these animals if you take a walk in the *macchia*. First you see a bale of hay which has been dumped over the fence and then an old abandoned bathtub, plug in place, which is there for water. Then you see a lone mare, or a mixed group standing solemnly two by two, head to tail so that the tail of one horse can flick flies away from the eyes of its neighbour.

The local breed of horse known as the *cavallo maremmano* is tailor-made for service in the rough, swampy Maremma pastures. This sturdy roan-coloured animal is rather low slung and has unusually wide hooves, which are said to have been developed for treading on marshland and mud. This horse is believed to be a descendant of the rough wild horses of the central European plain, and it can go through long periods of drought in summer and cold and rain in winter with no shelter and no sneezing. Thoroughbred horses have nowhere near this kind of fortitude. (A friend of ours brought a thoroughbred racer back from Ireland a few years ago, put it out with Maremma horses, and it immediately came down with pneumonia.)

It isn't only the *butteri* who keep horses. Massimo always kept two or three horses out in his fields and when we asked him why, he gave an odd lopsided smile and replied, '*Per passione.*' Aristeo, a retired mason who helps us prune our olive trees, has six or seven horses most of which have never been ridden.

'Horses are in my blood,' he once told us. 'My father kept them and his grandfather kept them. Without a horse we are lost.'

The Maremma has always been sheep and cattle country, and for several thousand years until the land reforms of

this century herds of Maremma sheep and the big white
Maremma cattle – most of them owned by the land-owning
princes – ranged freely from the sea all across the Tolfa hills
to the Apennines. The spectacle of thousands of sheep and
pure white long-horn cattle grazing among ruined castles
and classical ruins has inspired many artists, especially
Poussin.

These herds required not only shepherds on foot but also
mounted cowhands (known as *butteri*) with special abilities to
brand, rope and corral cattle, and over the centuries these
tough and resilient horsemen were able to carve out for themselves a special position in the community. The *butteri* refused
to take orders from the local *caporale* but dealt directly with
the landowners themselves who valued their special abilities
and paid them relatively well, realizing (like Genghis Khan
before them) that skilled horsemen could be used for a variety
of purposes, from hunting to warfare to mail delivery. Some
butteri were attracted to a lucrative sideline – brigandage. It is
not a coincidence that in the backward areas of Etruria where
horsemen flourished, the highwayman was often lurking in
the bushes.

The *butteri* achieved their greatest fame around the end of
the nineteenth century, and poems were written to tell of their
yearly travels. In the early spring when the grass began to
grow again they moved their herds from the barns and corrals
to the greening fields and pastures. New foals were born at
this time, calves were branded, and yearlings were rounded up
and broken – first at the end of a rope and then with a man on
their backs. By the feast of San Giuseppe (1 May) the animals

had to be taken away from the pastures to permit the hay crop to be cut in late May and baled for winter forage, and then came the move of the flocks into higher pasturage. This age-old operation, known as the *transumanaza* (transhumance), took place in the early summer, but in an area of great oak woods such as Manziana the *butteri* were allowed to browse their cattle all summer on the rich forest undergrowth. An ancient agreement, probably of Etruscan origin, permits residents of wooded areas to graze their cattle in the communal forest on payment of a small fee and to this day the woods of Manziana echo all summer to the lows and roars of browsing cattle.

In autumn the animals are brought back into the pasture-lands to graze again before the wet winter sets in and once the grapes are picked in the late October *vendemmia* they are also let into the vineyards to eat up the leftover grape leaves. No growing thing is ever wasted. The winter is spent fixing corrals, mending rough fences (often built around prickly bushes such as blackberry or *bianco spino*, hawthorn) and taking some of the young veal off to slaughter. Not infrequently the *butteri* are also called upon to organize hunting parties for cattle which have been stolen or have strayed or for shepherds who have gone missing. Only a few years back, a shepherd was found after a hunt of five days. He had apparently been attacked by a swarm of bees, fallen into a blackberry bush and died of a heart attack.

In the Fifties and Sixties it was possible to go into bars in Canale and Tolfa any Saturday evening and listen to the local shepherds and *butteri* singing their *stornelli* about their adventures. One *buttero* would begin improvising in a high nasal tone which gradually sank lower like a patter song, and after he had created several stanzas his friend would pick up the same story, with the same music, but give the tale an ironic or amusing twist at the end. In singing back and forth to each other, the two men were in effect engaging in a musical duel, and the audience listened with glee and applauded the winner with another litre of wine.

'*La bottiglia piange*' (the carafe is crying), they would bellow as they called on the *padrone* to fill up their litre measures with harsh white wine.

Historians say that these verbal duels had their origin in the Middle Ages, and led to grand opera; but a more perceptive scholar has pointed out that in Virgil's Eclogues there is a 'singing match between Corydon and Thyrsis'. The tales told in the *stornelli* were the stuff of great folk epics – but it is ironic that when the Italian director Sergio Leone decided to make films about cowboys (often called 'spaghetti westerns'), he forgot the Italian tradition and stole his plots and often his locations, and leading actors like Clint Eastwood, from Hollywood.

One of the climactic events in *buttero* history was the time when Buffalo Bill and his Wild West cowboys challenged the *butteri* to a rodeo contest, and the *butteri* won. This triumph came in 1919, when Buffalo Bill made his famous European tour bringing Red Indians and their chief Geronimo in his entourage. When the Italian horsemen won hands down the king was so delighted he entertained the Indians in the Quirinale, letting them park their ponies in the royal courtyard.

The dwindling of the herds, brought on by the land reform which encouraged fencing, means that today only a few *butteri* can find regular work, often as forest guards and game-keepers, but there is a growing population of young men who work as part-time riders and spend nearly all their weekends competing in the local tournaments and horse races. These freelance *butteri* are expert horsemen and prefer to ride bareback when they can. They wear typical *butteri* fedora hats and boots or sometimes rough leather puttees. If they do use a saddle, it is often the Maremma saddle which resembles the scooped-out Western saddle, rising sharply both fore and aft.

The horse-racing season in the Maremma starts in late spring after the hay is in and the biggest events are often scheduled at traditional cattle fairs – events which bring horse traders, including a good number of gypsies, from all over Italy. These are rough and ready races with amateur riders, having little to do with sophisticated big-city horse racing. The Canalesi favour an obstacle course where the *butteri* canter in big circles holding out spears with which they try to capture metal rings set on poles along the side of the course. Other contests involve getting off horses and completing the race on foot.

All of this feverish activity finds its climax in the two greatest *buttero* races of all – the Palio of Siena, held 1 July and again on the day of the Madonna, 15 August. It is no surprise that many of the winning jockeys at the Palio used to come from our area and indeed one of the greatest jockeys of all was a native of Manziana. His name was Beppe Gentile, and we

got to know him because he took part in some of the early
summer tune-up races run on the long stretch of dirt road near
our house.

Beppe stood out at once as a person to be reckoned with. He
was small and slender. He sat very erect in the saddle, which
was English (not the Maremma style), and he held his
head high. He had a kind of animal quickness about him
and he leapt on to his horse with one easy bounce. His face
had an aquiline sharpness that gave him a regal, almost
Aztec look and he rarely smiled. Other jockeys spoke to him
deferentially.

'That is the great Beppe Gentile,' our neighbour Jack said.
'When he's in a race, nobody else has a chance.'

Jack went on to explain to me that Beppe had won nearly all
the big races in the Maremma area, and had won the Palio of
Siena close to a dozen times.

'He is so good that they come down from Siena every spring
and beg him to race up there. But he won't do it unless they
pay him one million lire for every race. He's called "Beppe la
Lepre" (Beppe the Hare) he is so fast on the start,' Jack said.
'He never starts a race until he has the advantage.'

'But how can he do that?'

'It's all his tricks at the beginning,' Jack explained. 'The
jockeys start these races by moving their horses back and forth
until they are in line, and then the gun goes off.' (It sounded
like the way we started yacht races in Duxbury, tacking
back and forth to be first across the line.) 'He pretends that his
horse is out of control, so he makes a lot of confusion and
prances around in circles, and unless he is right out in front

and moving forward at the starting gun, he wheels his horse around again and claims a foul.'

I watched Beppe manoeuvre during the first races, and it was exactly as Jack described it. The races were being run in heats of three horses at a time, and whenever his heat came up, Beppe's horse, a big black mare, suddenly started to jump around in a wild and nervous fashion. Beppe made a great show of trying to calm the animal, patting it and pulling angrily at the reins while the big black reared and showed the whites of her eyes, but there finally came a moment when the three horses were more or less equal at the line, and then Beppe's horse would suddenly calm down and plunge across the line with a smacking lead. If he did not have a clear advantage, Beppe's horse would suddenly whirl away from the start, and the manoeuvring would have to start again. There was little the opposing riders could do about this business, short of wheeling and turning themselves, but in the end it was Beppe who had the stamina and got off first.

Once headed down the track, there was no stopping him. Tightly knit, with shoulders tensed, Beppe fitted his horse like a centaur. He carried a crop, which he occasionally waved by the nose of the horse so it could be seen but not felt, and he rarely yielded first place to any other rider.

In later years, some stories came back from the Palio that made us worry about our local hero. Once during an August race, the story had it, Beppe got off to a bad start and came in sixth and after the race the men from the Oca *contrada* (Goose ward) who had hired him, beat him up and broke his right arm. They claimed he had deliberately thrown the race. But he was called back to Siena after this incident, and he was never beaten again. When he died several years later, after his horse ran into a tree in the Manziana woods, several thousand people followed his coffin down the main street from the church, and the Sienese sent a squad of expert flag-throwers and drummers in Renaissance costume to accompany it to the cemetery. Even the Manziana mayor, who was a close friend of Signor Andreotti and owned the local bus line, didn't get such a turnout.

September

Of Etruscan Ghosts and Gardens

DOZING IN THE FRAGRANT BACKLANDS OF SOUTHERN Etruria are two strange gardens which have a distinctly oriental flavour to them – and whenever I visit them I have a feeling that they may be haunted by the ghosts of some long-departed Etruscan stone carvers.

The first of these gardens is an enchanted woodland at Bomarzo, not far from Viterbo, which was created by a wealthy Italian nobleman and soldier named Vicino Orsini around 1560. The ghosts here seem watchful but they are on the whole content. The second is the fantasy garden of a beautiful and eccentric French-American sculptor, Niki di Saint Phalle. It lies above the sea at Capalbio (on the borders of Lazio and Tuscany) and consists of twenty-eight huge polychrome statues of Tarot figures glimmering in the sunlight. This garden was completed only in the early 1990s, and the ghosts here are still nervous and uncertain. I fancy that when evening comes, I can hear them keening into the soft night air.

Oddly, these two gardens, one an accepted masterpiece, the other still a question mark on the art scene, have many things in common. Both are the works of talented but unconventional designers and both gardens have brought on to Italian soil an extraordinary element of oriental magic which was originally the hallmark of the early Etruscans.

Everyone agrees there is an exotic flavour to the Bomarzo garden, and some early reports insisted that Vicino Orsini brought stone carvers from India – or was it Etruscan ghosts? – to carve the giant statues on his property. The area he chose for his garden was a wooded valley at the bottom of the Bomarzo property which was filled with great tufa stones thrown up by a volcanic eruption. Here he set his carvers to work cutting out dozens of eccentric figures – two huge sphinxes inscribed with riddles, an enormous tortoise with a giantess on his back blowing a trumpet, a two-tailed mermaid sitting on the grass with her long scaly tails stretching out behind her, a great fountain with Pegasus flying over it, and a life-sized Carthaginian elephant dressed in full battle gear which is raising a Roman soldier on its trunk.

Orsini also ordered his workers to carve buildings out of the live stone and they turned out some ominous buildings indeed – a nightmarish villa that is tilted crazily over to one side, chapels with thick porticoes and no windows, and everywhere carvings of oversized monsters, gaping masks and weird cabbalistic symbols.

In an epigram, carved into the wall and watched over by a

seated sphinx, Orsini asked the mischievous question: '*Dimmi poi se tante meraviglie sien fatte per inganno o per arte?*' (Tell me, were these marvels made by trickery or by art?)

Niki de Saint Phalle was greatly influenced by Bomarzo, which was only an hour away from the Capalbio hillside where she built her sculpture garden, and she too took pleasure in flummoxing visitors with the obscure symbols and myths of her Tarot cards.

Born in Paris in 1930, daughter of a French father and an American mother, Niki worked as a model in Paris, appearing on the covers of both *Vogue* and *Life* magazines, and then while still in her twenties she became a leading light in the artistic avant-garde where she was controversial from the first. She made an early alliance with the Swiss sculptor Jean Tinguely, who remained her companion for many years, and the two collaborated on the statue of a huge nude goddess which raised eyebrows when it was shown at the Stockholm Modern Art Museum. In the Sixties Tinguely and Saint Phalle made headlines again with their 'shooting parties', which involved hanging their works on the walls of Parisian galleries and shooting at them with shotguns. Their celebrity status increased when they built a fountain dedicated to Stravinsky in the forecourt of the Beaubourg Museum in Paris.

Saint Phalle was a frequent visitor to Garavicchio, the Capalbio estate of her friend Prince Carlo Caracciolo, a well-known Roman publisher and supporter of the arts (and brother of her good friend Mirella Agnelli), and she soon fell under the spell of the ancient Etruscan countryside. In fact she told Caracciolo that she dreamed one night that she was

strolling in an enchanted garden near the villa when she
encountered mystical figures from Tarot fortune-telling cards,
who seemed to loom up out of the land clothed in fantastic
colours and decked with precious stones. The prince, encouraged by his sister, obligingly offered a hillside near Villa
Garavicchio to build the garden she had dreamed of and she
began work on it in 1982. The work was long and strenuous,
even with Tinguely bravely welding the armatures on the
spot, and a dozen leading artists and ceramicists working on
the team. When the garden was completed more than ten
years later Saint Phalle had put up twenty-two enormous
mirrored or mosaic-clad statues in Day-Glo colours ranging
from fire-engine red to cobalt blue, leaf green, shocking
pink, turquoise and gold. The project cost Saint Phalle
more than three and a half million pounds, much of which
came from the sale of her Niki de Saint Phalle perfume in
Paris.

For sheer bravado, there are few sculpture gardens anywhere in the world to compare. In fact, only Bomarzo shows
the same dizzying ambition combined with a fascination for
dream worlds and the cabbala, and critics who admire both
gardens claim that the same Etruscan ghosts who materialized
to help the stone carvers at Bomarzo came back four centuries
later to exert their spell on the Tarot garden.

Niki herself used to say: 'It was not by chance that I made
this garden. My hand was guided.' When asked why she chose
the Tarot cards for her subject she added: 'Although life often
seems to be like a game of cards, we were born without know-
ing what the rules are. But we should continue to play the

game all the same.' Because of their very mystery, she said, poets, philosophers and artists in all ages have been attracted to these magic cards.

Visitors who are driving along the Via Aurelia can see the figures from miles away sending out glittery shafts of red and green and pink light, like giant lighthouses or warnings from the Evil Eye. The car park for the garden is located at the bottom of the hill, and visitors are obliged to climb up the long dusty road towards these shimmering figures.

Near the top, visitors reach a large piazza where there is a splashing fountain faced with sky blue mosaics. From the fountain a stairway lined with writhing sea monsters leads up to a great gaping mouth. On closer inspection this mouth is revealed to be part of a big blue cement mask with bright red eyes; and on top of it is a second more menacing mask which wears outsized white spectacles. A white hand emerges out of the top of the head. Next to this stands a figure looking rather like a sailor with bow legs and rays spreading out from its head which is meant to represent the sun (see p.229). Other statues – varying from two to four storeys in height, some of them so big that a visitor can walk into them – represent an empress or a sphinx (with a face like Queen Victoria), a dragon or a space shuttle. Saint Phalle, always a dedicated feminist, said that she built the garden 'for women of all times and all ages who were not allowed to be creative'.

A circular path takes one up to the top level above the staircase, and here the statues become weirder still. There are some elongated shapes which look like stretched-out blue birds, or fish. Over to one side there is a huge lopsided mirrored courtyard where doors and windows are inlaid with occult inscriptions written in green. One window exhibits an intricate Tinguely machine, a cross between a bicycle and a water wheel. A vividly coloured basket in the centre of this space contains bits and pieces of mosaic dolls which appear to have been thrown out of a nursery: a headless Raggedy Ann in green, a torso with swollen arms in blue.

A friendly guard comes over to talk about the days when the garden was being built.

'It was very ugly when it was going up,' he says. 'There was cement dripping all over the hillside, and the whole thing looked like a big rusty mess. But now, with most of the mosaics glued on, it is quite different.'

Visitors to the sculpture garden are divided into two groups. First there are the art lovers, usually young, with sandals and backpacks, who sit for hours contemplating the scene and communing with the great brooding statues. Some sketch, some talk quietly among themselves, but when they sign the visitors' book, they never fail to show their enthusiasm.

'This was one of the great experiences of my life.'

'*C'est la huitième merveille du monde.*'

The nay-sayers are neither so quiet nor so appreciative. These include Italians from the towns around Capalbio, foreign tourists heading north along the Aurelia, and a few garden lovers who come hoping to see mixed grey borders with white roses. They charge up and down the hill expressing their disapproval and dismay.

One American points to the reactor tower of the atomic

energy plant (now abandoned) on the coast at Montalto di Castro which is the only building visible along the horizon. 'That's it,' he cries, 'this is the perfect garden for the Atomic Age. A mutation!'

As one wanders down the hill leaving all the bright monsters behind, one wonders what people will say who visit Garavicchio two or three hundred years hence.

One negative vote came a year or so back when Saint Phalle offered the garden to the Comune of Capalbio, to be organized and run by the local community. To her dismay some bureaucrats in the Comune not only rejected her offer but threatened to levy stiff fines because she had failed to apply for a building permit when she started the project. Saint Phalle promptly withdrew her offer, and gave the garden instead to a French organization which set about preparing for a major opening of her monumental work, billing it as 'one of the most important outdoor displays in all of Italy'. The inauguration was sponsored by the nearby Comune of Orbetello, and the opening event at an Orbetello museum went well. Photographs, films and models were displayed and leading Italian art historians presented admiring monographs. But on the following day, when a bus was supposed to take journalists to visit the garden itself, word went out that the opening had been cancelled. It appears that Madame Saint Phalle, reportedly in poor health in California, had stopped the inauguration because of some new difficulty and had ruled that the garden could only be visited by children.

Now, however, a foundation for the Giardini dei Tarocchi has been formed in Grosseto to run the garden, with Saint

Phalle as president. Members include Prince Carlo Caracciolo, his brother Nicola and his sister Mirella Agnelli, and happily the Comune of Capalbio. They have arranged for the garden to be open to the public on weekday afternoons in the summer. The Etruscan ghosts of Garavicchio are a bit quieter now, but occasionally their wailing can still be heard amid the shining mosaic towers.

Lavinia Taverna, the Accidental Gardener

A S A NEWCOMER STRUGGLING TO MAKE A GARDEN IN AN unfamiliar climate, I was lucky to meet the Marchesa Lavinia Taverna early on. She had been through the whole agonizing business of converting a burnt-over piece of land into something beautiful, and was full of advice for beginners like me.

Her garden at Tor San Lorenzo south of Rome began by accident in the Fifties when she and her husband bought a piece of land with the intention of making it into a cattle farm. The farm was never developed, but instead Lavinia more or less by chance turned it into a garden.

The problems facing the new garden-maker were enormous. For one thing she had never made a garden before; in the social group into which she was born, gardens were usually not made but inherited. In addition there was the problem of the land itself – a weedy bit of backland, dust-dry in summer, soggy in winter and lashed by damaging salt winds from the nearby Tyrrhenian Sea, and there was neither a tree nor a blade of grass nor a flower to relieve the monotony. The land was also dangerous; it lay right in the middle of the old Anzio beachhead, where Allied forces were pinned down by German firepower for several months in 1944, so it had to be cleared of unexploded bombs and mines before it was safe to work.

But somehow by trial and error and with lots of pluck Lavinia managed slowly to create La Landriana, one of the most beautiful and important gardens of twentieth-century Italy. She also put an end to the old cliché that all the best modern gardens in Italy were made by foreigners.

I went down to interview the Marchesa in the mid-1990s when word went out that she was considering opening La Landriana to the public. I had been warned that Lavinia might be difficult to interview as she was a formidable woman with strong opinions but I found instead a charming white-haired lady, probably in her early seventies, wearing a straw hat and carrying a notebook and accompanied by a brace of leaping hounds.

'I must tell you right away that I created this garden all backwards,' she told me. 'I had no intention of doing any planting here. In fact, I was very happy to spend my summers with our four children at the villa on Lake Como. This was strictly a business affair, and I came down to keep my husband company. My only attempt to improve the place was to put in two big white umbrellas in the front garden so that we could relax when we came for picnics. But then I started collecting plants for my own amusement and now I have this huge garden with thirty-three separate garden rooms and there is not a corner left for cattle.'

She suggested that we take a walk down to see the artificial lake, and as we walked she told me a little of her history. Her garden career began, she said, one sunny afternoon in March 1958 when she was rummaging in her pocket for the keys to the derelict farmhouse that came with the cattle farm. She didn't find the keys but she did come upon a small packet of godetia seeds which a friend had given her. Absent-mindedly she tore open the packet and scattered the seeds in an arc near the door. Not for a moment did she dream that this tiny spoonful of seeds would mark the beginning of her beloved garden.

But the godetia seeds bloomed so gloriously the first summer that the Marchesa ordered more seeds and began to redesign the farmhouse (which she had sworn never to live in). In a year or so she was receiving shipments of winter-blooming plants from Australia, antique roses from London and flowering cherries and crab apples from Japan.

Her problem, she said, was that she started her career as a collector of plants, not as a gardener. She kept ordering plants which took her fancy and when they arrived she and her maid Domenica set them out in clumps like exhibits at a flower show. She soon acquired the habit of studying her new plants in botany textbooks and encyclopaedias, and she eventually became such an expert on horticulture that she was able to write the best and most useful book yet written on Mediterranean gardening, *Un Giardino Mediterraneo*. She also steeped herself in the history and culture of the great gardens of Europe, especially her favourites in England, but oddly she never travelled to see any of the gardens she so admired.

'I was really very isolated out here in the country,' she told me as we walked. 'I had very few people to talk to about gardening, so I had to work everything out on my own. Fortunately I had one good friend, Donato Sanminiatelli, who was making his own garden near Lake Bracciano, and I asked him to come out to see what I was doing here. He came and told me that what I lacked was an all-over plan, an organizing principle for my garden.'

Sanminiatelli suggested that Lavinia might benefit from professional guidance, and he prevailed upon her to consult his friend, the English landscapist Russell Page who was working for him at Bracciano. In 1967 Page came to La Landriana, took one look at her garden and told the Marchesa, 'It's too chaotic! It needs cooling down.'

Then, to show what he meant, he built her a charming rock garden at the edge of her front lawn, putting in olive trees and umbrella pines as a background, with grey shrubs underneath. After this he spent long hours hiking around the property with a hammer and stakes, marking out a series of paths to be bordered by hedges, dividing the garden into a series of individual 'green rooms'. He also suggested that a fairly large pond should be dug at the bottom of the property to broaden the view with a sparkle of water, and to provide the resources for a much needed irrigation system.

Page, who became her good friend, managed to channel the Marchesa's formidable energies into a more disciplined approach to garden planning – but he was no sooner out of the gate than she began to rearrange the flowers and trees that he had planted.

'Page was my true maestro; he taught me nearly everything I know,' she told me, 'but I did not approve of some of his plantings – particularly his taste for conifers. I think most conifers, with the exception of cypresses and a few pines, are pompous and I cannot abide palm trees, cycads and cacti either. They are too heavy, too African.' Then she led me to a small clearing at the top of the hill.

'Here there was a big clump of Arizonica cypresses and spruce trees which my husband Fede [short for Federico] and Page had planted,' she said. 'I really didn't like them at all, so in the dead of night I had my gardeners cut them all down.'

I gasped inwardly. What could be more astonishing than a lady who dared to countermand the orders of one of Europe's most prestigious landscape architects, and at the same time to risk the wrath of a strong-minded conifer-loving husband?

As we approached the artificial lake, I half expected some kind of swamp lined with black plastic and piles of mud, but instead we came down to a lovely clear sheet of water blooming with callas and water lilies, with a fine old swamp cypress growing near the bank. Ducks were swimming in the deep green waters, and two grey herons rose from the opposite shore.

'Page had ordered a little lake, a swamp really, but I told the bulldozer men to make it larger, and then when they put up the dam I told them to lift the level by at least a metre. This took real courage because everyone in the family was boycotting my lake. But the workers were on my side and helped me secretly. Now I wish I had had the courage to dig it deeper.'

She led me over to the two rose gardens above the lake where I was immediately struck by the daring individuality of her design; for while most rose gardeners in Europe cling to the doctrine that roses are delicate plants and must be isolated in squared-off hygienic beds, like patients in an intensive care ward, Lavinia had had the temerity to fling her roses like confetti across the rolling pastureland.

The garden on the right was filled with one variety of rose, the China rose 'Mutabilis' which has the priceless ability to flower every day of the year. 'The "Mutabilis" has only five petals,' she said to me, 'but the flowers change colour every day, going from pink to pinkish yellow to a bronzy red. I was so pleased with this rose that I kept reproducing it until I had more than three hundred bushes. I can't imagine why I did this, but in the end I had no choice but to make a separate garden for them, as they don't go with other roses.' The English rosarian Peter Beales was so impressed that he included the 'Mutabilis' garden as one of the world's great rose gardens in his book *Visions of Roses*.

Not satisfied with this one triumph, Lavinia took an entirely different valley on the other side of the hill and filled it with five hundred bushes of old-fashioned roses, which she considered the most romantic roses of all. She limited the colours here to shades of pink, rose and white – and planted between the roses clusters of *Pavonia hostata*, an unusual South American shrub which shows quantities of pink malva-like flowers with deep pink centres in midsummer when the roses are not flowering. The bushes are underplanted with varieties of lavender.

After reclimbing the hill Lavinia took me to see the two most famous Page gardens on the top. The first, known as the Olive Garden, is set in a romantic glade below a sturdy cork oak, and features two rows of olive trees with two octagonal stone fountains. Page intended it to be a simple Mediterranean olive grove, but Lavinia decided it needed more colour and replanted the whole garden with masses of mauve and yellow flowers and bulbs to contrast with the glaucous tones of the olive leaves.

The second Page garden nearby was conceived as a rose garden and made up of six square beds, set on a diagonal. The designer filled these beds with a series of rose bushes which he thought would appeal to the Marchesa's painterly colour sense – it was to be her 'paintbox, palette and canvas' – but soon Lavinia tired of seeing the same roses in the same order and proceeded to replant the whole garden with standards of bitter orange trees, rigorously pruned like lollipops. Under these she put neat clumps of myrtle-like bushes pruned to resemble beach balloons. The resulting play between the little balls and the great globes of orange trees looks like some giant's bowling alley.

As we walked Lavinia explained to me that she probably made too many drastic changes in the Page arrangements after the maestro left, so that the garden went from a high in the post-Page Seventies to a low point in the Eighties when it was in such depressing shape that she seriously thought of packing up for good. Happily in 1985 she decided to make one last effort to pull the place together. She mercilessly removed all the plants that were too difficult to grow and for the first time she imposed a rigid design on the open garden, planting miles of laurel hedges to create the separate 'garden rooms'.

'What you see now is essentially a brand new garden. And this time I have been very rigorous,' she said with a sigh.

As we moved from one garden room to the next, I began to realize that most of the rooms had gone through two or three complete changes of scenery before Lavinia was pleased with them. The formal Spanish Pool Garden, for instance, had started off as a tropical Arab garden, then became a hydrangea garden, then a gardenia garden and ended up full of peonies. The long border of blue agapanthus which flourished under the *kaki* (persimmon) trees had to be transferred to a sunnier spot when the *kaki* grew up and made too much shade. A clump of climbing 'Cocktail' roses near the house, which looked neat when it was small, became increasingly vulgar in middle age and was banished to the chicken coop and a whole Red Garden which struck the Marchesa as aggressive was dug up and hidden away in a valley behind the lake. But she was always making plans to resurrect it.

The story of these meanderings was music to the ears of gardeners like me, who stagger from one blunder to the next, because we almost never find experts who admit that anything goes wrong for them. To hear them tell it, they plan their gardens perfectly, their plants settle into the soil as if they were born there and they live happily ever after.

Lavinia Taverna, however, was perfectly happy to share with me the stories of her failures. There was the collapse of her rock garden, for instance. She and Page had decided to build a large rock amphitheatre which they would fill to overflowing with Alpine flowers. The rocks were hauled to the spot and a band of workers toiled to dig proper drainage and to plant hundreds of the finest rock garden flowers shipped in from Switzerland. But alas, the plants just sat there next to the rocks and refused to grow. Desperate attempts were made to coddle them but one sad day it became clear that the garden was dying and should be given up for lost. The lower part was levelled and planted with fruit trees and the remaining spaces were filled with sunny Mediterranean shrubs, which promptly began to wither because the fruit trees gave too much shade.

The story of the grey garden by the front terrace is another cautionary tale. When Page planned this garden under a line of pine trees he failed to consider that the pines would eventually rob the grey plants of much needed sun, and also would drop acid needles which would poison the lime-loving plants. This garden struggled along for years, having to be completely replanted every year, but in the spring of 1996 the Marchesa decided to move it down the hill into a grove of olives (which have shallow and non-invasive roots). The result is an enlarged grey garden near the entrance of the estate, which glimmers under the dappled shade of the olives, as soft as a painting by Renoir. Its finest moment comes in April when great stalks of echium (from the Canary Islands) send their vivid blue spires up to mingle with the olive branches.

Lavinia explained to me that her aim throughout was to copy an English cottage garden but a close look suggested to me that just as a Tasmanian wolf resembles a European wolf only superficially, so her garden's resemblance to an

English cottage garden was more fanciful than real. Since she could not grow the tender perennials like delphiniums that fill English gardens, she achieved nearly all her effects with similar looking but tougher Mediterranean plantings. She used dozens of shrubs such as myrtle and rosemary and viburnum to create colour and mass, and she made her hedges of laurel rather than of box and yew which are harder to grow in Italy. To avoid the scorched earth and dust that make Italian gardens so dreary in summer she grew miles of bright groundcovers so that the bare earth is never exposed.

When I asked her about future plans, Lavinia told me she had decided to open her gardens to the public, not because she wanted to make money but because she hoped that by putting it on a paying basis her garden's future would be more assured.

'No one in my family has much interest in the garden,' she told me, 'and I am afraid that if it does not become self-supporting they will give it up.' Unfortunately Italy does not have an institution like the National Trust, which has the know-how and the resources to take over the care of important modern gardens.

Not long after this interview the Marchesa, who was busily planning new gardens for the twenty-first century, was taken to hospital with complications after a minor stroke and unexpectedly she died. Some reports have it that the garden may be taken over by her former partner, Mario Margheriti, who built the largest nursery in Italy right next door to La Landriana. At the moment the family are hoping that the garden will remain open to the public, as the Marchesa would have wished.

I well remember the last time I saw Lavinia and Margheriti together. It was an April morning, and the Marchesa was hosting a large outdoor lunch. The affair was to mark the opening of her Primavera Landriana, a garden bazaar which attracted growers and gardeners from all over Italy as well as critics and collectors from England and France. The guests were milling about in the warm spring sunlight looking for tables – deputies, diplomats and socialites from Rome, old friends, and garden experts including the landscapist Paolo Peyrone and rose grower Peter Beales. I noticed that far from mixing with her guests, Lavinia Taverna was huddled in a corner in deep consultation with Mario Margheriti and young Annalisa, her much loved head gardener. She called me over to join them.

'Maybe you can help us,' she said to me. 'I have just come from the Olive Garden and I am very unhappy. The latest clematis we planted next to the olive trees has started to bloom and it is not mauve at all as they promised me, but a dreadful shade of purple. What I need is a true mauve. It must go with the olive leaves and all those yellow tulips.'

I suggested trying some of the new larkspurs, but she shook her head.

'No, no,' she said, 'I have seen them too and they are not right. They are either royal blue or lavender, they are not mauve.'

Then Annalisa remembered that some new violas had just arrived from a grower in France, and she seemed to recall that some of them might be mauve.

'Would you mind going and getting one or two and bringing them to me?' Lavinia said to her. 'I will wait until you get back. If the colour is good, I would like to plant forty or fifty of them this afternoon.'

By the time she had reached her table where the British and American ambassadors were seated, they had already finished the lasagna and were starting on the fish course.

On one of my last visits she took me out behind the lake to see two new plantings which she expected to become mature in perhaps fifteen years. One which she baptized 'Sunset Boulevard' was then only a line of slender deciduous trees, but they were specimen trees which she had picked because they would one day make a vivid show of autumn colour (not common in Italy). Beyond this she had planted an even larger group of saplings which she hoped would grow into a thick woodland and provide a place for cool walks in summer.

'I know I may never get to walk through these woods,' Lavinia said with a smile, 'but you should never deprive a gardener of her dreams. If a garden stops changing, it is no longer truly alive.'

October

Chasing Pigs

SPRING AND AUTUMN ARE THE TWO SEASONS MARKED BY AN unfamiliar hazard, the arrival of footloose animals on our land. Our first spring we thought that all those cows and sheep and pigs must have wandered in by chance, but we gradually realized that it was a question of grass – and that there was a purpose behind it.

The problem of grass for the animals has for centuries been one of the main preoccupations of farmers and shepherds around the Tolfa hills. Since much of the land has traditionally been owned by absentee landlords, the poor shepherds and *butteri* have enjoyed little pastureland of their own. This imbalance has resulted in dozens of desperate stratagems to procure grass for animals, and the folklore is full of stories about 'flying cows', 'sheep who climb fences' and pigs who run wild on the night of the full moon.

We were unfamiliar with this folklore when, soon after we

had bought our land, we were approached by a rather be-draggled shepherd named Ascanio, who had a sly smile and a limp. Ascanio appeared suddenly on our field while we were picnicking under the almond tree one day in early spring. He was accompanied by two large Maremma dogs.

As he walked towards us across the field, Ascanio stopped several times to sweep up a handful of our grass and examine the seeds. He held this out to us as he came closer.

'Too bad about your grass,' he said. 'It is in terrible shape, I doubt if it will even be worth baling. The only thing that would save it would be manure – good sheep manure. If I put my sheep on it for the next few months, the manure would fortify the soil and make the grass grow better.'

'But wouldn't the sheep cause damage?' Robert asked.

'There is nothing on your property that the sheep can harm,' Ascanio replied with a sidewise glance at our olive trees. 'All they will do is keep the weeds down, and fertilize your soil for you at the same time.'

It sounded like a good proposal to us, but we pointed out to Ascanio that although we welcomed the sheep in winter and early spring, we would not want them around after the end of April because all our wild flowers would (we fondly hoped) be blooming.

'No, no,' replied Ascanio, 'I always take my sheep away late in April. It is too hot for them by May so I will either take them up into the hills or out into the forest.'

This seemed fine, so an informal deal was closed on the spot. Ascanio could put his sheep on our property in the cooler weather to nibble away and keep the weeds down but by late

April he would be gone. No mention was made of money, but he indicated that what we would gain in fertilizer no money on earth could repay.

As he headed back to his herd, Ascanio shook Robert's hand and murmured something about the right to graze for the rest of the winter, *erba compresa* (grass included).

'He thinks his sheep are going to eat grass,' Robert remarked to me as he went away, 'but the only crop here is rocks and thistles.'

A month later when we were starting to move some furniture into our half-built house, we were pleased to see a pretty flock of sheep grazing on our pastureland with the shepherd's son Gianni dozing under a fig tree. What a lovely picture, we thought, our own sheep on our own meadow!

But the picture was spoiled somewhat by the realization that the sheep were actually grazing in our olive grove, and several of them seemed to be nibbling the trunks and lower branches of the olive trees. 'They never did that before,' Gianni assured us, rubbing his eyes after we had woken him. 'I've had them here for a week and they never went near the olives.'

We inspected our trees and could find only a few branches that appeared to have been broken, so we did not make a fuss. And after that, every time we came to work on the house we found the sheep innocently browsing on the open meadows.

Then came April with its sweet showers, and at the end of the month Ascanio arrived to take his sheep away.

'I am moving them to the forest for a while,' he said, 'so the grass will grow very well here.'

We did not give much significance to these words, but he was quite right about the grass. It leaped up some 60 centimetres during the first weeks in May, and soon it was almost as high as our five-year-old son Henry, and showed no sign of slowing down.

Signor Fiorello, our site manager, remarked on our splendid grass crop, and said that if we didn't know what to do with it he could send his brother-in-law over who could cut it, bale it and lug it away, leaving our property clean for the summer. Among other things, it would reduce the fire hazard.

We were delighted with this offer, and a week later, on the very day when we were planning to spend our first night in our house, Fiorello's brother-in-law sent over a small tractor with a cutting arm and began systematically to cut down our hay. When we went to bed that night, the smell of new-mown hay filled the air and nightingales sang as if this was their final aria.

'This is the life,' I murmured as we settled down on our camp beds, 'new mown hay, nightingales and a gibbous moon.'

At that precise instant a wail of great intensity rent the night air.

'They have robbed my grass, they have robbed my grass,' someone shrieked.

We leaped from our beds and went out to the driveway, where a small Fiat 500 was parked near the pumphouse. The first person we saw was the shepherd Ascanio, who had thrown a raincoat over his pyjamas. He was followed by his wife, a large woman wearing a pink flowered nightgown with matching wrapper. She hurled herself in our direction with tears in her eyes.

'You have stolen our grass,' she wailed. 'We will denounce you to the Carabinieri.'

'It is true,' Ascanio chorused. 'Our neighbour Angelo just came to tell us that you have given your hay to the brother-in-law of Fiorello. He saw him going away in his tractor.'

'Why not? It's my hay,' said Robert somewhat stiffly.

'No, it's not your hay, it's our hay,' screamed Signora Ascanio, 'and you will pay for your perfidy.'

'Look here,' said Robert growing even angrier, 'I was nice enough to let your damn sheep on to my land where they chewed the bark off my olive trees, but I'm damned if I have to give you my hay too.'

'Yes you do, yes you do,' retorted Ascanio, eyes flashing. 'That was the agreement – *erba compresa*.' Grass included.

Robert threw a nervous glance towards me.

'He says I made a deal with him – he gets the hay too.'

'He doesn't get *this* hay,' I assured him, sounding more confident than I really was. 'It's *our* hay and we do what we want with it.'

The only trouble was that I was wrong.

We asked our builders the next day, and they confirmed that there are many ancient rules governing the contracts between a shepherd and a landowner, and one of these stipulates that if the shepherd grazes his sheep all winter, he can also cut and bale the grass and take it away after his sheep have left. In other words his sheep get the grass, whether it is growing green on the field or baled and packaged and served up dry like shredded wheat for breakfast.

The only thing that might work in our favour, the builders said, was the fact that the contract had been a verbal one, and the shepherd had not offered the usual remuneration, which was a milk-fed *abbacchio* (baby lamb) at Easter. There was also the matter of the gnawed olive trunks.

In time, it was agreed through intermediaries that the shepherd would withdraw his complaint against us if we paid him the outrageous sum of 50,000 lire, and we would withdraw our complaint against him if he promised to vacate our hayfields for ever.

'You got off lightly,' said our head builder. 'There is another law that says if a shepherd has his sheep on your land for more than five years, and you don't use it yourself to grow crops on, the shepherd automatically gets the land in his name. I have two cousins who lost two hayfields that way.'

After this, we had no more dealings with shepherds. But it seemed that whenever a shepherd passed down the lane that bordered our property, a few animals would invariably 'escape' on to our land and have to be chased out.

On all these occasions, the shepherd would rush in to retrieve the wandering sheep or cows, swearing that they had escaped his notice, but once in a while, especially if we had been away for some time, we would return to find fifty sheep contentedly browsing just inside our gate. And always the shepherd swore that the sheep had simply spilled through our gate while he was off retrieving a lost lamb.

In many of the little cattle towns in our area, it used to be considered an act of heroism to send your cattle to dine on the prince's grass. The farmers of the cattle town of Pisciarelli, which lies near the north shore of Lake Bracciano, kept their cattle alive by taking them off every night to graze on the rich pastures of the Principe Odescalchi of Bracciano, and although the prince had anti-poaching wardens on duty, they rarely managed to clap *manette* (handcuffs) on the Pisciarelli plunderers. This triumph of the local cattle men was not considered thievery by the Pisciarellesi, but was cheered as an act of courage and independence. The idea was that if the farmers couldn't graze their cattle, they would rapidly become impoverished, and in the end would have to beg for work from the prince on his terms. On the other hand, by sending their cattle off to eat the prince's pastures they remained free and independent, valiant fighters against the tyranny of the uncaring nobles.

I am not sure if the local cattle men regarded us as substitutes for the prince – I rather think they did not – but it remains a fact that we and many of our neighbours had to be constantly on the alert for intruding animals, especially in the autumn when our cabbages, tomatoes and zucchini were ripening and our fruit trees were yielding up delicious crops of pears, apples, figs, nuts and even guavas. All of these were highly favoured by sheep, cows, pigs and, on one memorable occasion, a full-grown ram.

One morning in early autumn Henry came running into our bedroom.

'Mommy, come, there are bulls in our *orto*. They are eating all our tomatoes.'

I dashed out in my dressing gown and there in our kitchen

garden next to the pumphouse were three hefty young *vitelloni* (calves not yet bulls) who were eating our tomato plants whole and trampling down everything else that was growing in the garden.

I rushed towards them, waving my arms and making threatening noises. Robert, already at work in the studio, came out on the double banging a plate of copper with his chasing hammer.

The *vitelloni* looked up at us with mild disdain and went on eating, so Robert raced up to the largest of the beasts and gave him a whack across the rump with the copper plate. The animal jumped in surprise and then trotted out into the field, destroying a row of ripe peppers as he went. Robert then turned on the other two, beating at them angrily, and one at a time they vacated the *orto* for the safety of the wider field, leaving deep and distressing hoof marks all over the well-watered earth.

At this point our neighbour Luigi, who had heard the rumpus, came running across our field yelling.

'Close the gate, close the gate. I have called the game warden and he is coming to impound the *bestiacce* (terrible beasts) before they do more damage.'

Henry sprinted off to close the gate while I stood guard in the *orto*. Luigi and Robert, with more shouting and waving of arms, managed to back the calves into a closed corner of the field, where they stood uncertain and somewhat rattled by all the excitement.

In a surprisingly short time we heard the roar of a large motorcycle and the Canale game warden, Lamberto, appeared at the gate. Lamberto was a familiar character around Canale, dressed in a trim khaki uniform with service ribbons on his chest and a long pheasant's feather trailing from his military cap. The whole effect was diminished when he opened his mouth because he spoke in a high squeaky voice.

'I have told Rodolfo to come over here at once,' he said, 'because I am sure that they are his animals. It's not the first time they have gone on a feeding spree.'

As he said this, an ancient mud-covered motorcycle hove into view, driven by Rodolfo who had the aggrieved air of a man wrongly accused. He took one look at the big calves and shook his head.

'No, they are not mine,' he said, turning his motorcycle round. 'I keep all my animals penned up and secure. They do not race around Prati Lunghi eating other people's cabbages.'

'OK,' said Lamberto, pulling a large hank of rope from the back of his motorcycle. 'I'll just take them down to the Canale lock-up for tonight and we'll sell them at auction in a couple of days.'

Rodolfo stopped dead when he heard this, and then went for a closer look at the animals.

'Well what do you know, they *are* mine after all,' he said. 'But someone else must have let them out just to get me into trouble.'

'Right,' said Lamberto. 'If they are yours, you better get a truck down here fast. And then come round to my office to talk about damages.'

That was the last we heard of the *vitelloni*, but in the next couple of weeks we had visits from a herd of four runaway horses, who amused themselves galloping around our field and eating fallen apples, and some cows who were more timid than the *vitelloni*, and turned and ran when we approached them with rakes and pitchforks.

Then one bright Sunday morning, as we were finishing our morning tea, we looked up to see a very large animal with long curved horns processing down the main walk to the house, as if he had been invited for tea. The children thought he was another bull, but since both Robert and I were born in April we knew a zodiacal ram when we saw one.

'No,' I said, 'he is an Ariete – a male sheep.' Robert reached for a piece of paper so that he could draw this extraordinary animal as he moved to the fig tree and began sampling the new dark purple figs. But the ram had hardly finished one when a man in a black suit came running down the path carrying a rope. It turned out that he was the owner of the beast, whom he rented out to service the ewes around Canale. On an average day the animal earned him as much as 100,000 lire. Needless to say he roped up the ram without further ado and hurried him away to get on with his business before the sun set.

If you were to count the damage done by animals on a scale of one to ten, there is little doubt that while horses rate only about four and *vitelloni* eight, the terrible herds of rampaging pigs rate a full ten. For the pigs are cleverer than other animals; they range around in family groups which consist of mother pigs who are very tough and will attack you if you disturb their young, and small pigs who are even tougher, built like tractors, and capable of tunnelling or kicking their way through a solid brick wall if there is food on the other side. Compared to these demons, even fierce German shepherds look like pussy-cats. Let loose in a flourishing *orto*, a mixed gang of pigs can reduce all the vegetables to compost quicker than a tree-shredding machine can shred one small oak in the Borghese Gardens.

The most frustrating aspect of the roving pig herds in Canale was that we all knew who sent them. Their owner was a foul-tempered Sardinian named Olera, who lived in a shack over in the Sasso hills and was so formidable that even the Carabinieri were scared of him. He was known to shoot at people who dared to ride by his property on horseback, and he had several times been involved in knifing incidents outside bars in Canale.

Olera apparently kept himself informed as to when our various crops were ripe, because his pig herds invariably arrived when we were ready to harvest the pumpkins or the peppers, or when the apples started dropping from our trees. One evening, just before sunset, we heard the usual gruntings from the field and found a larger than average gang of pigs rooting under the apple trees. Robert summoned Luigi, who also suffered from pig predations, and the two of them put a pre-arranged plan into operation. Luigi went after the female pigs with a large pole to stop them from attacking, and Robert grabbed one of the smaller piglets and shoved him, struggling like a wild tiger, into a burlap bag. Then both men grabbed hold of the kicking, wiggling bag and ran with it to the studio, with the mother pig in hot pursuit. They popped the bag into a strong wooden crate, useful for shipping statues. The piglet wasted no time in breaking out of the bag, and began kicking at the slats of the wooden crate, breaking the top with ease, so Robert found a big slab of oak to reinforce the cover. Then, fearful that the little demon would still escape, they moved the crate into the bathroom and locked the door. The next morning they drove the crate, piglet still kicking inside, down to the Carabinieri headquarters in Manziana, as proof of trespassing, and filed a complaint against Olera for wilful damage to property. The Carabinieri said they would take up the matter with the dreaded Sardinian, but we never heard from them again. We never heard what happened to the piglet either, although we doubt if it was returned to its owner.

In the end it was the local farmers who had to come to grips with the Olera menace. An American painter friend of ours, Ann Louise, used to rent a little house down in Santiori during the warm months, and she often went out at the weekends with her friend Josie to do some painting.

One autumn night when the moon was full, we were awakened around midnight by frightened calls at the front door. We went out to find Ann Louise and Josie, wrapped in blankets over their nightclothes and shivering with fear.

'Oh, it is awful down at Santiori,' Ann Louise gasped. 'There's a war going on. Lots of pigs are stampeding around, trampling down the flowers and grunting like mad; and there are lots of men hiding in the bushes, and every once in a while there is a blast from a shotgun and more pigs screaming. It is really so frightening we can't go back.'

We naturally offered the women beds where they could sleep for the rest of the night. The next morning Luigi reported that three dead pigs had been found in the Santiori area, along with hundreds of spent cartridges. Since the pigs had been killed only a few hours earlier, the local farmers were hard at work turning them into sausages, bacon, liver, pig's-feet and tasty pork chops. We also heard that Olera had filed a complaint against 'persons unknown' for the massacre of his animals, but after several weeks of investigation the Carabinieri reported that they were unable to locate the culprits, and assumed that they were the usual Albanian cattle-rustlers who had come from out of town.

Mushroom Madness

YOU HAVE TO LIVE IN THE COUNTRY A WHILE BEFORE YOU can understand the frenzy that the mushroom season produces among the locals. It is like an attack of malaria or hepatitis; it grabs you suddenly and can remain with you for life.

When I lived in the city, I was essentially indifferent to the mushroom. It was an odd kind of vegetable. I liked to order my pizzas *con funghi* and I was not averse to eating a dish of *spaghetti con funghi* if it was well prepared but I was not one to hang about gaping when a market vendor unloaded a basketful of mushrooms on his counter, nor did I much care whether he was selling big *porcini* mushrooms or plain garden-variety white ones. They were just *funghi* to me, and like spinach they moved me not at all.

But then came an afternoon in late September when all of our builders from Tolfa disappeared in one fell swoop. The only person who had seen them going was the well-digger.

'These people from Tolfa are not serious,' he said. 'They have gone after *funghi*.'

'How do you know? Did they tell you?'

'Not exactly,' said the well-digger, 'I just put two and two together.'

The Tolfetani had acted quite normally all morning, he said, but around lunchtime they were joined by one Lorenzo Sgriscia, a welder from Tolfa who had come over to measure our terrace for wrought-iron gates. Sgriscia had a reputation for being the most fanatical *fungarolo* (mushroom hunter) in central Lazio. During his visit he took aside Mauro, who had a girlfriend in Canale, to ask him if he knew of a watering trough in the area named La Fontana della Femmina Morta (fountain of the dead woman). The *macchia* between us and the Maremma is dotted with these country troughs which provide water for local herds, and a surprising number of them are named for women who have come to an unhappy end (a fact which suggests an extended history of uxoricide, or at least of femicide).

Mauro had confirmed that such a fountain did indeed exist at the end of a dirt road heading towards Sasso, and Sgriscia took off soon afterwards. He returned about eighty minutes later to salute his fellow Tolfetani, claiming he had gone to have his silencer fixed, but when his friends peered into the back of his truck, they spied three large baskets covered with a poncho.

That was all the Tolfetani needed, and as soon as Sgriscia was out of the way they piled into Vincenzo's Fiat 500 and took off for the Femmina Morta. The five men resurfaced late in the afternoon bursting with good fellowship, and in every corner of their little car, on the floor, in the glove compartment and in the tiny boot, there were mushrooms – hundreds and hundreds of them – white, pink, orange, brown and grey. Had they won the New Year lottery or picked the winning combination on Totocalcio, they could not have been more full of innocent joy.

The next day I remember as one of those golden days when all the birds had bells on them. Our Tolfa workers came back in two trucks, bringing with them five wives, seven children and two dogs plus a series of boxes and crates. Without even discussing the need for a holiday from work or school, we piled into our assorted vehicles and bumped off westwards towards the fountain of the Femmina Morta.

The scene around the fountain was enough to make a strong man weep with joy. It was as if an errant Giovanni Appleseed had gone berserk and spread fungus spores instead of apple seeds and the mushrooms had come up so thickly that the rabbits had to zigzag to keep from tripping. The Tolfetani said they had never seen better conditions for mushroom sprouting; it was warm but not too warm, the sunlight freckled the ground, leaving it half in shadow and half in sun and the grass underfoot was spongy, easy on the feet. There was also a heart-warming aroma of mushrooms in the air, like that tantalizing smell of wet leggings drying by the fire, combined with a whiff of roasting chestnuts and the odour of a damp country cupboard.

We set our crates on the ground next to the cars, and arming ourselves with stout sticks and baskets (never plastic bags), we set off on the treasure hunt. Gigetto, the sturdy stonecutter from Tolfa, explained the procedure to us newcomers.

'The important thing is to take only mushrooms which you know,' he said. 'Take the *porcino* and the *ovolo*, and leave all the others alone.'

The *porcino*, he explained, was a big brown or beige toad-stool with a huge cap on top, the kind of mushroom that babies are found under in nursery tales. The second mushroom he permitted was the famous *ovolo*, which popped out of the earth in the form of a little white golf ball, and then proceeded to throw off its filmy white cover to reveal a glowing orange cap underneath which opened out gradually like an umbrella.

Both the *porcino* and the *ovolo* were substantial mushrooms, the mature ones running to half a pound each; and according to Gigetto they could not be confused with anything really poisonous. Any other mushrooms we were absolutely not to look at.

So we set off and in no time at all we were deep into mushroomland. First I found a whole family of *porcini* nestled behind a bed of furze, and only a few steps beyond it, hiding at the edge of the chestnut forest, was a long string of *ovoli*. Some were just peeping up from the ground, glistening white and full of vigour, and next to them were some fully mature specimens whose caps had turned bright orange.

The great thing about this day was that everybody was lucky. Even small children filled their baskets. You couldn't walk for tripping over the mushrooms.

Shrieks of joy resounded through the autumn woods.

'*Che bello!*' ('How beautiful!')

'*Una meraviglia!*' ('What a marvel!')

'*A Mamma, vieni qui. Tu non lo crederesti.*' ('You won't believe it!')

The wife of Vincenzo, the head builder, was electric with joy.

'*Che soddisfazione, che soddisfazione,*' she chorused. ('How satisfying!') 'I have never had a day of mushrooming like this in all my life.'

The men, however, seemed to have less time for exultant shouts. They were old-time woodsmen who followed the ancient rules, moving swiftly and silently through the undergrowth, keeping quiet in case there were other *fungaroli* (mushroomers) in the area. They were collecting easily twice as many mushrooms as the rest of us.

Since it was obvious that Gigetto was the champion collector in the group I asked if I could follow him to see how he did it.

'Of course you can, if you can keep up,' he said with a sidewise grin. With this he plunged into the thickets with me scrambling after him.

His basic plan was to move fast, very fast through the edges of the forest, working in big circles. He slowed down a bit when he came to that soft area where sun and shadows mixed and the earth was moist and the moment he found a couple of mushrooms, he branched out very carefully from there, testing every suspicious clump of leaves with his stick. He also used his stick to turn back stones, but after he had picked his mushroom he made sure to put the earth and leaves back the way he found them. That way the mushroom spores would be able to develop for the next year. For the same reason, trained *fungaroli* avoid the use of plastic bags because these isolate the picked mushrooms and keep their spores from falling. Mushrooms packed in an open basket are more likely to leave a trail of scattered roots and other bits and pieces which will live to make lovely mushrooms the following year.

Another attribute of the great *fungarolo*, I discovered, is a very sharp eye. Like a good birdwatcher, a mushroom collector can spot a clump of mushrooms where other people see only bushes. All he needs to alert him is a tiny flash of beige or a suspicious bump by the roots of an old oak tree and he has discovered six more mushrooms. Memory also plays an important part. I have gone mushrooming with some *fungaroli* who remember where they found a certain kind of mushroom a year or even two years ago. Not infrequently they can tell you how they cooked that particular batch and how they tasted.

Another thing I discovered is that large country dogs are no help whatsoever in finding mushrooms. The Tolfetani dogs galloped happily around us enjoying the fun, but whenever we found a clump, they tended to bound over, sniff loudly at the mushrooms and then occasionally roll in them, but they clearly could not distinguish good mushrooms from bad.

When we all finally assembled by the vehicles after a morning at the Femmina Morta, we found we had accumulated five large crates of *funghi*. We drove them to our recently completed kitchen, and the women of Tolfa went to work to make lunch.

The first course was a raw mushroom salad, made from slices of the firmest and whitest *ovoli*, tossed together with chunks of good Gruyère cheese and a liberal handful of *rughetta* (roquette) salad. (This piquant mustard-like green has recently become popular outside Italy.) A salad dressing made with olive oil, crushed garlic and balsamic vinegar ties all this together.

When you are preparing a dish of raw mushrooms, it is essential to clean them thoroughly, and this is an art in itself. The Tolfa ladies warned against too much washing as the water tends to dilute the exquisite taste. Better to rub the mushrooms with a damp cloth to remove any dirt, or, if they are hard to clean, the dark spots can be cut off with a knife. Never soak mushrooms in water even for a short time.

For the second course, we had *spaghetti al porcino*, which was simply a spaghetti sauce made of slices of mushrooms tossed in hot oil along with a generous amount of garlic and chopped parsley. This rich sauce is poured hot over very thin spaghetti, known as *spaghettini*. Opinions vary on whether grated *parmigiano* cheese should be added to this kingly feast, but the ladies from Tolfa voted to include the cheese.

The third course (for those still hungry) was *porcini alla gratella*, which means quite simply big *porcini* mushrooms under the grill. To make this you use only the caps, leaving the stems for a spaghetti sauce. You dampen the caps with olive oil, then roll them in a preparation of breadcrumbs, chopped parsley and garlic, sprinkle them with salt and pepper and put them on a plate directly under the grill. They are grilled for only ten minutes, turned once or twice and a little oil added. If properly grilled, these *porcini* make a dish fit for a maharajah, soft and almost runny in the centre and crisp on the outside.

Mushrooms, it goes without saying, do very well with a fine white wine, preferably from Cerveteri or further north, wine from the Tolfa hills being somewhat harsh.

Once the serious business of eating was completed, the Tolfa women set about preserving the rest of the mushrooms. The very best ones were set aside to be boiled lightly and then preserved in olive oil, a procedure which always makes me somewhat nervous, bringing to mind the thought of botulism. All the rest are laid out in the sun on soft cloths, to be dried until they have almost no moisture left in them. These dried mushrooms are used in spaghetti sauces and soups for the winter.

We have never had another day quite like the first day at the Femmina Morta, but gradually we have become familiar with the mushrooms which grow in our own back yard – a little golden treasure more precious than pearls, known in Italy as the *galletto* (cockerel) and in France as the *chanterelle*.

We go hunting for this exactly ten days after the first autumn rains, and we find it always in the shadowy sunny spot at the edge of the oak woods, for this is one of the mushrooms which grows in close connection with tree roots.

At first we see nothing, and then suddenly someone calls out:

'There it is!'

We see a glint of gold almost hidden under an oak leaf. We carefully pull the leaves away to find a little funnel-shaped *galletto* about the size of an eggcup with solid meat very closely packed like a truffle. We push back the leaves around it and find six more clinging close to the ground. Then, walking delicately so as not to tread on them we find another little patch of gold, and then another.

Soon we have a basketful of *galletti*, so we take them up the hill, clean them carefully and then toss them into a frying pan with parsley and olive oil and make a dense spaghetti sauce. Say all you want about truffles, I'll take *spaghetti con galletti* any day.

Later in the autumn the common field mushrooms (*prataroli*) appear, not in the woods but out in the sunny fields, and we pick kilos of them. These are related to the cultivated mushrooms but their taste is earthier.

All other mushrooms are taboo. I am not even tempted by parasol mushrooms, although all the books claim they are as safe as mother's milk. They grow as big as butter plates near our pumphouse and one October I roasted them in the oven for two guests from Verona. Something was clearly wrong with them because in the night four out of five of us felt extremely woozy. We were later told that some mushrooms, even the so-called 'safe' ones, can be rendered poisonous if they are grown in the vicinity of poisonous ones.

Our neighbour Immaculata, whose husband is Armando the bus driver and metalworker, is a mushroom buff and spends most of October hunting mushrooms or drying them or bottling them in oil. One afternoon not long ago her son-in-

law Bruno came home with a basketful of blue-brown mushrooms which his friends swore were edible. Immaculata
roasted some and put them into sandwiches for her husband's
lunchbox. Next morning Armando had no sooner left for
Rome carrying the mushroom sandwiches than Bruno came
rushing in to report that his friends were now having second
thoughts about the blue mushrooms and had decided they
must be poisonous after all.

Immaculata frantically called the Rome office of the bus
company ATAC to warn Armando, and the ATAC people got
busy on their mobile radio. About an hour later Armando was
driving bus 202 down the Corso di Francia when a big orange
bus overtook him and blocked his way.

'Are you Colombo Armando from Canale Monterano?
Don't panic! It's your lunch! Don't eat it! The mushrooms in
it are poisonous.'

Armando assured him he hadn't touched his lunch, and he
was proceeding slowly towards the Olympic Village when a
second bus going in the opposite direction waved him to stop.

'Armando,' yelled the driver, 'be careful! Don't eat the
mushrooms!'

Several passengers sitting up front exchanged worried
glances.

When bus 202 got to the stop light at the Viale Tiziano,
Armando was again flagged down, this time by a motorcycle
policeman in boots and helmet.

'Are you Colombo Armando from Canale Monterano,
Provincia di Roma? Have you eaten your lunch? No? Then
throw it out. It contains toxic mushrooms.'

Several of the female passengers got up and descended from the bus.

When he had completed his rounds, Armando was feeling hungry because he hadn't eaten any lunch, so he stopped by a trattoria near the railway station for a bite to eat.

What did he eat? 'Spaghetti with garlic and oil,' said Armando. 'Why take chances?'

November

Tree-planting Time

LEADING MEMBERS OF THE MODERN GARDEN MOVEMENT in Italy are convinced that trees should be the backbone of any well-organized garden. But this is not the general Italian attitude towards trees. The average Italian farmer does not like trees at all, and the moment he buys or inherits a new property his first move is to go out and cut all the trees down. Trees are considered non-essential and wasteful; they clutter up the land which then cannot be planted with edible crops; they drop messy leaves in the autumn and offer cover for lurking marauders and snakes.

Occasionally a farmer may leave one big tree such as a plane tree to provide shade for his house, and sometimes a second one to shelter his car or his tractor or his cow. He may also allow a few trees to grow around the border of his land where they do not interfere with his crops but it is understood that he will cut these for firewood every five or six years, whenever he needs it. There are only a few exceptions to this universal rule; the olive tree of course is respected and even revered because of its produce, and so are fruit trees – apples, cherries, plums, figs and persimmons – and nuts such as almonds and hazelnuts. But if it isn't edible, it's expendable.

As far as ornamental trees go, Italians draw a blank. The only ones they recognize are the cypress and the plane tree and they have a low opinion of both. The cypress is abhorred because it is grown in cemeteries and the plane tree, which has been planted along the roads to provide shade, is regarded as an obstacle to fast driving. Italian car enthusiasts are engaged in a campaign to have most of the old trees that line country roads cut down.

Italian nurseries, if they sell trees at all, stock only the most traditional and socially correct species such as magnolias or cedars, or fancy conifers with metallic blue or yellow foliage. Thus if a village grandee like the local doctor or banker feels the urge to decorate his front lawn with a few 'ornamental' trees he invariably ends up with a magnolia or a cedar of Lebanon which soon grows higher than his villa, destroying any other planting and taking all the light from his house.

In recent years, however, trees have suddenly been put on to the government agenda. The Italian Agriculture Ministry has woken up to the deforestation problem which brings crippling floods along the river banks each autumn; and to encourage reforestation government nurseries now hand out tree seedlings to anyone who wants them (provided, of course, they come with the necessary signed documents and tip the right nursery officials). The Ente Cellulosa, a government office in charge of encouraging paper-pulp production, also offers larger trees – such as eucalyptus and Monterey pines – to all who are prepared to pay a token sum for each tree.

In addition the post-war prosperity has encouraged many young Italian professionals to build second homes in the country. These youthful nature enthusiasts, many of them members of the Green party, read *Maison & Jardin* and Italian garden magazines every month, and have travelled more than their elders so that they know there are more possibilities in the tree world than the plane and the cypress. They want to build leafy terraces where they can dine at night and they wish to surround these terraces with pretty flowering trees. So winter has become tree-planting time for many new Italian gardeners.

Since our first efforts at tree planting with the bulldozer and dynamite had been so traumatic, we had decided to do the rest of the planting slowly, and we swore that this time we would make advance plans about what to plant and where to plant it. The idea was to plant only a few trees every winter, and to dig most of the holes by hand. This way we could keep a close watch on the new plants every summer, and make sure they received enough water to get through their first season's heat. Once they were established, we would proceed with another small planting the next autumn. We actually weren't as badly off, tree-wise, as we had first thought. With the help of the bulldozer we had put in two lines of cypresses alongside our entrance drive so the house had a formal entry point, and we had also planted a second line of evergreens to the north of the house to serve as a windbreak from the tramontana wind.

We had ten cypresses left in pots, and we proceeded to plant them out one by one as accents around the house. One went on either side of the main pumphouse border, two were planted by the pumphouse itself and six more marked the corners of the lower terrace in such a way that they framed the long view out across the valley. These trees were among the best plantings we made as they gave a much-needed perpendicular accent to the long view into the valley.

Our Italian friends complained that we were planting cemetery trees that would bring melancholy and bad luck, but we reminded them that the more adventurous Tuscans have been dotting their countryside with cypresses for years. It also seemed to us that banning the cypress from Italian gardens is like banning spaghetti from Italian kitchens. In a hot, dry country where much of the vegetation is low and scrubby there is nothing like a vertical surge of deep green to add contrast and refreshment. The cypress is so beautiful and so dramatic that landscape painters are drawn to it as to a flame. Think of Cézanne who used the cypress to give height and colour to his Provençal landscapes; or Van Gogh who turned the tree into an agonized spiral that twisted about as if caught in the eye of a cyclone.

Oddly enough, the shape of the Italian cypress is not something that can be taken entirely for granted. Although all the trees we planted came from the same batch, some of our cypresses grew up narrow and slim as flagpoles, while others right next to them came up round and blowzy with branches extending horizontally for a metre or more.

I tried to find the explanation for this in the *Garden*

Encyclopaedia, but the discussion was inconclusive. At one point the encyclopaedia suggested that cypresses get fatter as they grow older, a complaint not unknown to other species; but this failed to convince me because I had many other cypresses that started slim and stayed slim all their lives.

The encyclopaedia also talked about two kinds of Italian cypress, one of which was *horizontalis* and the other *pyramidalis*, but the nursery had never heard of this distinction. All they had were two kinds of *pyramidalis*, one which they said was female (and chubby) and the second which they claimed was a 'grafted male' and guaranteed to be pencil slim. Needless to say the grafted male trees cost almost twice as much as the female.

Apart from being flagrantly sexist, this distinction is also botanically incorrect as all conifers, including cypresses, have both male and female flowers on the same tree, so there is no such thing as a male cypress tree. They are all defiantly bisexual.

None the less the Italians cling to this distinction and as an experiment I bought a couple of 'grafted male' cypresses and planted them in the lower garden. They are now very tall and they are definitely on the slim side, but they are still not the slimmest in the garden. That distinction goes to two regular cypresses which I moved out of our driveway years ago because they were crowded. After I moved them they were hit by a freak southern wind and blew over, and had to be propped back up with stakes. These two have remained ramrod slim ever since. Could it be that they remained skinny because of all their troubles; that the suffering they endured, being blown about by the wind, might be responsible for their extraordinary slimness?

I posed the question to Alan Mitchell, the British tree expert, and he shook his head. Some yew trees in the east of Ireland always keep their fastigiate form, he said, while those on the west coast remain stubbornly short and squat. The same happens to some poplars.

'It may have to do with the prevailing winds. It may be soil conditions,' Mitchell said. 'So far nobody really knows the answer.'

As for the other trees around the house, we decided to stick to evergreens because we had both grown up in New England and were fed up with bare black tree branches against the cold winter sky. In later years we were happy we had made this decision as many of our friends who planted big deciduous trees such as oaks or planes close to their houses complained that all of their gardening time in the autumn was taken up with raking and bagging the mountains of leaves that fell and had to be removed or burned.

Ever since I could remember I had had a secret yearning for a mimosa tree, so this was the first tree that we planted after the cypresses. The mimosa grew like a house on fire in our dooryard garden, a small planted area near the front door, and very soon it was brightening our February days with great sprays of foaming yellow flowers. But our joy was brief. The flowers started fading almost as soon as they came out, turning a dismal brown colour, and from then on the tree did little but shed dead flowers, seed pods and broken branches. It was a botanical oil slick. Nothing would live under the tree and the

more we weeded around it, the more the little mimosa
seedlings grew. After a year or so we sawed the blasted thing
down and planted peonies. Fortunately a few stray seedlings
rooted themselves out beyond the olive grove, so we can
always get a mimosa sprig for Italian Feminist occasions.

After my earlier remarks about the local craze for
magnolias, I am embarrassed to admit that I planted two of
them in our lower garden. One was the big pyramidal tree
Magnolia grandiflora which has lovely white flowers but leaves
that are rusty on the underside and seem to be forever dropping. The second was *Magnolia grandiflora var. gloriosa*. Not
quite so regular in growth, this had even larger flowers and
did not present such a leaf-clutter problem. When it became
apparent that there was not room enough for both magnolias
in our garden, we decided to keep only the *gloriosa* with its
huge platter-shaped flowers and eliminate the other.

The doctor in Canale heard that a magnolia was going
begging, so he sent down two workers who dug it up roots and
all and transported it to his garden where it now blooms
happily every June. Magnolias and olive trees seem to be very
easy to transplant in our part of Italy.

On the other side of our lower terrace we put in two nice
little persimmon trees, having admired a similar planting
scheme at Bernhard Berenson's villa, I Tatti, near Florence.
Officially known as *Diospyros kaki*, the trees were a fine choice.
They have a fluffy round shape like a child's drawing and
their heart-shaped leaves are pretty all summer. When the
leaves drop in the late autumn the shiny vermilion persimmon
fruits look like decorations on a Christmas tree. Often we do

not pick them until Christmas because unless they have ripened for a month, persimmons taste just like blotting paper. When ripe they are slippery as peaches.

On the edges of the lower terrace we also planted two fig trees. One is a special hybrid which gives us three crops of figs each summer, starting in June when figs are nearly as scarce as peacock's eggs. Our second fig is called *cuore* and gives us luscious heart-shaped green figs from September on. These figs are much too juicy to be dried but they make a delicious fig compote when baked in a sugar and cinnamon syrup. We have several other fig trees out in the olive grove which make small pinkish-white figs which obligingly dry in the sun before they are even picked from the tree.

To make sure that we have nuts to go with dried figs we have also planted several rows of hazelnut trees, *Corylus avellana*, in our back field. The hazelnut is a most obliging nut tree which has no enemies and requires very little upkeep. Picking it is also easy; the nuts simply fall to the ground when they are ripe, so all you have to do is pick them up, remove the outer round husk and then dry them in the sun for a few days. In Italy the trees are sold either as standards or as bushes, grouped around three large stems, and we chose those in bush form. Some of the larger bushes are actually small trees, which give good shade for picnic benches, and although the leaves drop in the autumn the trees put out pretty yellow catkins in midwinter. These nuts are a major crop in Italy and grow in large plantations in the Viterbo area where the ground around them is kept perennially cleared. They end up, as I understand it, in Hershey bars.

Another fruiting tree which we put right in the middle of our dooryard terrace was a small evergreen guava tree, *Feijoa sellowiana*. From a distance it looks exactly like a small olive tree with leaves which are silvery grey on the back and strongly glaucous. But the resemblance is deceptive. In June the tree suddenly erupts with a wealth of waxy white flowers which resemble orange blossoms except that their stamens are very prominent and bright red. The petals of these flowers are sweet and edible, tasting like candied violets, and they make a big hit in fruit salad. The only caution in picking them is to leave the centres, or stamens, intact so that they can develop into fruits in the late autumn.

The guava fruits are a greenish colour and look like rather small lemons. When peeled they reveal a smooth pinkish pulp which tastes halfway between a lemon and a banana and is rich in Vitamin C. These are the guavas which make the famous guava jelly, once featured as the main ingredient of the cream cheese and guava sandwich. (Schraft's on Boylston Street made the best in Boston.)

Another exotic fruit which is now attracting great attention in Italy is the kiwi fruit from New Zealand. This fruit, which looks like a fuzzy brown plum, actually grows on a vine like a grape, and when planted there must be at least one male bush for every three or four female ones. We never got around to planting kiwis because our arbour space was limited but a number of our friends have planted them and are now harvesting bumper crops.

When the kiwi was first introduced into Italian markets a few years ago it was as exotic as mangoes or avocados, and cost one or two thousand lire apiece. Slices of bright green kiwi fruits, dotted with black seeds, were the centrepieces for elegant fruitcakes. The whole kiwi market was blown to smithereens about two years later, however, when Italian farmers started stealing the black seeds off the fruitcakes and growing plantations of kiwis without asking New Zealand for permission. Now there are so many kiwis in Italian markets that the value of the fruit has dropped to a thousand lire for a whole kilo. Growers down under must be gnashing their teeth – not to mention the Italian seed hustlers.

One year the Cellulosa office gave us five little plants of *Eucalyptus globulus*, more commonly known as the blue gum, and we put them in a line behind the sculpture studio, hoping they would provide a wind shelter and also some privacy for the artist.

The little seedlings took off like sprinters and in only a few years they had billowed up to thirty metres, towering over the studio and everything else around us. The *globulus* is curious as it starts with little round leaves and then develops long thin greyish leaves as it grows older, and these sway gracefully in any summer breeze. The trees are essentially evergreen but they drop a lot of leaves and also the grey-white bark has an odd way of ripping off in large strips and dropping to the ground. This bark makes excellent kindling wood.

The charge has also been made that despite voracious roots, the eucalyptus will tend to blow over in a high wind. A number of eucalyptus wind-belts have suffered heavy storm damage near us, but in our garden our big trees have lost a lot of branches but have stood firm throughout even the strongest blows.

Our lower field, which rolls down to the crest of the river valley, is covered with an assortment of old olive trees which we have cultivated with care, pruned, and fed with both chemical fertilizer and manure. I never tire of looking down from our terrace to the grey-green olive trees; and my favourite time is early evening when they seem to be silhouetted with great precision against the paling sky and the grey-blue hills of Sasso off in the distance. For a while at twilight the olives take on a one-dimensional look like the most delicate filigree work and remind me of the white marble tracery on ancient Muslim tombs. They also give us lovely green oil in the autumn, although we have gradually become tired of picking them on cold November days and now let them out to any farmer who will pick them all and give us a few litres of oil in return.

Some clever gardeners I know – an Austrian couple who garden near Lake Bracciano – have managed to make a whole garden, or perhaps it should be called a park, just out of olive trees.

What they do is to cut the grass around the olive trunks until it is very short and very neat. They then water it regularly so it takes on a pleasant light green colour. The combination of light green grass with the twisted grey tree trunks and pale olive-grey leaves is very peaceful and they enhance this symphony of grey-green by putting in a few clumps of narcissus in spring, and pink geraniums in the summer.

The park looks like the beautifully kept white and green garden room of a stately villa. I would love to try something like it myself, but I worry that constant watering might eventually damage the drought-loving olive trees (as happened in the Olive Garden at La Landriana) so we have left our olive grove unimproved. It now gets mowed once a year, in May, when the hay is at its best. In spring the fields grow poppies and wild lupins and daisies, and in the autumn they bloom again with Queen Anne's lace and toadflax and meadow sage.

We wanted to plant some larger evergreen trees out near the borders of the property to provide some of the bulk and substance that the olives lack. Fortunately there were already two large holm oaks just below the olives, and we cut down all undergrowth around them so they would stand out. The holm oak, known officially as *Quercus ilex*, is considered by many to be the greatest of the Mediterranean trees, and I would put it very high on my list. It is a slow-growing tree which starts off looking like a holly bush, but as it grows it gradually fills out until it presents a huge rounded dome that is so solid and symmetrical it looks as if it has been clipped. The evergreen leaves of the holm oak are the size of olive leaves, but they are round and leathery, and when new leaves develop in the spring they are a soft whitish green which gradually turns very dark.

As for other large evergreens, the forestry people gave us a rather interesting assortment. One of the most handsome of these was the *Pinus pinea* or stone pine which appears in all the postcards of the Bay of Naples. This pine is a tree of true nobility and like a great cathedral it takes a long time to reach its full size. It starts life as a little fuzzy seedling, then goes through a young Christmas tree stage, but finally as it grows taller it starts to lose its lower branches, and eventually after fifty or sixty years (or even more perhaps) it takes on the classic umbrella shape. Its pine cones are much in demand, as they can be cracked open to yield the little pine nuts known as *pignoli* which are used for spaghetti sauces (especially in *pesto*) and also in elaborate pies and cakes.

For those who do not have the patience to wait for the stone pine to develop, the Forestry Department now offers an incredibly fast-growing pine that comes from America. The *Pinus radiata*, known to Americans as the Monterey pine, is a warm-climate pine from California which grows like a rocket. When we got our first seedlings they were about fifteen centimetres high. After a year they had grown to sixty centimetres; a year later they were over a metre, and then they spurted to four metres and then twelve. In less than fifteen years our Monterey pines had become the tallest trees in our valley while still maintaining the lovely symmetrical shape of the Christmas tree. Owls, magpies and golden orioles make their nests in the wide spreading branches.

Because these pines were given to us free, and because they grew so fast, we decided that they were necessarily inferior trees. Anything that grew so fast was bound to be short-lived and weedy, we decided, and we were convinced that the wood, which the Forestry Department recommended for paper, was bound to be tacky.

We were wrong on all counts. On a recent visit to the gardens at Dartington Hall in Devon, we admired some noble pines which we were told were more than two hundred years old – the oldest trees on the property. Imagine our surprise when we learned that they were our old friends the Monterey pine.

These ancient beauties had a nobility that can only come to a tree of great age. There they stood with giant trunks, so wide it would take two men's outstretched arms to encircle them. The trunks rose bare and unadorned for about eighteen metres and then fanned out into huge domes, very much like the domes of umbrella pines.

Alan Mitchell later explained to us that the English have long cherished the Monterey pine (it may have been sent back to England by David Douglas in the 1820s) and accord it the same respect that they give to the yew and the beech. A survey made after the devastating hurricanes that hit England in 1987 and 1990 showed that one of the most successful evergreens in withstanding the storms was the *radiata*. Long live Monterey.

No one seemed to know when the trees at Dartington took on their extraordinary umbrella shape but it seems likely, since they are such fast growers, that they reached this bobbed state at a relatively early age. The trees in Italy are still too young to start shedding their lower branches but we now look at them with new respect, realizing that unless some cruel soul chops them down they will still be hale and hearty in two hundred years' time.

Unfortunately their new status as Grade A trees cannot hide one defect which we have noted on all the *radiatas* in our area; they attract a particularly virulent type of pine moth known as the processional moth *Thaumotopoea pityocampa*. This moth lays its eggs in the top branches of the *radiatas* every autumn and the eggs hatch into black and yellow caterpillars which chew their way into tender pine buds, causing much damage to the trees. Their presence can be seen by the big tent-like cocoons which cling to the upper branches. Eventually, before pupating, the almost fully grown caterpillars descend from the trees and walk across the countryside in long straight lines like Roman legions, nose to tail, then have a final feed and change into moths.

I made the mistake of picking up one of these cocoons which had fallen from a tree, to see what it looked like. Within minutes my hands began to itch and the itching spread to my face and neck; great welts developed which were uncomfortable for several days. Subsequently I was told that these insects are so poisonous that farmers have often been hospitalized after touching them, and many people develop allergies if they breathe the air near the infested trees.

The Italian way to handle them is to get a shotgun and shoot the cocoons out of the trees and then burn them, wearing protective clothing the whole time. We have not resorted to this desperate stratagem so far because we do not have a gun, and our trees are so large that the caterpillars can't seem to do too much damage. However, I have seen many smaller *radiatas* which have been very badly chewed up by this ominous insect.

One other conifer which has had almost too much success with us has been the Norwegian spruce, a glorious tree which our paediatrician brought to us after he had used it as a Christmas tree. We had been given other Christmas trees which had invariably expired by Valentine's Day, so we paid little attention to the spruce as we popped it into a shallow hole behind our kitchen door. Lo and behold it began to grow, and now that our children have grown up too and left home it towers higher than our three-storey house. When they come back for holidays, Henry from Boston and Jenny from Mexico, they look up at our giant spruce and say:

'My goodness, where did *that* come from?'

Tomb Robbers

DEDE WAS THE FIRST COUNTRYWOMAN I MET WHO KNEW the difference between a tulip and a dahlia. Most of the farmers' wives around Canale professed to be great lovers of flowers and were happy if I offered them a cutting of a shasta daisy or a striped geranium, but they took no interest at all in the finer points of horticulture.

All bulbs, whether they were lilies or irises or amaryllis, were just bulbs to them and all composite flowers were *margherite* (daisies) whether they were chrysanthemums or sunflowers. They had a special fondness for roses and they were quite adept at starting new plants from cuttings which they put into the ground in November, but they were not prepared to spend any money at all on buying new varieties. Thus every village tended to specialize in only one variety of rose, and cuttings were handed on from one housewife to the next. The Canalesi favoured 'Queen Elizabeth'.

The rest of their flowers were grown in pots or old oilcans so as not to take up any space in the far more rewarding *orto* (vegetable garden) but the women knew enough about horticulture to weed carefully and to nourish their seedlings with ample doses of rich manure.

There was one garden, however, which seemed to me to be somewhat out of the ordinary in this narrow world, and this was a patch of land hard by the Quadroni road which exploded in late May with a superb display of giant poppies. These were not the common red poppies which turn European cornfields crimson in spring, nor the yellow and orange varieties so prized in California, but instead, great pink, mauve and grey poppies which are listed in the encyclopaedias as *Papaver somniferum* or, to put it simply, opium poppies. Now these lovely things, twists of Tiffany tissue paper in the very finest pastel tones, are to my mind the queens of the poppy world, prettier by far than the flamboyant reds and pinks of Oriental poppies, and a universe away from the rather timid Shirley poppies developed from a mutant corn poppy by a Scottish clergyman named Shirley. I used to detour around the Quadroni road in mid-May just to gaze longingly at these fringed opium poppies and ask myself where the owner got them, and how she ever got away with planting them. For as any close reader of English seed catalogues can tell you it is illegal to grow opium poppies in Europe.

I got my answer only a day or two later, when our friend Franco, the plumber who lived in Quadroni, brought the owner of the poppy garden to see my greenhouse.

'Here is my neighbour DeDe,' he said. 'She is the signora who grows those poppies you keep talking about. I told her about your garden and she wanted to see it.'

Signora DeDe (short for Deborah) didn't look like an opium grower to me. She was a tiny woman of late middle age, with jet black hair, and when we shook hands I could feel that her nails were rough and her skin was chapped – the hands of a genuine gardener. The most startling thing about her was her cough; it was deep and it was chronic. She started coughing when we were introduced, and she immediately began fishing around in her pockets for her cigarettes and lighter.

'Wait a minute,' she gasped, 'I have to take care of this cough.' She took a long drag on her cigarette, wheezed a minute and then her coughing stopped.

I asked if she would like a glass of water or a cup of coffee, but she brushed this aside as superfluous.

'No, no,' she said, waving her hand, 'I came to see the garden. So let's get on with it.' I knew at once that we would be friends.

We did a thorough tour of my garden, both outside and in the greenhouse, and she studied every plant and every flower with the greatest concentration, lighting up a new cigarette for every blossom. I asked her if she would like to try some cuttings and she admitted that she would, so we gradually filled a plastic bag with cuttings of *Pelargonium odoratissimum*, *Brugmansia arborea* (datura) and *Lavatera* 'Barnsley'. Unlike most garden watchers who tire after gazing at one or two flowering daturas, Signora DeDe was just as fascinated by my secondary plants and spent a long time surveying modest little bushes of veronica, clumps of *Convolvulus mauritanicus* in flower and patches of primrose. She even stopped for fully ten minutes to study my boxes of seedlings and to my great surprise she asked if she could have a few of them too.

I assured her that I was happy to spread the seedlings around as a kind of insurance policy.

'That way if I lose all of one variety there's a chance I can get it back later from a friend,' I said. Little did I realize, as I dug up two tiny seedlings from the Paulownia tree which I had obtained in China, that in ten years' time Signora DeDe would give one of them back to me as a thriving sapling.

As we were transferring the plants I ventured a comment about her outlaw poppies.

'Oh, those,' said DeDe. 'A friend of mine gave me a handful of seeds. Next September I will let you have all you want.' It was like an offer of diamonds. I asked her if there was any danger in growing plants on the forbidden list but her face was blank so I decided to drop the matter. If DeDe didn't know she was growing illegal opium poppies, chances were the local Carabinieri wouldn't know either.

She lit up another cigarette as she got into the car.

'You have a very nice garden, Signora Giovanna,' she said. 'Very nice, but there is just one thing that surprises me. Your geraniums are weedy and frail as if they had rickets. You take a lot of trouble with most of your plants so I am surprised that you have fallen down on such a simple matter.'

I felt like a schoolgirl who had failed her six-times table.

'I know,' I said, 'what should I do?'

'*Stabbio*,' she said, '*stabbio, stabbio*' (farmyard manure). (I had been brought up to believe that pelargoniums flourished in poor soil, the poorer the better.) Then she ground out her cigarette, wheezed for a minute and made me promise to come and see her garden the next day.

'Isn't it wonderful!' I said to Robert. 'Now I have someone I can gossip with about flowers.'

I went to see DeDe the next day and from then on we exchanged visits about once a week in the growing season. Her garden wasn't really a planned garden at all, but simply a back yard with a few grapevines and climbing roses, and around the edges she had an assortment of pots, old boxes and tin cans where she grew all manner of strange and exotic cuttings. Two cans were turned over to *Campanula pyramidalis*, a form of bellflower which shoots up to about a metre in summer and then produces an unending series of bright blue bellflowers. She also grew fancy lupins, and some very odd amaryllis that she claimed she got in Sorrento. They were smaller than the Dutch bulbs, coppery red in colour and I found them irresistible. She had also found seeds for some very strange morning glories which came up striped like zebras.

Our visits were so involved with flowers and growing hints that we had little time for any superfluous conversation. Our habit was to march directly around our gardens for an hour, exchange whatever cuttings or seeds were available and discuss propagation methods, weather and pests.

Families were rarely mentioned during these tours – least of all husbands – but I did manage to glean that she had a

husband named Lorenzo who had spent most of his life working as an usher in the Ministry of Transport. He had retired to
Quadroni quite recently (this was where he had grown up)
and it was obvious to me that he occupied a place in her heart
somewhere between the Japanese beetle and the rose borer.

One day when I went to call on her, I found her hanging out
on her clothesline twelve dripping red and yellow sets of football kit, plus twenty-four high white socks.

'It's all the fault of my husband,' she sputtered, taking time
out for a cigarette. 'He's been made a director of the Superior
School which means he has to coach the football team, and
guess who has to wash the kit? It's all because of this wretched
mayor.'

I couldn't make much sense of this outburst, but it came
into focus a day or so later when I met Lorenzo for the first
time. He was a smallish man with grizzled hair, a quick way
of speaking and a very nervous smile, and there was something about his ingratiating manner that made me think of a
special category of bureaucrats in Italy known as *porta-borse*
(briefcase carriers). In Britain he might have been a political
errand boy, in Russia a party hack; but in whichever ambience
you found him he would invariably be hovering like a
dragonfly around some important politician.

Lorenzo was quick to tell me that he was a distant cousin of
the mayor of Manziana, an ambitious type who had come to
the town thirty years ago as a Carabiniere and had gradually
risen to be the biggest landowner in town, the owner of the
only bus system and longtime mayor (a theoretically unpaid
job). As the right-hand man of this distinguished citizen,

Lorenzo performed a series of functions which had no apparent connection one to the other. He drove the school bus, he ferried the mayor to party meetings in Lazio, he worked as purchasing agent for the Manziana school system and he coached the senior-school football team (hence the dirty kit). On Fridays, for reasons which I have never understood, he showed up at the local outdoor market where he could be seen slicing swordfish, and cleaning and wrapping fish for some fishmongers from Civitavecchia. Franco the plumber also hinted that some of his income came from the buying and selling of Etruscan objects uncovered by the local *tombaroli* (tomb robbers).

In due course Lorenzo drove DeDe down for one of her weekly visits to my garden, and he took the opportunity to visit Robert in his studio. The two hit it off from the start; Lorenzo was impressed by a big waxworker who had statues on five continents and Robert, in turn, was fascinated to meet a local politician who knew all about the refuse collection tax and the new bypass to Bracciano. So the visits from Lorenzo and DeDe became part of our weekly routine and even when we went away on trips, they fell into the habit of driving down to have a look round and make sure that our property was intact. It was understood that they were free to pick figs or sour cherries or any of our other fruits that happened to be ready when we were absent.

Thus it came to pass that one Saturday afternoon, Lorenzo arrived in a gun-metal black Mercedes accompanied by two men. One I recognized as Gianfranco, his cousin, who ran a big farm over on the Sasso road and grew grapes and excellent melons. Gianfranco was younger than Lorenzo, a big hand-some fellow with grey-blond hair and a permanent suntan. The third man was even bigger than Gianfranco but he had no suntan at all. He might have been a car mechanic or a bus driver.

Lorenzo ushered these two visitors up to Robert's studio, where I was pruning roses, and Lorenzo suggested to me that this was to be a private conference with Cook. I started to back away but Robert, to his credit, said: 'No, no, Giovanna can stay. Anything you say to me you can say to her.'

All three visitors threw me a look of some surprise, for very few Italian wives would get that kind of support from their husbands.

Then Lorenzo sat down, lit a cigarette, and began telling the story to Robert. It was a matter concerning Etruscan pots, he said. Gianfranco and his friend had been shown some very fine pots by a 'farmer' who lived between Sasso and Cerveteri and had dug up the pots on his own land when he was plough-ing. Gianfranco was convinced that he could make a great deal of money from them if he could sell them to an important go-between named Claudio who was an antique dealer in Rome. Claudio, who had some kind of a connection with a truck driver who went regularly to Switzerland, had already seen one of the pots and said that, if the other four were of the same quality, he was willing to pay 250 million lire (£86,500) for the five of them. There was only one problem – Claudio, not having been born yesterday, was reluctant to buy Etruscan pots from a farmer, because even if they had been dug up on the farmer's land, they were still the property of the Italian

State. There was also the dreadful possibility, Claudio said, that the pots had been dug up by tomb robbers. The idea was to find a 'foreigner' who lived in the area and who was prepared to claim that the pots had been in his collection for a long time, and Lorenzo had suggested that his good friend Cook might be willing to act the part of the pot owner. Claudio was pleased with this arrangement, but said that he would like to meet the 'foreigner', and also to see all five pots before concluding the deal. So an appointment had been made for noon the next day at the home of Lorenzo's daughter.

That was all I needed to hear.

'We were warned when we first moved into this area that we should have nothing to do with Etruscan pots,' I said. 'Our *geometra* warned us, and our friends warned us that the Carabinieri keep a close watch on all this tomb robbing and they especially resent foreigners like us getting involved. It is very dangerous and also illegal.'

Our visitors exchanged glances, and stepped forward as if on the offensive.

'Who is asking you to break any laws?' Lorenzo exclaimed. 'All we want is for Cook to come over for ten minutes – five minutes – and tell this antique dealer that the pots used to belong to him. What law are you breaking just to do that?'

He then turned to face Robert directly.

'Roberto,' he said, 'I am asking you this as an old friend, just this little favour. I have had some financial reverses of late. My old Fiat is breaking down and I need a new one.'

'I am still against it,' I said as I headed for the door.

Twenty minutes later Robert came down to the house.

'Look, honey,' he said, 'I told them I couldn't say the stuff was part of my collection. I said it just wasn't true.'

'So then what?'

'So Lorenzo went outside to get his mobile phone, and he came back in a minute to tell me that he had contacted another friend, an Englishman who lives in Bracciano, who was willing to claim that the pots once belonged to him. Lorenzo said all he wanted me to do was to come over to have a look at the pots the next morning when the dealer was there, and to tell him if I thought they looked authentic.'

At a quarter to twelve the next morning we parked our car in front of the house of Lorenzo's daughter and went inside. The house was an Italian version of a monastery in Shangri-La, featuring wide cement terraces around every floor and overhanging eaves.

Lorenzo and the two friends were waiting for Robert at the front door and he was hurried into a private meeting room while I was told unceremoniously to go upstairs and join La Signora DeDe. My friend was hovering unhappily in the kitchen drinking black coffee and smoking cigarettes, and when I asked her what she thought of the proceedings, she replied: 'I don't know what they are doing but I wish they would stop.'

We leaned over the rail to see what was happening downstairs and from time to time the four men came out to enquire if Claudio had arrived. Robert looked up at me.

'They've only got three pots here,' he called up, 'but they look pretty good to me. Don't worry about anything.'

Eventually there was the flurry of a big foreign car out

front, and a dark burgundy BMW flashed past on the small country road, then turned round and drove past the house. Eventually it parked about fifty yards beyond the house. Like detectives in a thriller movie, DeDe and I watched, gaping, as a young man with bright red hair in a well-cut suit hurried towards the entrance, carrying a large pigskin briefcase.

'That's the money man,' said DeDe with a tone of disapproval. 'They say he could smuggle his mother-in-law into Switzerland and the customs guards wouldn't notice.'

I felt a frisson of excitement as Lorenzo opened the front door and let the new arrival in. The two went at once to the meeting room, while DeDe and I retreated to the kitchen where we had yet another cup of coffee.

'I wish Lorenzo would just work with the football team and the school bus and forget all these other things!' DeDe said darkly.

Some fifteen minutes after he had arrived, there was a slam of the front door and we rushed to the balcony to see the red-headed art dealer hurrying down the front path. In a minute the BMW revved up like a 747 and raced off down the street.

The four men came out of their room and Robert called up to me.

'You can come down now, honey, the man has gone.'

We went downstairs to find the four men looking glum.

'Is it all done?' I asked. 'Pots on their way to Switzerland?'

Gianfranco and his big friend glared at me, and Robert smiled and gestured to a package on the table.

'The pots are still here,' he said. 'He's going to take them tomorrow.'

Lorenzo cleared his throat and looked at me with great concentration.

'There's been a slight hitch,' he said. 'We only have three pots to show him, and Claudio says he wants all five or it's no deal.'

'So *get* all five. What's holding you back?'

'The farmer who found the pots. He won't give us all five of them until we give him a down-payment of 50 million lire [£17,300]. Of course we'll get our money back tomorrow. But he wants the cash tonight.'

I got up.

Lorenzo hurried on, 'I have a little savings account for my two granddaughters of about eight million lire. I can't tell DeDe about this, but I could get that money out tomorrow morning. After all, it's only for a few hours.'

'That leaves 42 million more,' said Gianfranco. All three men then looked at Robert. 'We'd even give the pots as security to anybody who would put up the money for a day.'

Robert remained impassive.

'Too bad, I don't have that kind of money around,' he said.

Lorenzo darted a quick glance.

'I thought you said you had an account at the Banco di Santo Spirito right in Canale?'

'All I've got there is a couple of million,' said Robert in a non-committal tone.

I started for the door and Robert soon joined me in the car.

'Lorenzo was very insistent,' he said. 'He asked me as a friend to try and raise the 42 million just for overnight. He offered to give me the three pots right away to hold as a guarantee against the loan.'

'You didn't agree, did you?'

'Hell, no. I'm not crazy. But he thanked me anyway and said he would call to tell me how it came out.'

I waved goodbye to DeDe who was hanging nervously over the balcony.

'What did you think of the pots?' I asked Robert.

'They looked fine to me.'

'So what did you say to the dealer?'

'I just told him that the pots looked pretty good to me although I was no expert. And he said something funny: he said that I should know because they had been part of my collection. Of course I told him I had never *had* a collection.'

'And then what did he say?'

'He kind of nodded as if he didn't hear me and then he opened his briefcase to get out some photographs, and there he had strapped to the bag – just like in the movies – great big stacks of 10,000 lire notes.'

So we went home and had lunch. We rather expected to hear from Lorenzo later in the day but he didn't call that night, or the next night either. Signora DeDe did not help matters by calling on the third day to tell me in a worried voice that she and Lorenzo were beginning to fear that the go-between, Claudio, was really an undercover agent of the Carabinieri and he might arrest us all for conspiracy. This news, needless to say, put us in a panic.

Perhaps the antique dealer, Claudio, had a tape recorder on him and would threaten to expose Robert for dealing in stolen

Etruscan pottery? Or perhaps he really was an undercover Carabinieri agent? Or perhaps we were just being warned to keep quiet.

We took the problem to some of our Italian friends and they were all of the firm opinion that we had been the intended victims of an old-time confidence trick. Claudio, they said, was not an antique dealer, but neither was he a detective in the Carabinieri. He was the fourth man on the sting team and his role was to convince Robert that he was ready to disburse 250 million lire as soon as he was given the five pots. The trick was to persuade Robert to 'loan' the necessary 42 million for overnight payment to the farmer, and he would be given the three pots to hold as surety against the loan. We were supposed to believe that the three pots were worth far more than the paltry 42 million, but all of our Italian friends were confident that the pots were fakes. They also believed that the Englishman who had reportedly claimed to have owned the pots was a figment of Lorenzo's imagination.

About three months later, when we were buying fish at the Friday market we realized that our trout was being cleaned by our old friend Lorenzo. As soon as he saw us, he hurried us around to a quiet spot behind the fish stand.

'I have bad news, terrible news,' he hissed, cleaning his fish knife on his trousers. 'Those two fellows from Ladispoli, the two who were trying to sell those five pots, they have both ended up in jail! For extortion and selling stolen goods.'

We gasped.

'They were finally denounced, first by a man in Oriolo who had loaned 150 million to them to buy the pots, and then by a doctor in Barbarano who had lost about 85 million in the same way. And they say that there were two more complaints from people who didn't want to give their names because they might be charged with complicity.'

We stared at him open-mouthed.

'What can I say?' Lorenzo hurried on. 'I was a fool. I was taken in by them, trying to do them a favour. I really believed them when they said they just needed an American to claim that he was the owner of the pots. I was stupid, very stupid.'

We nodded, but I don't think either of us really believed his story. The only statement we really believed was Lorenzo's admission that he had been a fool. He had been a fool to get involved in the business, and he had also chosen his victim foolishly. Robert was not a man to involve himself in complex Levantine intrigues. He was willing to participate in a small and harmless charade as long as it helped his friend and yielded good will. But the idea of putting up the overnight money – the 42 million – never entered his mind, even remotely. Thrifty he most certainly was. Foolhardy he most certainly was not.

We did not hear from Lorenzo or DeDe for nearly two years, and then she called to tell me about the Paulownia tree which had finally bloomed about four years after I had given her the seedling. Strangely enough it was that phone call which convinced me that DeDe was not involved in the pot scam. If she had been, I doubt if she would have had the courage to call me about a long-ago gift of a very small seedling.

December

Joy and Sorrow in the Winter Greenhouse

IT SEEMS TO BE A PRACTICE IN THE WORLD OF HORTI-
culture to record the flowers you have in bloom over the
Christmas holiday season. The English owners of the famed
Hanbury Botanical Garden at Ventimiglia were in the habit of
sending off to the *Gardener's Chronicle* in London a list of all
the plants that were blooming at the beginning of the New
Year. In 1875 they sent off a list with 103 names, and by 1886
the number had jumped to 500 species. In 1985, when the
garden had been turned over to the Italian government which
left it half-abandoned, the count at the New Year was down to
232. (It is now apparently on the rise again.)

I have never presumed to send out any list of the flowers
that bloom in our greenhouse in midwinter, although I admit
I have spent a good bit of time trying to find plants that will
bloom there every month of the year. There is no doubt, as I
said earlier, that the datura (*Brugmansia suaveolens*), a member

of the potato family, is the most dramatic and eye-catching tree that we have. We started with a few random cuttings from Amalfi. They survived, but only just, in the garden outdoors but they never flowered. But when we brought them indoors and planted them in semi-shade, it was like bringing eels to the Sargasso Sea – they had found a perfect home and they have been thanking us ever since.

The daturas usually are smallish trees with big green leaves, and their astonishing trumpet-like flowers are often more than thirty centimetres long. They are most commonly white, though by hunting around you can find some that are pink and yellow and lavender. These beauties usually open their new flowers just as the sun goes down; they begin rather stiffly as furled white umbrellas and they seem to weave back and forth in a kind of tropical dance – lithe and sinuous – and then slowly they unfurl, one pleat at a time, pop, pop, pop. Once it is fully open, the datura flower projects outwards at a right angle from the branch. The most extraordinary part of all is the scent which is strong and sweet and faintly sinister; a fact not to be wondered at as the datura contains a strong narcotic, stramonium, and all its parts are highly poisonous. According to Theophrastus, one bite of a datura petal or leaf brings a slight narcotic effect, but a whole mouthful can be fatal.

The plants originate in South America, and archaeologists tell us that the Incas made datura plantations within their temple walls and took small bites of the leaves to relieve pain, rheumatism and epilepsy. The datura was also known to the early settlers in America. Captain John Smith mentions in his journals, published in the early seventeenth century, that some of his men ate seeds of a 'strange apple' which they found in Jamestown and began to act in a peculiar fashion as if intoxicated. The plant subsequently became known as 'Jamestown weed' or 'Jimson weed', a weedy annual that still grows in waste places throughout the South.

You would think that this success with the white daturas would have satisfied me, but not at all; I soon began yearning for daturas in other colours. In time I found a little plant at the Chris Harries nursery in Nairobi which the sales lady assured me was a pink datura. She trimmed it neatly so I could fit it into my knapsack and I set it out carefully in the front row of the greenhouse when we got home.

The little plant seemed reluctant to take hold, so for many months we coddled it with special helpings of manure and rations of manure water; and then one May evening after a long struggle the first timid flower bud began to unfold. We watched with excitement as the petals began to pop open, and then came the disappointment.

'But it's not pink,' my husband exclaimed, 'it's white!'

The long-awaited flower was indeed an unfortunate blend of white and off-yellow.

We had been invited out to dinner that night so we naturally regaled our hosts with tales of our pink datura which wasn't pink, but since tales of flower failures do not rate as high as local gossip, our story brought little sympathy.

Returning home about midnight, I went to bid good night to my failed pink datura.

And lo and behold, in the three hours we had been gone, our datura had changed colour. It was not exactly a pure pink.

It was a soft pinkish-salmon colour, brightest along the outer edges and fading into a very pretty shrimp pink in the interior. But still it was pink and since that night it has grown so big that it brushes the roof of the greenhouse.

I have done some research on this plant, and believe that it is a hybrid known as *Datura × candida* 'Grand Marnier' which was developed by the French hybridizer Marnier-Lapostelle in the botanic garden at Saint Jean Cap Ferrat. What he apparently did was to cross a standard white tree datura with the orangey-red *Datura sanguinea* which has narrow tubular flowers and originated in Peru.

To add to their other charms, daturas are prolific bloomers. They begin putting out their flowers as soon as the weather warms up in the spring, and they bloom one after another throughout the summer and autumn. Some say they bloom best when the moon is full. Last year the salmon datura was in triumphant bloom from Christmas to the middle of January.

The datura isn't the only bright-coloured flower that has succeeded in the greenhouse. I have also had surprising luck with the clivia, a sturdy bulbous plant from South Africa which has broad strap-shaped leaves and flower umbels bearing from twelve to twenty bright scarlet funnel-shaped flowers with clear yellow throats.

Clivias like shade, lots of water in the growing season, and very rich soil. Whenever I have trouble with a clivia which won't flower, I repot it, putting in a stronger dose of rotted manure, and it generally makes flowers the next season. Clivia bulbs must be carefully potted so that more than half of each bulb remains above the earth while the fleshy roots are covered. (If they are not covered they tend to get a white mould, which inhibits growth.) New plants can be made by separating offshoots from the main bulb.

I have now managed to grow eight large clivia plants which put out an amazing display of flaming stars throughout the spring. In one season the first pot began to bloom early in March, and the four last pots were still in full bloom at the end of May.

The South Pacific has also provided its share of hot weather plants for our greenhouse. We were invited on a cruise to explore the smaller islands of the Society of Islands group and the last ten days were spent seed collecting in Tahiti. I cannot imagine any place on earth that could be more exciting for a plant lover. Just walking down the streets of any Tahitian village was like walking through a great tropical greenhouse, with tree ferns ten metres high and clumps of pink and orange cannas blooming beside the roads. There were jade vines curling around the banana plants, huge caladiums with pale green and white leaves spilling over front hedges and flamboyant trees lighting up every back yard and garden.

I collected bagloads of seeds, but looking back I think my greatest success came with two trees, a pink bauhinia and a yellow cassia. I found the cassia tree, *Cassia corymbosa*, in full flower with its golden racemes sparkling in the sunlight just outside Papeete and I collected all the seed pods I could find.

When I got them home I soaked these in water overnight, and then nicked them with a knife to let the humidity in, and in short order I had several nice little cassia trees growing in pots on the terrace. I knew they were something special when

I saw that the delicate fernlike foliage arranged in geometrical patterns up and down the stalks had a habit of closing up tight the moment the sun went down.

Three of these trees grew to be quite tall but the winter cold caught up with two of them, killing them straight off; so I hastily moved the survivor to a shady corner of the greenhouse and it began to bloom within months. I can now count on it to give a shower of yellow to my greenhouse every July and it often flowers again in September.

The bauhinia is a more delicate tree which I found close to a little coffee shop near Gauguin Bay on Tahiti. This is an appealing tree with odd heart-shaped leaves like the cloven hoof of a bullock. Its splendour is in its flowers which are very sharply cut, like pink orchids. I managed to scrounge a handful of seed pods one moonless evening and I now have two bauhinia trees growing in the sunniest part of my greenhouse. One of them has bloomed, giving us four delicate pink and white flowers which caused considerable comment.

But of all the plants I grow in my greenhouse, the ones that most ignite my imagination are the passionflowers, and recently their appeal has been doubled with the discovery that they may indeed contain some chemicals which help fight cancer. The first passionflower I came upon almost by chance – a plain brown packet in my seed store labelled by hand 'passiflora'. It seemed unlikely to me that such an anonymous item would ever sprout but I soon had a vine over a metre high which was creeping all over the back wall of the *serra*. There were no flowers at first, but suddenly two years later in June I caught a glimpse of white and blue in the midst of the greenery and saw my first flower. It was quite a sight. The passionflower is built in layers like an old-fashioned lace valentine. The bottom layer is like a daisy, with ten outstretched waxy white petals. On top of these is an odd blue corona from which sprouts a circular blue fringe. Then come five green stamens which project out like the spokes of a wheel, and sticking out beyond this are three large waxy stigmas. It is not surprising that this complex four-level flower should set people's imaginations to work. When European missionaries first came upon the flower in the jungles of Brazil, they took one look at the wreath-like halo that surrounds the flower and decided that the whole thing represents the Passion of Christ. The petals were the apostles, but since there are only ten of them it was decided that both Peter and Judas were absent. The stamens were decreed to be the five wounds of Christ, the stigmas were the nails used in the crucifixion and the corona represented the crown of thorns.

My favourite passion vine is a tropical version of *Passiflora edulis* which makes the fruit used in tropical drinks. I started several vines from seeds and the following May I was delighted to find a number of flowers which were blue and white in the centre and had a white fringe which was creased like a tightly pleated skirt. This vine now gives us about twenty or thirty nice purple-green fruits about the size of lemons which make excellent passionflower jelly, a conversation stopper at any Sunday brunch.

My most recent greenhouse discovery was a rather uncommon member of the salvia family which it took me close

to a dozen years to acquire. I saw it first on a chilly November
day blooming its head off outside a greenhouse window at the
Cambridge University Botanic Garden. It was a big plant, and
the flowers which it bore in profusion were a riveting shade of
royal blue which I believe is the finest blue in the whole floral
kingdom. The name, which I copied at once, was *Salvia
guaranitica*.

The great plantsman Graham Thomas was equally enthusiastic about this beauty. 'To see this plant in full flower in
October, next perhaps to *Hypericum* "Rowallane" or some
silvery foliage, is to taste the fullness of gardening,' he wrote.

My problem was not only that I could not find any nursery
that sold it but it wasn't in any catalogues either. I knew that I
had the name correctly as they are serious people at the
Cambridge Botanic Garden, and I continued to dream of my
guaranitica.

Finally, a good ten years after my historic sighting at
Cambridge, I was having tea in the garden of my friend
Giovanna Ralli in Olgiata and my eye was caught by a vivid
blue in the corner under a cherry tree. It was *guaranitica*
flowering! I told Giovanna of my struggles and asked her if
she would try to take a few cuttings for me, and she went over
immediately and broke off four or five large branches.

'No need to wait for me to take cuttings,' she said. 'Just
poke these into the ground and they'll grow roots.'

We were leaving the next day to spend a month in England,
and since the border would be getting very little water I
decided to pop the branches into one of the big pots in the
greenhouse where I habitually put cuttings. Since I keep a dish

of water under this pot and it contains a lot of sharp sand it almost never dries out and provides a good climate for would-be cuttings.

We returned from England early in August and as soon as I looked into the *serra*, I caught a glimpse of something blue in the cuttings section. My four branches of *guaranitica* had not only taken root but had grown about thirty centimetres each, and three of them were in full bloom. They continued to flower conspicuously all autumn, and at Christmas they made a marvellous display, giving a much needed accent of blue in a greenhouse that had previously shown mainly pink and white and yellow.

To me, there are mysterious forces at work here. Was it some ancient instinct which made me recognize *Salvia guaranitica* as a future friend the first time I saw it? Or was it only coincidence? And why had it taken me so many years to find it and actually see it growing in my garden? From this experience, there 'surges spontaneously', as the Italians say, another question: how many other salvia guaraniticas are out there waiting for me to discover them?

We usually close our *serra* door some time in November and reopen it in April, and aside from watering it occasionally the greenhouse does not get much attention during the winter months. But there was one Christmas season not so long ago when the greenhouse required all the attention we could give it.

The alert came – as it often does when trouble strikes – in an early morning telephone call to us in Rome. It was Luigi,

our neighbour in Canale, who reported in his usual abbrevi-
ated style that we had better get out to the country in a hurry,
as a southern gale the day before had ripped our roof off. He
was very short on details except to say that the storm, which
had rocketed in from the Sahara, had knocked down trees and
power lines (but fortunately not telephones) and from what he
could see at a distance our top roof had half disappeared.

We had not planned to go to the country for the holidays as
the weather had been wet and nasty all week, but the call sent
us out to Canale on the double. It was still raining and blowing hard as we left Rome, and the roads going north were
strewn with broken branches and debris, and we had to detour
once or twice around road-crews who were sawing up fallen
tree trunks which blocked traffic.

The moment we turned into our entrance drive, however,
we could see the worst. The whole top roof of our house had
simply been picked up at the southern edge and rolled neatly
back upon itself, like a big duvet on a bed. Driving closer we
saw that the roll-back had created a large hole on the front of
the roof, into which the rain was gently falling; but it had also
thrown down hundreds and hundreds of large ceramic roofing tiles, which now lay smashed in heaps all around the
house, crushing under their weight broken iron porch chairs,
flower pots, and a good assortment of tree peonies, rose
bushes, lavender and viburnums. We had to knock aside a
heap of tiles to get the front door open. Once inside the house
we were relieved to see that most of the water coming through
the roof-hole was falling into the *altana* (attic) which I used as
my studio, and only a minor streamlet was running down the

stairs where it was being sopped up by the fireplace rug and the sofa.

We climbed quickly up to the *altana*, which was inundated with broken tiles and water, but aside from flooding some books which I had left on the floor, the damage was not irreversible.

But when we glanced out of the western *altana* window, a new horror presented itself – for while the blown-back tiles had landed on the ground on three sides of the house, to the west they had fallen directly on to the glass roof of the greenhouse and completely smashed three of the four big glass roof-windows. In other words, my beloved greenhouse was completely exposed to the wild and freezing winds of winter. I felt slightly faint.

What to do? It was Christmas Eve. We telephoned our trusty builder Vincenzo in Tolfa, and he informed us that he had let his whole crew off for the holidays, and they would not be reporting back to work until after the Befana (6 January). However, he said that he would come himself to see what should be done.

I have no solid recollection of how the salvage operation was organized but I do recall that within two hours we had a substantial crew at work. The first helper to arrive was our neighbour Luigi, who said our biggest job was to cover over the hole in the roof to keep the rain out. He therefore put himself to work digging among the fallen tiles on the ground to find those that were big enough to put back – even in temporary fashion – on the wooden roof supports. He was joined soon by the bus driver and metalworker Armando, who started carrying usable tiles up the stairs to the roof. Then came Franco the plumber, who offered to go to the woodyard (before it closed for Christmas) to buy some rolls of tarpaper and vinyl plastic to help cover the holes. Soon after this came Immaculata, who as usual wasn't speaking to her husband Armando, but she offered us a bowl of spaghetti with garlic and hot peppers, which warmed us up.

By early afternoon we had at least ten volunteers helping us to shore up our open roof. Vincenzo had arrived from Tolfa, with two long ladders and a carload of big tarpaulins and plastic sheets of all sizes which he started to tack over the hole in the greenhouse roof. Then came Gino, the street-cleaner from Canale, to help him. Luigi Triossi, our horse-riding friend from Pisciarelli, showed up with two bottles of grappa and a box full of tubes of a substance you squeeze on to glass like toothpaste to repair cracks. And soon after came Renzo Sgriscia, the welder from Tolfa, who brought a whole truck-load of roof tiles which he said he kept in his back yard in case of emergency. He immediately began to carry them up to the roof piled on his shoulders. And finally, to my enormous surprise, I saw my old gardening friend DeDe carrying two thermoses of hot coffee and a hot apple pie. She was followed, reluctantly I suspect, by her husband Lorenzo, who gave me a big embarrassed hug. As he did this he murmured, '*Amici come prima*' (Friends like before), which is an expression used in our parts when friends end a quarrel. Well, why not?

The interesting thing about this heterogeneous crew was that they worked in perfect harmony and every man seemed to find useful work to do. Somehow, without anyone bossing anyone else, they got the broken tiles taken away, the new tiles placed, and the extra holes covered over with lengths of plastic, tarpaulin and even cloths used to collect olives.

I had the feeling as I watched them work that this was a perfectly natural occurrence in their lives – that they had been doing this kind of thing for years. If a friend's roof blew off, even on Christmas Eve, you went over and helped put it back on. That was the way things were done. Period.

At sunset, by the time our kind helpers had finished, the roof was covered. Nearly all of them invited us to come over and share their Christmas Eve dinner at their homes, even though most of them had no light or heat. But we thanked them politely and said vaguely that we had other plans.

We lit a fire in our dampish hearth, put on two more sweaters and moved over two wooden chairs to take the place of the soggy sofa. I found a match and lit a dozen candles that gave off a nice holiday glow.

Robert meanwhile foraged in the empty kitchen and came back holding a bottle of what we call 'blue champagne', a local sparkling wine made at the nearby Torre in Pietra farm.

After he poured the wine he raised his glass.

'Guess what we have for our Christmas Eve banquet, madame. Two tins of borlotti beans and tuna fish. *Buon appetito!*'

Eels for Christmas

ACTUALLY THE ITALIANS HAVE NEVER BEEN WILDLY enthusiastic about Christmas celebrations. They tend to favour pagan holidays involving horse races, or football championships accompanied by bottles of chilled Prosecco and platters of raw ham. If they must suffer a holiday based on a religious figure, they prefer someone like San Giuseppe whose birthday is celebrated with charcoal-grilled snails or San Martino whose name-day, 11 November, is the day when the new wine is ready to drink – *a San Martino ogni mosto è vino* (on San Martino the must becomes wine).

Though the birthday of the new wine merits reverent attention, a festival centred around the birthday of a baby lying in a stable in Jerusalem is not exactly the Italian cup of tea (although they do enjoy making crèches about the Nativity, as long as they can fill them with Botticelli angels and shepherds wearing eighteenth-century Neapolitan costumes).

Italians are equally non-committal about the presiding saint of the northern Christmas, a large figure like a bearded Norwegian troll, who wears an unstylish outfit of scarlet felt edged with white fur and who spends his working hours riding around the skies in a sleigh drawn by eight tiny reindeer. A figure whom Italians feel more at home with during the holiday season is a hook-nosed crone named La Befana, traditionally shown wearing a long black cape and carrying a bag of coal. The Befana is the person who brings gifts to children on the Epiphany (whence the name Befana) of 6 January, but children who have behaved badly during the year are given blocks of coal (*carbone*) instead – so although the witch is a favourite of parents she is regarded by most children with misgiving.

A few well-travelled families try to combine both the Nordic and the Mediterranean Christmas; they start off in early December with a spree of frenzied shopping *all' americana*, followed by weeks of feasting *all'italiana*, and end up with dyspepsia, a cupboardful of broken electronic toys and a living room littered with fallen Christmas tree needles.

Cleverer (or more realistic) Italians are far more selective and manage to pick out only the Christmas festivities that are to their taste. They renounce Santa Claus and the boring Yankee feast of roast turkey, sweet potatoes and cranberry sauce, and instead throw their energies into their traditional Christmas Eve dinner. The church calendar lists this as a *cucina di magro* or fasting menu. Meat is forbidden on this fast day, but since fish is permitted the Italian Christmas Eve dinner is not so lean after all (the Italians call it *falso magro*).

Starting with *spaghetti alle vongole*, it goes on to pious delicacies such as raw oysters and finishes with ten-pound eels fresh caught at Lake Bolsena, grilled or roasted with a tomato sauce and washed down with the best *vernaccia*. (After this 'lean' repast few Italians are hungry on Christmas Day, so they spend the day either walking in the park, taking the kids to visit relatives or watching TV.) They then organize a few scattered feasts until New Year's Eve when they once again organize a major-holiday repast, which may start with an antipasto of bottled eel and go on to hefty plates of lentils (lentils bring money) cooked with *cotechino*, an Italian version of pigs' trotters. The New Year celebration used to end when all hands united to throw most of the year's supply of broken or cracked dishes out of the window, a tradition which was finally curbed when pedestrians complained of being hurt by flying glass.

The insistence on eels during winter holidays is more than a bit surprising as eel is no longer a basic item in the standard Italian menu, and indeed you could go to three dozen trattorie before you found the word *anguilla* (eel) spelled out among the fish dishes.

According to my anthropologist friends, whenever you find an unexplained or eccentric custom which has no obvious raison d'être but seems to be implanted in the psyche of a group, you can assume that it is very old indeed. In fact scholars have shown that the tradition of eels for the mid-winter holiday goes back not just to the Romans but to the Etruscans, and as proof of this they point to an ingenious eel trap which Etruscan fish fanciers built around 600 BC at the mouth of the Marta river near Lake Bolsena.

I can personally vouch for the existence of this trap, known locally as La Cannara, as it is owned by friends of ours at Marta and we have partaken of a delicious ten-pound female eel caught in the trap, and roasted on an outdoor spit in their charming year-round garden.

In case the concept of an 'eel trap' seems improbable, be assured that it is not only unusual, it is unique and the one in Marta could well be the biggest and oldest eel trap in the world. What the Etruscans did was to build a kind of water-mill, complete with a watchtower, just half a mile downstream from the spot where the river Marta rushes out of Lake Bolsena towards the sea. The mill straddles the river like a bridge (and the foundations of this bridge are certified as pure Etruscan) but instead of putting in a waterwheel to harness the downward-rushing water and grind corn, the Etruscans channelled the water into two narrow sluices and in the middle of this mini-waterfall they placed two great pallets of interwoven reeds where eels, heading south to the sea, could be conveniently trapped in a kind of sieve.

We have, unfortunately, no wall paintings showing the Etruscans trapping eels, and no fables either, as the jealous Romans destroyed most of the Etruscan literature, but there is no doubt that the eel has been much cherished in Italian culinary history for more than two thousand years.

Henry VIII may have preferred the breast of swan for his banquets, but the ruling nabobs in Italy, starting with the Etruscan kings and going on to the princes of the Vatican, have always had a special hankering for the succulent flesh of an eel. One of the first eye-witness reports on the eel trap comes to us from 1462 when the then Pope Pius II went to Marta to try to resolve a dispute between squabbling Bolsena fishermen and stopped at La Cannara on his way home to give us a vivid description of the way the trap worked:

> When the south wind ruffles the clear water [the eels] retreat to the end of the lake and, following the course of the river, fall into a trap. For where the river drops the inhabitants have built a tower with a wooden receptacle at its foot which lets out the water through many small holes in the floor but keeps the eels in. Since they cannot climb up again against the force of the water flowing down from above they are left high and dry and are caught. The tower is kept under guard and returns a very considerable revenue.

The Pope reportedly left instructions at the eel trap to have a goodly supply of the biggest eels sent to the Vatican at Christmas and to this day the good citizens of Bolsena send a brimming bucket of live eels to the Vatican for the holidays.

Cookery experts say that eels have an unfair reputation for being both fatty and oily. This fat, they claim, is collected mainly in the outer skin, and if this is peeled off the remaining flesh is muscular and tasty. At Christmas the eel is generally stewed in a rich tomato sauce. On other occasions it can be roasted, or left with the skin on and made into kebabs with bay leaves and crusty bread. Lucrezia Borgia had a fondness for eel done in pastry and fishermen around Bolsena still preserve it in glass jars with garlic, pepper and hot peppers and eat it all year round.

One Pope, Martin IV (a Frenchman originally called Simon de Brie), reportedly was so fond of the huge Bolsena *anguilla* drowned in *vernaccia* that he ate too many and expired on the spot. This prompted Dante to send Martin to hell as a glutton.

Despite bad publicity like this, the eel trapping at Marta went swimmingly for close to two thousand years, and records show that as late as 1900 the Cannara could trap up to three or four quintales of wiggling eels in a single day, which is a lot of eels even if you calculate that some of the larger females weigh six kilos each. (The males are less than half as large.) The recorded annual income for Cannara eels ran to around 300,000 lire in 1903 which at current rates would be about £8.4 million a year – enough to enable the happy owners of the trap to travel widely and build themselves glorious villas all over Tuscia (southern Etruria).

But the end came suddenly soon after the Second World War, when nylon thread was introduced into Italy and fishermen on Lake Bolsena – always furious about their limited eel catch – discovered to their joy that while cotton nets and traps had not been strong enough to hold many of the biggest wriggling eels, nylon traps were. All at once eel fishing on the lake became big business, and the poor fish factory on the Marta river saw its haul drop from thousands to hundreds to a handful of eels a year. This meant that the Cannara was no longer profitable as a protein factory although it still produced a modest quantity of fish each year.

The trap was saved from oblivion in 1980 when Marcello Faggiani, who had been born in Marta, became aware of the Cannara's plight and bought it for conversion into a summer home. The job was tricky as the old watchtower was crumbling and the assorted sheds which abutted the trap had all lost their roofs. But in a short time the Faggianis had reroofed the whole structure, putting together a charming series of winding rooms and corridors which all have windows looking out at the fresh and foaming waters of the Marta – and the house is invigorated at all hours of the day and night by the muted thunder of galloping waters.

Faggiani's wife Mirella, a piano teacher by profession, decided to organize the clean-up of the grounds which had become an all-purpose village dump, and after the debris was hauled away, she set about removing the bristling weeds and thistles which towered two metres high beside the river. Once this was accomplished she made the momentous decision to plant a little garden. Like all beginning gardeners, Mirella had no inkling how engrossed she would become with the garden but now, two decades later, she has created a riverside garden of inestimable charm, which stands out as one of the rarest beauty spots of the Tuscia area.

As you enter from the main gate on the road from Tuscania to Marta, the visitor walks towards a pretty whitewashed cottage which is guarded by a massive chestnut door and two prosperous camellia bushes, and over everything there is the sound of rushing water. Out to the left there is a promise of what is to come – a long view of the river Marta framed by a curtain of willows, bamboos, ilexes, and waving tufts of reeds and flowering grasses which remind you of a hidden river in a child's fairy tale, and a huge loop of the lovely 'Albertine' rose swoops down as if trying to touch the waters.

The river plunges straight under the house from north to south and while the trap is actually under the sitting room, there is a spill basin on the far side of the house, surrounded again by roses and water irises, where the river tumbles down about a metre to continue its longish trip to the sea.

Mirella has taken advantage of this centrepiece of flowing water to build a long flowering path running parallel to the river and fill it with mixed yellow and orange day lilies and a dramatic row of cerulean agapanthus. The garden path ends at a shady arboretum where she has planted an exotic assortment of shrub mallows with showy crimson, pink and yellow hollyhock-like flowers blooming in late summer. This area is bounded on one side by a thick stand of black bamboo and is underplanted with white violets, pink autumn crocuses, tiny daffodils and masses of pink bergenia flowers, which start to show their colour in February.

Behind the house are two large freshwater basins originally built to keep trapped eels alive until they were delivered in big wooden barrels to fish markets all over Italy on Christmas Eve. (Invariably a few of the most enterprising eels managed to escape and slithered around the wet pavements of the Christmas markets, scaring susceptible shoppers half to death.) The basins have now been converted into outdoor pools full of flourishing water lilies and big goldfish; and they are visited now and again by local ducks and kingfishers, and an occasional pair of blue or white herons.

Mirella has arranged tree peonies around the tanks and close to the water she has planted dozens of *Amaryllis belladonna* bulbs which send up delightful scapes of sweet-smelling pink lilies from early September on. By the time her late autumn flowers have faded, some of her early-flowering fruit trees are almost ready to burst into bloom, so that her garden by the rushing water can boast something in flower all year long.

An odd sidelight to the eel story is that even after two thousand years of eel trapping, and great advances in science, leading fishing experts are still not sure about the logistics of eel reproduction. The good old Etruscans, instinctive ecologists from the start, were well aware that when the eels became mature in Lake Bolsena, they felt a strong desire to move down the Marta river to spawn in the salt water. They also realized that these mature eels never returned to their home in the lake. The only fish that came back were swarms of tiny baby eels about two inches long known as elvers, who seemed mysteriously to know that Lake Bolsena was the place where they belonged. The Etruscans also realized that the elvers were not strong enough to swim through the fast-moving eel trap to get back to the lake, so they dug a second, re-entry channel which goes outside the eel trap and joins the Marta river later on, and permits the elvers to travel safely from sea to lake where they spend five or six years before they mature. Little eels go home in style.

But the big question that no one has really answered is, where do the big eels go once they get out of the Marta river and into the sea? Most people assume that they go to the Sargasso Sea, which is two thousand miles out into the Atlantic beyond Bermuda. But in truth hardly anyone has ever seen a big freshwater eel swimming through the Straits of

Gibraltar. Even the greatest of the fish experts, Sir Alister Hardy, claims that the only person who ever reported sighting an eel in the mid-Atlantic was the Prince of Monaco, who found a full-grown eel in the 'stomach of a sperm whale near the Azores 1898'.

Hardy does not explain whether the prince acquired the whale while on a fishing expedition, or whether he was collecting it for his famous aquarium in Monte Carlo. (But he does report in a footnote – presumably added later – that a few more adult eels have been taken twenty or thirty miles south of the Devon and Cornwall coast.) This may make ten or perhaps twenty eels sighted in the Atlantic in the last hundred years, which is not a lot of eels. What happened to the rest? The most common suggestion is that they swim in very deep waters, so they are never sighted by regular fishermen.

Sir Alister admits he had trouble with all the ramifications of this migration – how, for instance, do the elvers sort themselves out so that some go home to Spain and some home to Italy? – but he bravely concluded: 'The adult eels are seen leaving the rivers for the sea, and their eggs and newly hatched fry are found in only one spot in the world [the Sargasso Sea]; we cannot doubt that they make the journey.'

Some sceptics, however, think there might be other solutions. Could it not be, they suggest, that Italian eels have worked out a secret system of spawning deep in the Mediterranean, where they do not feel the culture shock that comes of travelling all the way to the Bermudas?

Wily Bolsena fishermen offer a slightly different explanation for eel survival. They claim that they frequently catch pregnant eels in the spring – and when they cut them open to make fillets they find them full of tiny slithery fishlets. The idea is that Bolsena eels have become viviparous – an adaptation which ensures reproduction in Lake Bolsena and not in the Atlantic and cuts travel time by 95 per cent.

Whichever fish story you fancy, the eels of Bolsena appear to be thriving and Italians, who don't worry too much about the why and the wherefore of their provenance, are perfectly happy to sit down every Christmas Eve to enjoy a heaped (*cena di magro*) dinner of barbecued eel, washed down with a robust bottle of Pinot Grigio. Fortunately for them there is no censorious Dante around these days to look over their shoulders and send them off to hell as gluttons.

Epilogue

NOT SO LONG AGO I USED TO DREAM ABOUT A GARDEN
that I could not quite place. It was not my kind of
garden at all; it was a minimalist garden, full of muted greys
and greens and rounded shapes – chic and under control – and
I used to wonder what this dream had to do with me. Was it
perhaps a warning to me to get my act together? Or was it a
yearning for a garden that I might like to build next time
around?

I finally realized that I was dreaming of a garden in the
Lubéron, in the south of France, which I had visited the
previous summer with a group from the Rome Garden Club.
Tucked high on a hillside near an ancient farmhouse of grey
stone, La Loupe was not so much a garden as a collection of
low evergreen bushes cropped into neat balls, their smooth
domes rolling softly down towards the horizon. The overall
tone ranged from blue green to olive green to grey. It was

neat, controlled and very stylish, and it has had an astonishing impact on garden lovers all over Europe. Many of the ladies in the group rushed back to Italy to redecorate their gardens in the same starkly elegant style, and I admit that when I got to Canale I found myself clipping away at some of my lavender and rosemary bushes.

But it didn't take me long to realize that I could never bring myself to embrace the kind of discipline that I had seen in the Lubéron. If I were creating another garden, I would probably do it in my standard hugger-mugger fashion; rushing the plants into the soil as fast as I could and then sitting around crossing my fingers (not always green ones) and willing them to survive. Half the fun of a garden, I believe, is to try out odd plants from all over the world, and if we deliberately banish experiments we risk losing a lot of pleasure. Worse, to outlaw yellow or pink or crimson from a Mediterranean garden is like banning colours from an Impressionistic painting. As Cézanne put it, 'Colour is the place where our spirit and the universe meet.'

Furthermore, I have come to realize that, as we enter the third millennium, gardening is turning a sharp corner. The old elitist gardens of the aristocracy – reserved for the privileged few – have shown themselves to be out of date, and the endless debate between those who favour classical garden designs and those who prefer informal landscapes seems a bit on the frivolous side.

We are beginning to realize that the main task for humanity today is not to design charming gardens but to solve the ecological crisis; to come to grips with the problems of over-population, industrial pollution and destruction of the natural eco-systems upon which our lives depend. We realize too that our unnatural lifestyles – revolving around fast cars, obsessive over-consumption and passive entertainment – are quite literally killing us. Unless we change our ways and clean up our planet, we may not make it into the twenty-second century at all, to say nothing of the fourth millennium. By then the only surviving animals may well be alligators, cockroaches and magpies.

This planetary emergency is surely one of the reasons for the astonishing leap in gardening enthusiasm in the last decades. People everywhere have decided that life on the fast track, cut off from nature and from green and growing things, is not the answer, and they are seeking ways to re-engage with the natural world and also to preserve it for future generations.

Visible proof of this new attitude can be seen in some of the new gardens in Italy which are hidden away in unexpected places. There is a lady in Palermo, an officer in the local chapter of the Legambiente (League for the Environment), who believes that nature must be defended at all costs. In her costume of blue jeans, jacket and trainers, she is always at the forefront of public battles with the speculators and contractors who are trying to lay a blanket of cement over her beloved Palermo.

Practising what she preaches, she has created a wild nature garden in her own back yard where, instead of a lily pool, she has built a pretty little bog-pond to encourage frogs and snakes. No chemicals are allowed to pass her portals; instead of raking up the leaves and burning them, she lets them rot slowly on the ground where they make excellent compost, and whenever possible she allows the weeds and grasses to grow untroubled along with nettles and cabbages.

One of Italy's best-known garden writers, Professor Ippolito Pizzetti, has been insisting for years that the emphasis in Italy must switch from private gardening to public gardening, so that everyone can enjoy and even help to promote the glories of nature. The average citizens of the future will have neither the money nor the land to build themselves a private garden, Pizzetti says, so it is essential for their health and the health of the whole of society that public green spaces be created where people can lie down under a tree or take their children to ride bicycles.

An example of the public interest in green spaces can be seen in Garbatella, a little enclave beyond the Protestant Cemetery in Rome, where residents volunteer to tend the flourishing central gardens and courtyards of their neighbourhood. Garbatella was originally designed as a slum clearance project in the Twenties, and has now become a proud refuge for natural beauty and harmony, with its citizens constantly on the alert to ward off the attacks of greedy speculators.

If you were to ask me to give an award to the Best Gardener of 1999, I would consider nominating a lady (whose name I do not know) who grows a fetching garden on the grassy verge of a North London railway line. The railway engineers recently built a new underpass where this line goes underground but they left an ugly orange-red brick wall between the underpass and the street, and children began smashing bottles on the wall and dumping litter. Undaunted, the lady gardener moved over from her grassy verge with a pickaxe and a wheelbarrow, and soon she was growing rambler roses up the wall and brightening the surrounding terrain with flowering cherry trees, clumps of oriental poppies and jolly patches of coreopsis. People going down the street on the way to the bus now stop to admire the garden which runs beside the pavement, and no one throws bottles or rubbish there any more.

Reports like this suggest to me that one group of people who may be counted on to work for a more ecological future are the gardeners themselves. For digging in a garden has a way of instilling down-to-earth values; it teaches people to slow down and relax, to be more patient and less grasping. It also helps to increase their awareness of the natural world, and encourages them to form links with other people who share their interest in green growing things and healthy air and water.

I have felt these changes, perhaps in a somewhat superficial way, in my own limited experience with a garden. When I started with my little plot in Canale I was in a big hurry. I wanted to get all the seeds in early, and I got up at dawn to see if my plants had bloomed. I felt rushed and anxious to build a successful garden, and it seemed as if I never had time just to sit down and enjoy what I was doing.

Occasionally when I was weeding, I used to drag a wooden stool along with me where I could put my tools so they wouldn't get lost, and now and again as I worked I brushed the tools aside and sat down on the stool so that I could enjoy the flowers blooming around me. In these stolen moments I saw things that I had never noticed before – a pretty combination of pale blue iris and purple lavender, or a little wild meadow sage that had wandered in from the fields.

An even better time for contemplation came when I began to water my garden in the evening, and I grew to enjoy this pastime so much that I resisted the idea of putting in an automatic watering system. This permitted me at the day's end to stand hot and sticky over my beloved plantings while the cool well water trickled from my hose, and I could greet my flowers one by one as I gave them a deep and welcome drink.

Gradually, as I learned to relax, I realized that up until then I had really been on a treadmill, trying to perfect a flowery stage set so that my visitors would speak kindly about it (after studying it for thirty seconds). And so with relaxation came tranquillity and a hopeful frame of mind. Even small triumphs brought joy.

For real gardening can be one of the most rewarding of all human occupations. We live in an age of anxious haste and mindless grabbiness. We have to hurry to finish our education and get a job; we have to hurry to find a husband or a wife or we won't be 'marketable' any longer. We have to hurry to make money fast because there may be a new slump coming tomorrow. Our brains will not be so sharp next year, we will have lost our looks and our health and everything that we want in life will be made of polyester and cost double.

But the world is not like this for the experienced gardener. Time is our friend; everything will be prettier and greener tomorrow; every seed we plant is a thrilling promise and every tree will grow nobler and stronger with each passing year. We look forward to the next year and the next five years in our gardens with happy anticipation, not dread. This waiting and watching is a hopeful and not a fearful thing and we become, while watching our seedlings grow, philosophers.

This relaxed attitude has also brought another dividend – my garden no longer lays claim to my exclusive attention. There is another world out there and if I want to find out how the daturas bloom in Amalfi or how they prune lemon trees in Sicily I can go to see for myself. And when someone suggests a trip to Puglia or, better yet, to Karnataka and Kerala, I can be packed up and ready in a matter of days with lots of empty envelopes waiting for seeds.

A garden should not be an anchor, it should be a spinnaker ready to catch the best winds that blow, and if the wind is right it can blow you to places of breathtaking beauty. Actually when we travel, which we do a lot, I do not abandon my garden at all, I take it with me in my knapsack or in my mind, and it makes all the other spots much more enjoyable. Gardeners when travelling have a special visa – an invitation, you might say – to refresh their spirit in the world of nature. They go to all the gardens they can find, and fall into the habit of wandering off the trail in search of rare plants or new colour combinations. They get to bathe in the shade of tree ferns.

Being a member of the worldwide clan of garden fanatics enables a traveller to make friends with people who would otherwise pass unnoticed on crowded foreign streets. It was our enthusiasm for the great ironwood trees of the Borneo jungle that in Kuching brought us together with Dr Danny Kok, expert on everything from acupuncture to pitcher plants to orangutans. And since we are keen fruit and nut growers, we happened to strike up a lunchtime conversation with an Indian planter of pineapples, coconuts and cashew nuts, Dr Livingston Soans. We now go regularly to stay with Livy on his pineapple plantation in Moodbidri in the state of Karnataka, India, and we have spent long night-time hours sitting with him beside his irrigation tank in the midst of his pineapple plants while he shows us the course of the planets through the heavens.

We have done a lot of plant swapping with Livy too. A dozen little olive-tree suckers which we brought from Canale in plastic bags are now growing well in Livy's experimental plantation, a temperate-zone farm high up in the Western Ghats, and one of our Italian hazelnut trees is already producing hazelnuts there. In our garden in Italy some small cashew trees given us by Livy are struggling to survive, although Canale cannot give them the heat and humidity they enjoyed in the monsoon jungles.

I realize as I look back that, although my garden and flowers are very dear to me, I am fonder still of the people around the globe who grew them – a group I know as the Clan of Passionate Garden People.

This is a very odd clan indeed. It has no president, no constitution, no uniform, no lapel insignia; but its members recognize one another instantly without any badges. They are people who wander about with secateurs in their pockets, and when they reach for a coin they are likely to come up with a *Caesalpinia* seed or a red runner bean. When they walk in public gardens they absent-mindedly twitch off the dead flowers of geraniums and dahlias even though there are signs saying 'Don't touch the flowers'. They simply cannot stop themselves. When they go out driving in other people's cars, they are apt to call out 'Stop!' in front of every roadside stand, nursery, florist, herbalist or garden centre, not to mention flower markets and botanical gardens. On beaches, these people do not look ahead towards the waves, but backwards at the flowering dunes; in the mountains their gaze does not rise towards the snowy peaks but drifts down to the meadows.

Their night tables are covered with seed catalogues and garden books and they generally subscribe to *House and Garden* or *Gardenia* magazine, and watch nature programmes on television. Floral arrangements attract them like moths no matter how mediocre they are, and a flower they do not recognize is enough to secure their complete attention at even the most entertaining cocktail party.

These people show an unusual, often manic, interest in charts and maps about annual rainfall and early frosts. And if they see a bulldozer or a cement mixer moving towards an open field, they stop to ask what it is doing. If they hear a power saw cutting down trees in their local woods, they go out to investigate.

If you ask them for a nail file, they may offer you a grafting knife. Their keys are held together by bits of green grafting tape, and their broken duffel bags, wallets and shoes are secured by green plastic-covered wire suitable for holding up peonies.

There are, naturally, a few secret passwords that unite this clan. If you talk about soil temperature or your PH rate they will leap to attention, and if you are concerned about the ozone layer or implanting wheat seeds with genes from North Sea herrings, they will invite you home for dinner and offer you their best gardening boots. They may be nuts but they are my kind of nuts, and when the crisis comes they can be counted on to lend a helping hand.

About the Artist

THE DRAWINGS OF CORINNA SARGOOD HAVE CHARMED ME from the day I first saw them illustrating *Honey from a Weed* by Patience Gray, a new kind of travel memoir which paved the way for many of today's most popular travel volumes.

It was clear from Corinna's drawings – and also from *Rustic Structures* (Downhill Press, 1984) which she wrote and illustrated while bicycling through Apulia – that she knew and loved the Mediterranean landscape with its figs, flowers, gnarled olives and classical ruins, and I was delighted when she agreed to do the drawings for my own book.

Corinna visited us in Canale so that she could see everything at first hand. She made dozens of drawings of our garden and greenhouse, our wrought-iron bed and flowering terraces complete with birds and small animals, as well as scenes from the Etruscan countryside. These warm-hearted sketches, drawn with such precision and care, have become family heirlooms and whenever we look at them we are taken back to the day when we were invaded by killer bees, or the time when we found so many mushrooms out in the *macchia* that we had to make a special trip back to the house to get more baskets.

JM

Bibliography

Beales, Peter, *Visions of Roses*, Little, Brown, 1966.

Goold-Adams, Deenagh, *The Cool Greenhouse Today*, Faber and Faber, London, 1969.

Gould, Stephen, *The Panda's Thumb*, W. W. Norton and Co., London, 1982.

Hardy, Alister, *The Open Sea*, Houghton Mifflin, Boston, 1964.

Kennet, Wayland, and Young, Elizabeth, *Northern Lazio: An Unknown Italy*, John Murray, London, 1990.

Lawrence, Elizabeth, *A Southern Garden*, University of North Carolina Press, Chapel Hill, 1942.

Menninger, Edwin A., *Flowering Trees of the World*, Hearthside Press Inc., New York, 1962.

Nuese, Josephine, *The Country Garden*, Charles Scribner's Sons, New York, 1970.

Taverna, Lavinia, *Un Giardino Mediterraneo*, Rizzoli, Milan, 1982.

Wharton, Edith, *Italian Villas and Their Gardens*, Century Co., New York, 1904, reissued by De Capo Press inc., New York, 1988.